DATE DUE			

REPRODUCTIVE BIOLOGY
RESEARCH FOUNDATION CONFERENCE

ETHICAL ISSUES IN SEX THERAPY AND RESEARCH

A CONFERENCE SPONSORED
BY THE REPRODUCTIVE BIOLOGY RESEARCH
FOUNDATION, ST. LOUIS, MISSOURI

PROGRAM COMMITTEE

WILLIAM H. MASTERS

VIRGINIA E. JOHNSON

ROBERT C. KOLODNY
Conference Coordinator

REPRODUCTIVE BIOLOGY
RESEARCH FOUNDATION CONFERENCE

Ethical Issues in
Sex Therapy and Research

EDITED BY

WILLIAM H. MASTERS M.D.
Co-Director, Reproductive Biology Research Foundation

VIRGINIA E. JOHNSON
Co-Director, Reproductive Biology Research Foundation

ROBERT C. KOLODNY, M.D.
Associate Director, Reproductive Biology Research Foundation

Little, Brown and Company
BOSTON

PARTICIPANTS

JEAN APPERSON, Ph.D.
Clinical Psychologist, The University of Michigan Institute for Human
Adjustment, Ann Arbor, Michigan. Designated conference representative,
American Psychological Association

MAE A. BIGGS, R.N., B.S.N., M.S.
Senior Clinical and Research Associate, Reproductive Biology
Research Foundation, St. Louis, Missouri

MARY S. CALDERONE, M.D., M.P.H.
President, Sex Information and Education Council of the United
States, New York, New York

HELEN DARRAGH, M.S.S.
Director, Professional Services, Family and Children's Service,
St. Louis, Missouri. Designated conference representative, Family Service
Association of America

**H. TRISTRAM ENGELHARDT, JR.,
Ph.D., M.D.**
Associate Professor, Institute for the Medical Humanities,
and Department of Preventive Medicine and Community Health,
University of Texas Medical Branch, Galveston, Texas

PAUL H. GEBHARD, Ph.D.
Director, Institute for Sex Research, Indiana University,
Bloomington, Indiana

ROBERT GORDIS, Ph.D., D.D.
Professor of Bible and Professor in the Philosophies of Religion,
Jewish Theological Seminary of America,
New York, New York

RICHARD GREEN, M.D.
Founding President, International Academy of Sex Research;
Professor, Department of Psychiatry and Behavioral Sciences and
Department of Psychology, State University of New York,
Stony Brook, New York

SEWARD HILTNER, Ph.D.
Professor of Theology and Personality, Princeton Theological
Seminary, Princeton, New Jersey

R. CHRISTIAN JOHNSON, Ph.D.
Office of Population Research, Princeton University,
Princeton, New Jersey

VIRGINIA E. JOHNSON
Co-Director, Reproductive Biology Research Foundation,
St. Louis, Missouri

HELEN S. KAPLAN, M.D., Ph.D.
Clinical Associate Professor of Psychiatry, Cornell University
Medical College; Director of the Sex Education and Therapy Program
of Cornell University, The New York Hospital—Cornell
Medical Center, New York, New York

JAY KATZ, M.D.
Professor (Adjunct) of Law and Psychiatry, Yale Law School,
New Haven, Connecticut

MIRIAM F. KELTY, Ph.D.
Psychologist, National Commission for the Protection of Human
Subjects of Biomedical and Behavioral Research,
Bethesda, Maryland

ROBERT C. KOLODNY, M.D.
Associate Director, Reproductive Biology Research Foundation,
St. Louis, Missouri

JUDITH LONG LAWS, Ph.D.
Assistant Professor of Sociology and Psychology, Cornell
University, Ithaca, New York

HAROLD I. LIEF, M.D.
Professor of Psychiatry, Director of the Division of Family
Study, and Director of the Center for the Study of Sex Education in
Medicine, The University of Pennsylvania School of Medicine,
Philadelphia, Pennsylvania

RUTH MACKLIN, Ph.D.
Associate Professor of Philosophy, Case Western Reserve
University, Cleveland, Ohio; Staff member, Institute of Society, Ethics and the
Life Sciences, Hastings-on-Hudson, New York

JUDD MARMOR, M.D.
President, American Psychiatric Association; Franz Alexander
Professor of Psychiatry, University of Southern California School
of Medicine, Los Angeles, California

WILLIAM H. MASTERS, M.D.
Co-Director, Reproductive Biology Research Foundation,
St. Louis, Missouri

JOHN MONEY, Ph.D.
President, Society for Scientific Study of Sex;
Professor of Medical Psychology and Pediatrics, The Johns Hopkins
University School of Medicine,
Baltimore, Maryland

EMILY HARTSHORNE MUDD, Ph.D.
Member of Board of Directors, Reproductive Biology
Research Foundation; Emeritus Professor of Family Study in Psychiatry
and Consultant in Behavioral Sciences, Department of Obstetrics and
Gynecology, The University of Pennsylvania School of Medicine,
Philadelphia, Pennsylvania

FRITZ REDLICH, M.D.
Professor of Psychiatry, Yale University School of Medicine,
New Haven, Connecticut

CHARLES REMBAR, LL.B.
Lawyer specializing in First Amendment issues; tried and argued
the cases on *Lady Chatterley's Lover*, *Tropic of Cancer*, and *Fanny Hill*
(U.S. Supreme Court); author of *The End of Obscenity* (1968),
Perspective (1975); New York, New York

SALLIE SCHUMACHER, Ph.D.
Associate Professor of Clinical Psychiatry and Director, Center
for Study of Human Sexual Behavior, Department of Psychiatry,
The University of Pittsburgh School of Medicine, Pittsburgh,
Pennsylvania

PEPPER SCHWARTZ, Ph.D.
Assistant Professor of Sociology, University of Washington,
Seattle, Washington

MARY JANE SHERFEY, M.D.
Psychiatrist, Cornell University Medical College, New York,
New York

CARL S. SHULTZ, M.D.
President, American Association of Sex Educators and
Counselors; Director, Office of Population Affairs,
Department of Health, Education, and Welfare,
Washington, D.C.

ALAN A. STONE, M.D.
Professor of Law and Psychiatry in the Faculty of Law and the
Faculty of Medicine, Harvard University, Cambridge,
Massachusetts

ROBERT L. STUBBLEFIELD, M.D.
Member of the American Medical Association Council on Mental Health;
Medical Director, Silver Hill Foundation,
New Canaan, Connecticut

JACK WIENER, M.A.
Social Problems Research Consultant, National Institute of
Mental Health, Rockville, Maryland

JEROME F. WILKERSON,
M.Div., Ph.D.
Director, Newman Center, Washington University Medical
Campus, St. Louis, Missouri

PREFACE

The recent past has witnessed a remarkable upsurge of interest in sex therapy and research among both professionals and the public. The burgeoning number of health-care professionals treating sexual problems today contrasts sharply with the relative handful practicing a decade ago, and there has also been a quieter but significant surge of activity in the scientific investigation of human sexuality. As in many other scientific fields, the initial rapid growth of a new discipline has been accompanied by problems of public acceptance. Since sexuality is so central to human identity, public scrutiny has been justifiably intense. Our awareness of the need for public accountability precipitated plans for a conference to discuss the ethical concerns of sex therapy and research.

Years ago, when our private discussions of ethical responsibilities began, we hoped that an established national organization would organize such a meeting. Because this responsibility was not accepted at the national level and because public awareness of ethical issues in sciences generally has been mounting rapidly—apparently more rapidly than corresponding awareness in many professional groups—the Reproductive Biology Research Foundation decided to ·organize and sponsor a conference, which was held January 22–23, 1976.

Early in the planning stages, it was decided that the aims of this conference should be restricted to identifying and discussing the fundamental ethical issues in therapeutic and investigative approaches to human sexuality. It was also agreed that the participants should include responsible representatives of all the health-care sciences, theologians, philosophers, and lawyers, in an attempt to achieve the broadest possible perspective.

We had no illusions that this initial meeting could generate meaningful guidelines or rules for ethical conduct. However, we did—and continue to—believe that, once problems have been identified and the recorded discussion of them has been widely disseminated to concerned professionals and the general public, it will be possible to take the further steps necessary to formulate a cohesive and responsible set of ethical guidelines for this field. Toward this goal, a subsequent meeting of broader scope is currently planned for January, 1978.

W. H. M.
V. E. J.
R. C. K.

St. Louis

ACKNOWLEDGMENTS

Wᴇ are deeply indebted to the many individuals who participated in this endeavor in a variety of ways. Those who attended the conference generated an exciting interchange of ideas in a friendly and professional atmosphere. The thoughtful contributions of Raymond Waggoner, Emily Mudd, Fritz Redlich, and Richard Hedrich to the planning of this meeting deserve special mention.

Valuable suggestions and partial financial support were received from the National Science Foundation and the National Institute of Mental Health, under contract number 278–76–0004 (ER). The views expressed at this conference are those of the individual participants and do not represent the positions of participating federal agencies.

Able secretarial services were cheerfully provided by Wanda Bowen, Anne Bibbo, Chris Busby, and Lynn Strenkofsky throughout thousands of hours of letter-writing, transcription, and editing. Editorial work was competently assisted by Nancy Kolodny.

CONTENTS

PARTICIPANTS vii

PREFACE xiii

ACKNOWLEDGMENTS xv

1. The Historical Background of Ethical
   Considerations in Sex Research and Sex Therapy 1
   Emily Hartshorne Mudd

   DESIGNATED DISCUSSION: Paul H. Gebhard 11

   GENERAL DISCUSSION: R. Christian Johnson
   (Chairperson), Wiener, Sherfey, Mudd, Macklin, Lief,
   Schwartz, Rembar, Gebhard

2. Theological Perspectives on the Ethics of Scientific
   Investigation and Treatment of Human Sexuality 20
   Seward Hiltner

   DESIGNATED DISCUSSION: Robert Gordis 32

   DESIGNATED DISCUSSION: Jerome F. Wilkerson 38

   GENERAL DISCUSSION: Mary S. Calderone 46
   (Chairperson), Lief, Schwartz, Hiltner, Gordis, Wilkerson,
   Shultz, Johnson, Stubblefield, Rembar

xvii

3. Ethical Requirements for Sex Research in Humans:
   Informed Consent and General Principles   52
   Robert C. Kolodny

   DESIGNATED DISCUSSION: Ruth Macklin   69

   GENERAL DISCUSSION: Charles Rembar (Chairperson),   74
   R. C. Johnson, Macklin, Engelhardt, Kaplan, Gordis, Stone,
   Masters, V. E. Johnson, Shultz, Kolodny, Lief, Wiener, Money,
   Stubblefield, Schwartz, Green

4. Ethical Issues and Requirements for Sex Research
   with Humans: Confidentiality   84
   Miriam F. Kelty

   DESIGNATED DISCUSSION: Richard Green   106

   GENERAL DISCUSSION: Pepper Schwartz (Chairperson),   114
   Stone, Rembar, Lief, Kolodny, Calderone, Wiener

5. Issues and Attitudes in Research and Treatment
   of Variant Forms of Human Sexual Behavior   119
   John Money

   DESIGNATED DISCUSSION: H. Tristram Engelhardt, Jr.   132

   GENERAL DISCUSSION: Alan A. Stone (Chairperson),   137
   R. C. Johnson, Money, Kolodny, V. E. Johnson, Stone, Engelhardt,
   Gordis, Lief, Stubblefield, Katz, Darragh, Calderone

6. The Ethics of Sex Therapy   143
   Fritz Redlich

   DESIGNATED DISCUSSION: Judd Marmor   157

   DESIGNATED DISCUSSION: Jay Katz   161

   GENERAL DISCUSSION: Virginia E. Johnson   165
   (Chairperson), Rembar, Money, Kaplan, Redlich, Kolodny,
   R. C. Johnson, Green, Engelhardt, Wiener, Schwartz, Masters,
   Calderone, Laws, Marmor, Apperson, Katz, Lief, Hiltner, Stone

7. Training of Sex Therapists   182

   Helen S. Kaplan

   DESIGNATED DISCUSSION: Carl S. Shultz   189

   GENERAL DISCUSSION: Harold I. Lief (Chairperson),   193
   Biggs, Kolodny, Stubblefield, Kaplan, Schwartz, Green, Mudd,
   Marmor, Calderone, Shultz, Schumacher, Darragh,
   V. E. Johnson, Masters

8. Summary and Future Considerations   206

   William H. Masters

INDEX   221

REPRODUCTIVE BIOLOGY
RESEARCH FOUNDATION CONFERENCE

ETHICAL ISSUES IN SEX THERAPY AND RESEARCH

THE HISTORICAL BACKGROUND OF ETHICAL CONSIDERATIONS IN SEX RESEARCH AND SEX THERAPY

EMILY HARTSHORNE MUDD

Every culture prescribes for its population rules of conduct. Members of the group who deviate from the accepted regulations are subject to a variety of possible chastisements: social, moral, and legal. Exploration of the ethical issues in sex research and sex therapy in the United States implicit in this conference is timely, of great potential usefulness, and should undoubtedly be provocative.

How do we define ethical consideration? *Dorland's Medical Dictionary* states that ethics is "the science of right conduct, also the rules or principles governing the professional conduct of medical practitioners." *The American Heritage Dictionary of the English Language* defines ethics as "the study of the general nature of morals and of the specific moral choices to be made by the individual in his relationship with others."

The incidents in my professional experience that I will touch on illustrate attitudes and reactions to the moral quality of a course of action as it may interrelate with the rules or principles governing the professional conduct of practitioners. In sharing these episodes with you, I ask that you forgive me if my present sense of distance introduces humor to a subject that deserves, and indeed demands, serious and dignified consideration. I identify with Jacob Bronowski [1] when he tells us, "History is not events but people. And it is not just people remembering, it is people acting and living their past in the present" (p. 438).

REMEMBRANCES

After our marriage in 1922, I served as research assistant to my husband, Stuart Mudd, a microbiologist. While working at the Rockefeller Institute with Dr. Simon Flexner, we became friends of Margaret Sanger and her search for workable contraceptives. As a result, during part of our experimental work on cell surfaces, we attempted to develop serum to immobilize sperm from a variety of species—an attempt that, unfortunately, did not produce the hoped-for results [2]. When rumors of this research reached the administration, Dr. Flexner advised us clearly and firmly that such subject matter was not considered appropriate within the ongoing research programs of the Institute. This was our first venture counter to ethical procedure—"the rules and principles governing the professional conduct of medical practitioners."

After moving to the University of Pennsylvania School of Medicine, we served in our off-duty time on a committee of six to open Pennsylvania's first birth control clinic on the outskirts of Philadelphia in 1927. Since the drastic state obscenity laws of the time forbade the dissemination of contraceptive information, nurses were afraid to assist the physician who had volunteered to advise patients in the clinic. This fine man, Dr. Victor Janvier, was prepared for legal action and even for possible arrest. Attempting to be helpful, I found another old state law that a pregnant woman could not be incarcerated. Being very obviously pregnant at the time, I volunteered to assist our courageous physician. Suffice it to say that we both escaped arrest. Later, when interviewing at the clinic the middle-aged, poverty-stricken mothers of many unwanted children, I heard over and over "I only hope my daughter won't have to go through what I have"—a definite verbalization of changing values in spite of legal restrictions on controlling the outcome of sex relations.

The next question seemed logically to be: How can we help the daughters not to "go through" what their mothers did? This led to the initiation in 1933 of the Marriage Counsel Service "for those about to be or recently married" [3]. It emphasized prevention of unhappy marriage through education and counseling.

The next episode involving ethical conduct was at the first annual meeting of the Marriage Counsel Service. Prominent members of the board of trustees invited leaders of the community to their beautiful suburban home to hear about this new venture. An eminent professor from a recognized New England university was to bring us status, prestige, and we hoped, financial support by speaking at the dinner. Before sitting down, the hosts, a leading feminist and her illustrious lawyer-husband, asked to speak to me. We retired to a private corner. "Emily," they whispered, "this is very important. We know these people and we want them to back us. You must tell the speaker that he cannot use the word *sex* during his talk." Somewhat stunned, I argued, "But this is a meeting on marriage counseling." "You heard what we said," was the answer, "and we need money for the work." Once again ethical values made consideration of sex, even in marriage, a deterrent to community support.

My third vignette dates from a decade later. By 1947 the Marriage Counsel Service had progressed. It had more clients, more staff, and more premarital education groups, and was even beginning evaluative research. The board recommended incorporating to enhance our financial potential. The articles of incorporation were presented to the Court of Common Pleas of Philadelphia. The assistant district attorney assigned to the case sought an opinion from the Ethics Committee of the Philadelphia Bar Association, which concluded that we were using the name "counsel" illegally— only lawyers gave counsel. The name was then changed to the Marriage Council, but at this point the district attorney sought an opinion from the Committee on Ethics of the Philadelphia County Medical Society. Marriage Council was accused of being an abortion clinic, of giving information about sex, and of soliciting fees illegally. Staff, medical supervisors, and members of the board were subpoenaed and put on the witness stand; the huge record of evidence is, I suspect, still available in city hall.

Fortunately, Dr. Lewis Scheffey, then Professor of Obstetrics and

Gynecology at Jefferson Medical College, a liberal and a scholar, was president of the Philadelphia County Medical Society. He appointed a special committee of the County Medical Society, which studied the situation and reported, "There should not only be a Marriage Council in the city, there should be branches in all nearby areas." In spite of this positive rating, the Marriage Council was prevented from obtaining incorporation in Pennsylvania; it finally achieved this goal in the neighboring state of Delaware.

EVOLUTION OF SOCIAL ATTITUDES TO SEX

At this conference we must ask, "What influences produced the attitudes, convictions, and prohibitions reflected in the legal and societal reactions these incidents portray?" A brief review of the development of the American social climate in relation to sexuality seems indicated. This review moves from the puritanical concepts of the early settlers and the Victorian influence, through the revolutionary impress of Freudian psychology and the later social-psychological and behavioral theorists, to the impact of systematic research surveys on sexual activities and, more recently, the basic physiological and biological studies initiated by our hosts here in St. Louis.

The cultural milieu in the early New England settlements reflected the Calvinistic attitudes of a group of religious protestors known as the Puritans, who sailed to these shores in 1620. Scholars believe there was considerable variance at that time between the behavior that was publicly acceptable and that which was privately in vogue, but systematic exploration of the realities behind the atmosphere of the times would have been unthinkable.

Woman as the personification of sex was considered the incarnation of evil. She was presumed to have no sexual feeling. As man's property, her main function was to breed sons so that estates could be inherited. The act of adultery was considered so heinous in early New England that men as well as women were punished—in three cases by the death penalty. Modesty, decorum, and restraint were imposed as essential values, with little or no recognition of the normal biological urges of healthy, active men and women.

In the early twentieth century the advent of the Freudian psychology of sexuality as a basic force in personality undermined the rigidity of the Calvinistic, Puritan, and Victorian standards. According to Beck and Stein [4], "Freud postulated that sexuality provided the cornerstone of human personality development and that certain distortions or deviations in the sexual development predisposed to neuroses and psychoses." His concepts opened new vistas and challenged the then-accepted sexual dualism. The essays of Havelock Ellis [5] and the writings of D. H. Lawrence [6] in the early 1900s found acclaim in America and were permitted publication—a fact that attested to changing mores.

The so-called sexual revolution followed World War I and largely buried the Victorian era. By the 1920s the "Flaming Youth" depicted in the writings of Fitzgerald [7, 8] were praising sexual freedom. The relation of sexual activity to health and illness was considered in new terms. If sex as an integral part of each human being did not need to be denied, then distribution of available knowledge in this field was warranted and necessary. Thus, a new ethical approach was countenanced and educators became involved. A series of written materials resulted, some containing a combination of information, "facts of life," good sense, and good taste that kept them in circulation for several decades.

It soon became evident that knowledge of anatomical and physiological facts was only a partial step toward understanding or resolving the complexity of sexual attitudes and behavior, with their concomitant anxieties, guilts, maladjustments, and conflicts. Into this situation of personal and social ambivalence entered a few pioneering medical practitioners dedicated to systematic exploration of the sexual behavior of American men and women, single and married, and to publication of their findings. Among these early studies are those of Davis [9], Dickinson and Beam [10, 11], and Hamilton [12]. This era also introduced the informative sex manuals. These "how to do it" guides were concerned with techniques for effective, orgasmically satisfactory sex relations for husband and wife—by this period an apparently accepted ethical approach that encountered little legal interference.

Gradually, psychologists and psychiatrists began raising questions concerning the emotional aspects of sexual functioning. In the years following World War II, the importance of women's sexual response for marital happiness was emphasized. The ensuing controversy as to the type of orgasm, clitoral or vaginal, that "emotionally healthy, mature" women should experience was primarily initiated by men. The varying aspects of this "man-made" dilemma, which precipitated much unjustified conflict and unhappiness for many women, were summarized ably in 1953 by Albert Ellis [13] in his article questioning whether the vaginal orgasm is a myth.

During the next decade gradual modifications of Freud's original concepts of sexuality and personality were suggested by students of human behavior and the social order, notably Horney [14, 15], Erikson [16], and Parsons [17]. Horney questioned Freud's concepts of the origins of male and female sexuality and the importance of social factors in psychoanalysis; Erikson formulated the growth process of sexuality as concurrent with all stages in the development of the personality; and Parsons emphasized the continuing role of the common culture in the development of men and women, with obvious implications for sexual attitudes and behavior.

THE KINSEY ERA

Into this more open atmosphere entered an entomologist armed with a missionary zeal to discover and bring to "healthy daylight" systematic information on the sexual activities of men and women. Alfred Kinsey's studies of men [18] and women [19] presented basic new information on sexual behavior. Kinsey's early difficulties in being introduced to medical groups, and their reactions to his findings, seem hard to believe in light of the current prevalence of topless waitresses, "how it is done" films, and centers and weekend seminars for "sexual awareness."

I was first invited to meet Alfred Kinsey in 1945 by Dr. Robert Dickinson and Dr. Alan Gregg with a small group at the New York Academy of Medicine. After hearing him, I believed that his approach and findings were uniquely important and relayed this information to our medical associates in Philadelphia. They then organized an invitation-only meeting for physicians. There was obvious concern as to the response of the medical group to such a research program. Did it conform to medical ethics? Invitations were sent to professors whose clinical work might involve them in such matters: members of the departments of medicine, obstetrics and gynecology, pediatrics, and psychiatry at the five city medical schools. This meeting brought Dr. Kinsey into contact with individuals from professional associations, colleges, and schools who, in response to his request, volunteered to be interviewed on their sex lives. Dr. Kinsey and his staff stayed on in Philadelphia for two months, obtaining much data for his two books.

Following the wide distribution of Kinsey's books, and the myriad articles in lay journals about his work, the word *sex* became a byword from subway trains to elite dinner parties.

About the same time, 1952, Marriage Council became the operational unit of a new Division of Family Study in the Department of Psychiatry at the University of Pennsylvania.* It was our privilege "to teach medical students something of the relation of marriage problems to health and illness." So a course was to be offered to senior students. How to list it? The catalogues of all the medical schools in the United States were studied. In none did the words *sex* or *marriage* appear! The less the word *sex* was used, the more acceptable this course would be to the medical faculty. In 1952 the new elective "Family Attitudes, Sexual Behavior and Marriage Counseling" was listed. Ninety of our 110 seniors signed up [20].

Twenty years later, as you well know, Dr. Harold I. Lief, under a sizable six-year grant from the Commonwealth Fund, has cooperated with the medical schools in this country to orient medical teachers to the physiology and psychology of sexuality so that they, in turn, may orient their students [21].

Reflecting changes in mores and an obvious widespread interest in all aspects of sex and sexuality, the decade of the 1960s saw the publication of a variety of learned and less-learned books and reports dealing with male-female interrelatedness. Articles on morals in popular magazines summarized these changes and maintained

* This undertaking was implemented by generous five-year funding from the Grant Foundation, New York, New York.

that the 1960s ushered in the second sexual revolution, which sees
in sex both personal and social salvation—the last realm of freedom
in an industrialized society.

BEYOND KINSEY

Into an activated societal atmosphere in 1966 came Masters and
Johnson's carefully documented and purposely impersonal scientific
research report, *Human Sexual Response* [22]. This volume, which
pioneered and substantiated as yet unknown information on the
physiology of sex, was followed four years later by publication of the
equally striking and vitally important research, *Human Sexual
Inadequacy* [23]. The combination of the much-publicized and
-discussed process of obtaining data and the innovative knowledge
made available by these books shook any complacency remaining
on the subject of sexual ethics. Perhaps the greatest impact of the
new material was its focus on women and their sexual potential
[24].
    The 1975 publication by this outstanding team of *The Pleasure
Bond* has made much of their knowledge available to the lay public
in easily accessible form [25]. Through the use of such words as
commitment and *mutual fulfillment*, it in part placates those still-
reserved elements in the community that resent the overall impact
of sexuality. This book, in its own comforting way, seems to offer
an answer to a very pertinent question raised nearly twenty years
ago by the sociologist Nelson Foote [26]. "Why" he asked, "do
Americans have such difficulty in recognizing sex as a legitimate
form of relaxing pleasure or play?" He made an important point,
namely that "play—any kind of play—generates its own morality
and values. And the enforcement of the rules of play becomes the
concern of every player, because without their observance, the play
cannot continue." Foote pointed out that this kind of obligation
and commitment regulates a freer sexual morality in other countries, and that for the most part it was not as yet incorporated into
the transitional sexual standards in evidence in this country. "Our
rules governing sexual behavior," he added, "whether legal statutes

or informal codes, are often incongruent with human behavior, and need revision."

How can I summarize the examples and impressions of the experiences shared by me and, in varying degrees, by all participants in this seminar, of the changes in attitudes and behavior, in values and ethics, so evident in this century? As I reminisce and as I think and dream of the future, I find great comfort in the words of Jacob Bronowski [1] in his classic book, *The Ascent of Man.* "Self-knowledge," he states, "at last bringing together the experience of the arts and the exploration of science, waits ahead of us. . . . Our actions as adults, as decision makers, as human beings, are mediated by values, which I interpret as general strategies in which we balance opposing impulses. . . . We shape our conduct by finding principles to guide it. We devise ethical strategies or systems of values to ensure that what is attractive in the short term is weighed in the balance of the ultimate, long-term satisfactions" (pp. 436–437).

REFERENCES

1. Bronowski, J. *The Ascent of Man.* Boston: Little, Brown, 1973.
2. Mudd, S., and Mudd, E. B. H. The specificity of mammalian spermatozoa with special reference to electrophoresis as a means of serological differentiation. *Journal of Immunology* 17(1):39–52, 1929.
3. Mudd, E. H. Is preventive work the next step? *Birth Control Review* 16:42–43, 1932.
4. Beck, A. T., and Stein, M. Psychodynamics. In *Cyclopedia of Medicine, Surgery and Specialties.* Philadelphia: Davis, 11:422C–422K, 1961.
5. Ellis, H. *Little Essays of Love and Virtue.* Garden City, New York: Doubleday, 1930 (out of print).
6. Lawrence, D. H. *Lady Chatterley's Lover.* New York: Knopf, 1928.
7. Fitzgerald, F. S. *Six Tales of the Jazz Age.* New York: Scribner's Sons, 1922.
8. Fitzgerald, F. S. *Tender Is the Night.* New York: Scribner's Sons, 1933.
9. Davis, K. B. *Factors in the Sex Life of Twenty-Two Hundred Women.* New York: Harper & Row, 1929 (out of print).

10. Dickinson, R. L., and Beam, L. *A Thousand Marriages*. Baltimore: Williams & Wilkins, 1931 (out of print).

11. Dickinson, R. L., and Beam, L. *The Single Woman—A Medical Study in Sex Education*. Baltimore: Williams & Wilkins, 1934.

12. Hamilton, G. V. T. *A Research in Marriage*. Lear Publishers, 1948 (out of print).

13. Ellis, A. Is the Vaginal Orgasm a Myth? In M. F. DeMartius (Ed.), *Sexual Behavior and Personality Characteristics*. New York: Citadel Press, 1963.

14. Horney, K. *The Neurotic Personality of Our Times*. New York: Norton, 1937.

15. Horney, K. *New Ways in Psychoanalysis*. New York: 1939.

16. Erikson, E.H. *Childhood and Society*. New York: Norton, 1950; 2nd ed., 1963.

17. Parsons, T., Bales, R. F., and Shils, E. A. *The Superego and the Theory of Social Systems in Working Papers in the Theory of Action*. Glencoe, Illinois: Free Press, 1953. Pp. 13–28 (out of print).

18. Kinsey, A. C., Pomeroy, W. B., and Martin, C. E. *Sexual Behavior in the Human Male*. Philadelphia: Saunders, 1948.

19. Kinsey, A. C., Pomeroy, W. B., and Martin, C. E. *Sexual Behavior in the Human Female*. Philadelphia: Saunders, 1953.

20. Appel, K. E., Mudd, E. H., and Roche, P. Q. Medical school electives on family attitudes, sexual behavior, and marriage counseling. *American Journal of Psychiatry* 112(1):36–40, 1955.

21. Lief, H., and Karlin, A. (Eds.). *Sex Education in Medicine*. New York: Prentice-Hall, Spectrum, 1976.

22. Masters, W. H., and Johnson, V. E. *Human Sexual Response*. Boston: Little, Brown, 1966.

23. Masters, W. H., and Johnson, V. E. *Human Sexual Inadequacy*. Boston: Little, Brown, 1970.

24. Mudd, E. H. Changing Attitudes Toward Sexual Mores and Behavior: Their Effect on Premarital and Marital Counseling. In D. W. Abse, E. M. Nash, and L. M. R. Louden (Eds.), *Marital and Sexual Counseling in Medical Practice*. New York: Harper & Row, 1974. Pp. 513–533.

25. Masters, W. H., and Johnson, V. E. (in association with R. J. Levin). *The Pleasure Bond*. Boston: Little, Brown, 1975.

26. Foote, N. N. Sex as Play. In E. Larrabee and R. Meyerson (Eds.), *Mass Leisure*. Glencoe, Illinois: Free Press, 1958. Pp. 335–340.

DESIGNATED DISCUSSION

PAUL H. GEBHARD

While it will surprise no one to learn that ethical considerations were prime concerns of Kinsey and of the Institute for Sex Research he subsequently founded, few people know that the genesis of the Kinsey research was an ethical struggle between science and social tradition. Scientists with a strong sense of responsibility, such as Robert Yerkes, Alan Gregg, and George Corner, felt that science could no longer avoid the obligation to study human sexuality and, with this as one of their goals, helped establish in 1922 the National Research Council Committee for Research in Problems of Sex. This goal conflicted with social tradition, which held sex a taboo subject. Corner [1] describes the situation nicely: "Because of this long-standing aversion in our culture to the open consideration of sex matters, sexual conduct was viewed only in reference to established codes, not as a natural phenomenon suitable to be studied with the same detachment as digestion, muscular activity, or nerve function."

The struggle impeded and in some cases aborted early research efforts, even those supported by the Committee. For example, Roger Lee surveyed Harvard medical students about their sexual lives, but the university felt that the results should not be published. Adolf Meyer did a similar survey of students at Johns Hopkins and, despite the fact that he was one of the proponents of sex research, decided not to make his findings known lest they damage sexual morality. Consequently, when Kinsey appeared on the scene with a substantial number of case histories and an obvious desire to publish, the Committee welcomed him, especially since he shared their belief that research was imperative if one was to ameliorate social and individual sexual problems. In brief, he, like they, felt this to be an ethical obligation.

While this sex research arose from high moral and ethical motivation, subsequent ethical considerations generally presented themselves in the guise of problems.

First, who was qualified to do sex research and promulgate the findings? A dean of the Indiana University Medical School strongly expressed his opinion that such research should be in the hands of physicians. The local Ministerial Association also expressed concern over the "moral and social implications" of sex education provided by scientists rather than clergy. Almost 40 years later we are still wrestling with this problem.

A continuing ethical consideration was the effect on impressionable youth of being interviewed or taught by us, or of reading our publications. A physician sex educator, Thurman Rice, at the beginning warned Kinsey that he would sexually stimulate the young with his unnecessarily explicit questions and statements, that they would consequently fall into evil sexual habits, and that when the state legislature learned of the damage, not only Kinsey but the entire university would be punished. Years later, after the publication of the Institute's first two volumes, the same basically ethical complaint was loudly voiced by prominent persons. Reinhold Niebuhr [2] spoke of Kinsey's "moral anarchism, and the vulgar quality of his hedonism." Millicent McIntosh [3], President of Barnard College, wrote, "I am concerned about the effect of the Kinsey Reports on young men and women of high school and college age . . . no one in his wildest dreams would say that they provided constructive reading for the boy or girl of sixteen." Billy Graham [4] added, "It is impossible to estimate the damage this book will do to the already deteriorating morals of America."

In our present times, when nearly every campus has its committee for the protection of human subjects and the matter of informed consent is paramount, it is interesting to look back over the decades and see that this ethical matter of consent resulted in one of Kinsey's few defeats, ironically administered by his friend and supporter, Herman B. Wells, President of Indiana University. Wells gave Kinsey the choice of continuing a sex-education course Kinsey had formulated and giving up his research interviewing, or pursuing the research and giving up the course. Wells was acutely aware that when a professor asks students in his course if they would like to volunteer as research subjects, there is unavoidably an element of duress. Kinsey abandoned the course—which, deprived of his leadership, soon died.

Aside from such historical instances of how ethics were interwoven with the beginning and development of the Institute, there have always been several ethical considerations that do, or could, plague us. Despite our general policy of complete honesty, one problem involves the deception of subjects. In order to obtain cooperation and maintain rapport, one must empathize rather than conflict with one's subjects. To pretend overtly to share a subject's values and interests would be a hypocrisy contrary to our research ethics. On the other hand, a truly objective scientific approach would be so cold as to repel some people, and if carried to extremes would become absurd (for example, "We make no value judgments about rape."). Our solution to this dilemma consists of avoiding judgmental statements, making seemingly supportive ambiguous remarks, and expressing an interest in and sympathy with the respondent. The subject almost invariably assumes we share his or her attitudes and values, although we never say so. While one can call this efficient interviewing and good public relations, an objective scientist must also label it deception. We feel it is warranted as a necessary adaptation to human diversity.

A second ethical problem involves the absence of informed consent, as well as the element of deception that frequently characterizes participant observation. For example, the habitués of a homosexual bath are not asked whether they consent to be scrutinized by a researcher masquerading as another gay individual. The opponents of sex education listening to a fervid harangue by a member of the John Birch Society would not have consented to our presence, let alone talked with us freely, had we revealed ourselves.

A third and extremely important ethical matter centers on confidentiality. We have always insisted on maintaining confidentiality, even at the cost of thereby becoming amoral at best and criminal at worst. Examples of amorality are our refusal to inform a wife that her husband has just confessed to us he has an active venereal disease, and our refusal to tell parents that their child is involved in seriously deviant behavior. An example of criminality is our refusal to cooperate with authorities in apprehending a pedophile we had interviewed who was being sought for a sex murder. Nevertheless, without an ironclad guarantee of confidentiality we would never have been entrusted with the vital information ordinarily denied researchers who cannot make such a guarantee.

Lastly, there is the inescapable quagmire representing a mixture of ethics and law. The sex researcher is in an awkward and potentially dangerous situation. If he learns of a felony and does not report it, he is an accessory after the fact. If he knows that a felony (for example, adultery or homosexual activity) is to be committed and neither reports nor tries to prevent it, he is an accessory before the fact. If he is physically present when the felony occurs, he could be charged as an accomplice. The sex researcher does not enjoy privileged communication rights, as does the attorney or priest, and his records as well as his memory are subject to subpoena. The question remains: Does one owe one's primary ethical obligation to one's subjects or to the statutory law? Considering the nature of the majority of laws dealing with sex, we find this question easy to answer.

In summary, sex therapy and sex research exist in a matrix of ethical considerations, which, like all man-made things, change according to circumstances and with time. The researcher cannot escape the task of deciding which ethic will be honored and which sacrificed in the process. Each researcher must establish his or her own ethical hierarchy and decide as problems present themselves whether the ultimate good resulting from the research or therapy supersedes a particular ethic.

REFERENCES

1. Aberle, S., and Corner, G. *Twenty-Five Years of Sex Research.* Philadelphia: Saunders, 1953. P. 2.
2. Niebuhr, R. Kinsey and the Moral Problem of Man's Sexual Life. In D. Geddes (Ed.), *An Analysis of the Kinsey Reports on Sexual Behavior in the Human Male and Female.* New York: Dutton, 1954. P. 67.
3. McIntosh, M. I am Concerned . . . In D. Geddes (Ed.), *An Analysis of the Kinsey Reports on Sexual Behavior in the Human Male and Female.* New York: Dutton, 1954. P. 139.

4. Graham, B. The Bible and Dr. Kinsey. In E. Daniels (Ed.), *I Accuse Kinsey*. Orlando, Florida: Christ for the World Publishers, 1954. P. 103.

GENERAL DISCUSSION

R. CHRISTIAN JOHNSON: As both Drs. Mudd and Gebhard have suggested, the ethics of sex research involve three crucial elements: professionalism, confidentiality, and consent. These elements developed historically and did not spring up overnight. To understand the ethics of sex research at the present time, we might first turn to the development of "professionalism." We may define a professional as one who can be truly involved with the confidentiality of the relationship with his or her clients. Only a professional would have the presumed expertise necessary to inform his clients about the elements of therapy or a given research project so that the client would be able to give informed consent either to receive therapy or to participate in such a project. Historical inquiry is very helpful here because we are concerned with matters of policy—policy that is conceived at one time, implemented at another time, matures at still a further time, and, as we all too often discover, becomes obsolete. In order to discover the rationale for or basis of a policy, we almost have to go back into the past and see if we cannot understand the policy in terms of those who first conceived it. In our session this morning, we are fortunate to have several people who participated in the early professionalization of sex research, who themselves have been intimately concerned with the problems of the profession and also with the very practical problems of ensuring the professional treatment of both the client for therapy and the subject of sex research.

JACK WIENER: I wonder, Dr. Gebhard, if you could tell us if you or the Institute have actually been involved in any legal suits or legal cases?

PAUL H. GEBHARD: We have had a number of threatening situations. The only one that really became acute was one case in which the prosecution in a homosexual sadomasochism case in California insisted that I appear, and I was handed a subpoena. When I refused to appear, they put out a bench warrant for my arrest, but I returned to Indiana and told them they would have a hard time extraditing me and made it so difficult that they finally decided they would let the warrant drop. But that's the closest we've come. We did, however, write in a little unspoken contract in our research code to the effect that if any of us were in jail on contempt of court, our salaries would still be paid.

MARY JANE SHERFEY: I would like to ask Dr. Mudd why she thinks that review committees don't function appropriately.

EMILY HARTSHORNE MUDD: I guess I've just been exposed to that situation in some of my professional associations; this probably is not the place or the time to go into more specific details. One of the things that I have experienced, however, is that when a member of an accredited professional association has overstepped what are considered the ethical boundaries of that association, many very difficult options present themselves. Very often the situation is not followed up in accordance with the existing carefully devised written statement of the committee on ethics.

RUTH MACKLIN: I have a question for Dr. Gebhard. You gave two examples in discussing confidentiality, not telling the wife that her husband has a venereal disease and not telling parents that their child engages in some deviant behavior. There is a considerable difference between the two, and in any discussion of confidentiality, in medicine generally or in psychiatry, questions are raised about when it is justifiable to break confidentiality. My moral intuition would suggest that if considerable harm might come to an individual, such as the wife, perhaps the breaking of confidentiality is justified.

PAUL H. GEBHARD: In the early days, we went around and around on this issue, and we finally came up with this truly ironclad rule:

We would keep confidentiality even if life itself were at issue. We simply would not break confidentiality for any reason whatsoever. So, in many ways, we are rather amoral, but we simply set ourselves to one side and say, "We are scientists and observers, and we are not willing to get involved in this thing one way or another."

HAROLD I. LIEF: Dr. Gebhard, you know that there are special ethical considerations in the cases of certain groups, such as prisoners or children, where informed consent is questionable itself. I know that your group interviewed prisoners. I don't think there were any children involved in those early studies, but interviewing of children is an issue now even if it wasn't then. I wonder whether you would comment on that.

PAUL H. GEBHARD: I think you mean the element of duress in interviewing prisoners.

HAROLD I. LIEF: No, I mean the situation itself. You may get informed consent, but the very atmosphere might produce subtle pressures. You mentioned, for example, the issue of students in a class who might be seeking favor with the professor by volunteering to be interviewed.

PAUL H. GEBHARD: Yes, there is an element of duress if you're working in prison because they know that this matter might be subsequently brought up with the parole board and thus want to appear cooperative. The prisoners themselves, however, weren't disturbed by this ethical consideration; they just said they didn't feel under any great duress, they'd just go along, and they'd tell whatever they felt like. But prisoners want their parole boards to think of them as cooperative inmates, and that is the pervasive element of duress. The inmates did not seem disturbed by the ethics of an interview. So, since they didn't feel threatened by it, they didn't feel they necessarily had to reveal themselves or tell the truth. Our problem was not getting access to them, but getting the truth out of them and persuading them that we were alright to talk to. This, then, is the situation (going back to the previous question) in which confidentiality must be maintained.

When we began first interviewing prisoners in the California system, the prisoners checked us out; thank heavens, their test hit Pomeroy and not me. After one of the first interviews Pomeroy conducted, the inmate reached into his jacket and pulled out a file which had been turned into a ten-inch knife. The man announced that he was going to kill another inmate, whom he named and who was notorious for not paying his gambling debts. After having brandished this file, the interviewee put it back in his coat and left. Pomeroy realized that if he told the authorities, we would have no chance to get truthful interviews in the prison system, and yet if he didn't tell them, someone might get stabbed. We decided that the man might get stabbed anyway, probably for not paying his gambling debts, and that it was not up to us to tell anyone. So we didn't. We kept perfectly quiet. It turned out subsequently that it was purely a test, and that they were just waiting to see if the cell of the man with the file would be shaken down that night, or whether the intended victim would be removed from his cell block and put somewhere else. Had that occurred, we would never have gotten another prison history. There was a case where, in order to facilitate the research, we had to literally gamble with someone's life.

PEPPER SCHWARTZ: There is often a trade-off between one's humanistic concerns and the arrogance of scientists, that is, that we above all know what the greater good is in relative terms, that we can assume that our own research findings will justify consequences for the informant or for the public's right to know. It seems to me that this is a delicate balance, especially when we adhere to the rule of confidentiality above all.

CHARLES REMBAR: Dr. Gebhard shocked me with what seems to me to be an oversimplification of confidentiality. I know a bit about this because lawyers deal with rules, and one of the things every lawyer finds out about rules is that they must have exceptions. If not, they are simply inhuman abstractions and you wind up with the church of the Inquisition, the theocracy of the Massachusetts Bay Colony, or the imperviousness of the American Stalinists of the 1930s. I would suggest that, while confidentiality is terribly important, there simply have to be exceptions. Take the lawyer's case, since the lawyer-client relationship is the confidential relationship on which most others are modeled. A man comes to your office and says, "I want some legal advice. I'm about to murder my wife, and I want to know: (a) how many years I'll get, and (b) is it possible to get off altogether?" What's a lawyer to do then? He should call the cops; it's not going to destroy the social value of the ordinary use of privilege and confidentiality to make exceptions in cases like that.

PAUL H. GEBHARD: I've been thinking over some of these remarks. My position basically is that one owes one's allegiance to science, or one owes one's allegiance to the society in which one happens to live. Perhaps my attitude is fashioned by my training as an anthropologist, and as such I don't owe allegiance to any one society. If I went into the field as an anthropologist and I discovered that the tribe I was investigating practiced headhunting, I would not say, "Hey, that's murder, and you have to stop it." I would not go to the neighboring village and say "Look out, that tribe is after your heads." I would not call the authorities and ask them to send in a gunboat and watch these people. Instead, I would sit back and count the heads as they came in. In many ways, although that's a simplistic analogy, that's the way I look on my role in my own society. I just see what's going on.

2

THEOLOGICAL PERSPECTIVES ON THE ETHICS OF SCIENTIFIC INVESTIGATION AND TREATMENT OF HUMAN SEXUALITY

SEWARD HILTNER

The planners of this conference, in their invitation to me, posed four leading questions. Although they did not intend these necessarily to serve as a structure for my discussion, I have found them sufficiently discriminating to be used in that way; however, I have made one change in the order of their presentation. Those four questions, restated in my own way, are as follows:

1. What is meant by ethics when considered from theological perspectives?
2. In what ways, if at all, do theological perspectives on human sexuality agree with one another; and what points of difference are found among them?
3. What position or positions are taken or implied about the scientific study of human sexuality by theologically based sex ethics?
4. What specific issues are raised by sex therapy or sex research from the point of view of theologically based sex ethics?

Recently the Vatican, through its Congregation for the Doctrine of the Faith, and with the reported personal approval of the pope, issued a brief but comprehensive statement on human sex ethics [1]. Since the statement represents the official view of the largest body of Christians in the world, and since Christians are at least nominally the largest body of religious adherents in our nation and indeed in the West, this recent position paper provides a convenient starting-point for discussing each of the four questions. It should be noted at the outset, however, that the Vatican views on specific issues, and the theological and ethical principles and assumptions underlying them, are by no means necessarily shared by all Roman Catholics, or Catholic theologians and ethicists today, to say nothing of Christians other than Roman Catholics, or Jews, or theologians from other so-called universal religions of the world.

ETHICS FROM THEOLOGICAL PERSPECTIVES

Beginning with the Vatican statement, we may note first that, although it uses the term *sexual ethics* on two occasions, the central concern is set within the framework of morals and morality rather than of ethics. Although *ethics* as a term may be used to suggest norms of conduct, it may also connote a disinterested study of possible norms without necessarily adopting a prescriptive position. By speaking of morality, the statement obviously makes no concession to such a possible interpretation of ethics. Actually, the preferential use of *ethics* over *morality* today in intellectual circles is mainly an indirect result of the critique by Protestant forms of Christianity, at the time of the Reformation and afterward, of what was believed to be the excessive legalism of the Roman Catholic moral theology of that time. If one looks today in the card catalogue of a Protestant theological library for the category of "moral theology," he will find himself referred to the Roman Catholic literature; whereas the categories of ethics or Christian ethics will be spelled out in dozens of headings and subheadings. Those of us who do not begin where the Vatican does, therefore, should note that our preferential use of *ethics* over *morality* or *morals* may itself represent an implicit position differing from that of the Vatican.

Historically speaking, Christian ethics or Christian morality took its initial form from the encounter of the Jewish and the Hellenistic or Greek elements that were represented in its membership. In a broad sense the Greek side assumed ethics to be the search for the good, while the Jews saw the guideposts for their living in the covenant that a living God had made with them. Except in the hands of masters like Plato, the abstraction of the Greek view often led to elitism, to a denigration of the body, and to both asceticism and libertinism. The more concrete and dynamic Jewish view, except when it was crystallized into legalism, regarded the body as standard and indispensable equipment and found asceticism and libertinism equally alien. The inherent tension between these approaches has caused one or the other (usually the Hellenistic) to take precedence in Christian history; seldom if ever has there been a merger doing justice to the separate ingredients. It has usually been the Jewish side that has been neglected.

If we ask what ethics or morality has meant in traditions other than the Jewish or Christian, we are struck first by a very wide range of differences in the norms of conduct. With the important exception of Islam, however, it appears that the morals or ethics of the other universal religions, noble as they are, tend to be characterized by two levels, one for the elite and the other for the common people. Thus, a particular faith may advocate celibacy or detachment for a few and sex activity, although not libertinism, for the many. The philosophical basis for such apparently contradictory views ordinarily rests in a conviction that the world of existence in general and the body in particular are, so to speak, temporary human equipment, but not part of essential and continuing reality. In such contexts, ethics or morals guide conduct according to the levels of aspiration of the persons involved. Such a view of ethics is close to the Greek side of Christian ethics but is alien to the Jewish side.

AGREEMENT AND DIFFERENCE IN THEOLOGICAL VIEWS OF HUMAN SEXUALITY

The recent Vatican statement is based on the articulated premise that what is moral or immoral in the realm of human sexuality is given in "the moral law," and that the moral law is "the natural law" and has "an absolute and immutable value," implying and partly alleging that the church has indisputable knowledge of that natural law. Before we bring out the arguments against any ethics based on natural-law theory, it seems wise to be reminded of the potential power of that claim. Kinsey found, for example, that relatively well-educated men considered certain sexual activities by applying the standard of right and wrong [2]. Relatively uneducated men, in contrast, appraised the same activities according to their being natural or unnatural; hence, if the activities were believed to be natural, they found no need to apply criteria of right or wrong; if the activities were believed unnatural, they were not in effect tempted by them. Since *morals* as a term is derived from *mores*, in the original sense of customs, the criterion of what is and is not done is a deeper, more primitive, and more effective guide to conduct than the standard of right and wrong. The latter implies some conscious weighing of alternatives, while the former filters out the taboo behavior before it is seriously contemplated as a possible course of conduct. Even though many Catholic theologians do not base their ethics, sexual or otherwise, on the principle of natural law, it seems probable that the framers of the recent Vatican statement are aware of the possible threat to the influence of the church if alternatives to natural-law teaching are explicitly recognized.

The content of the Vatican statement appears, at first glance, to be just what might be expected. There is a general viewing with alarm. There is held to be a "corruption of morals" and an "unbridled exaltation of sex." We are not surprised at the assertion that the church, in its "teachings" and "moral criteria," has always stood against such tendencies. Our historical realism is, however, stretched by the allegation that what the church has taught has, in "modes of living," been "hitherto faithfully preserved."

The statement's discussion of marriage next is also expected, as is the focus on reserving sexual activity until after the marriage ceremony, on the part even of engaged couples. Although the Bible is referred to at other points in the document, its omission at this point is noticeable; for in the Old Testament, which is regarded as part of the sacred writings of Christianity, there are no prohibitions on this matter, since the view of what constitutes a marriage differs in part both from Catholic teaching and from the modern view within the law [3]. The transition from the marriage reference to other forms of sexual activity is provided by the sweeping statement that "every genital act must be within the framework of marriage."

From there, homosexual activity can be universally judged negatively; the Bible is cited here because its sole and few references to homosexuality involve acts, not orientation, and such reference does not allow for ambiguity as in the case of premarital sex relations between engaged couples [4]. The importance of the natural-law criterion is apparent in that the ultimate reason for a negative view of homosexual acts is that they are "intrinsically disordered" and "lack an essential and indispensable finality." "Finality" refers, of course, to a procreative intent in heterosexual activity.

Six paragraphs are then devoted to masturbation. Such activity is "an intrinsically and seriously disordered act," so that the most basic reason for appraising it negatively is also the natural-law character of the moral law. We need to recall that, in some previous periods of Catholic history, masturbation was almost the sole viable temptation for many of the faithful; and it was, therefore, more explicitly inveighed against than any other type of possible sexual activity. In today's climate, no doubt the framers of the present statement reasoned that an omission of reference to masturbation would be construed as approval; hence the present statement points the finger of blame at this "solitary pleasure" from which "loving communion" is absent, and which is finally wrong because it is "seriously disordered."

The Vatican statement does acknowledge some findings about human sexuality from modern scientific sources—for instance, that some masturbation may be compulsive and that at least some persons with a homosexual orientation may have little or no complicity in their orientation. Limited and concessive as these remarks are, their significance should not be underestimated.

Is there any sense in which the Jewish view of sexuality, Protestant views, or views of Roman Catholics that differ in many ways from those of the Vatican statement, can be said to accept anything in the Vatican view? Except for some small right-wing groups of Protestants, which take a natural-law view but call it something else and claim its ancestry in the Bible, there is a divergence at most basic points. A point of agreement would be, however, that sexuality in human life is a serious matter from at least three perspectives: the personal, the interpersonal and social, and in the context of God's intent for human beings. "Serious" does not, of course, have to mean solemnity without joy. But if any culture or time period treats sexuality reductionistically as casual, as divorced entirely from the allegedly real values of human life, as a kind of humorous mistake or joke on the part of the Creator, or as merely incidental to the human sense of identity, there might be agreement among the various groups that the meaning of human sexuality is being distorted.

In addition, we must note that some segments of Protestant theological opinion would agree with the Vatican references to the orders of creation, with a similar result, for example, in appraising homosexual acts negatively because such acts and the relationships that produce them do not serve purposes of completion in the sense that heterosexual acts, undertaken in love and commitment, are believed to do. Such is the position, for example, of both Karl Barth and Emil Brunner, and partly, though in a much more qualified way, of Helmut Thielicke [5–7]. Other Protestants, like myself, reject such reasoning, holding that a theological understanding of creation as continuing and in process exposes a preoccupation with the "orders of creation" as a backhanded version of natural-law theology.

Subject to correction by Jewish scholars, I suggest that the whole tone and approach of Judaism differs from that of the Vatican by first giving a positive appraisal of sexuality in human life, and only then specifying the conditions that will prevent the realization of the positive values. To modern as to ancient Jews, a human being is not conceivable without being body. A human being is an animated body. There is no essence of human being from which body is dispensable or detachable. God himself, who should even be nameless on human lips, works toward his benevolent ends through things of the common life, of which sexuality is one significant dimension. Sexuality is no divine concession to human weakness. It is an intrinsic part of God's creative intent.

Modern biblical scholarship tends to suggest that the absence of references to masturbation in the Old Testament means that it was regarded indulgently as an aspect of child development, although

clear proof is not possible. The few biblical references to homosexuality are all negative judgments of homosexual acts. Homosexual behavior is known to have been relatively widespread among
the groups surrounding the ancient Jews, and it is unlikely that it
was absent from Jewish life. To theologians like myself, however,
biblical statements about homsexual acts, plainly made without
understanding of the meaning of a homosexual orientation, are not
normative in their details. An increasing number of Protestants
hold a view similar to mine; so also do a number of Jewish and
Roman Catholic scholars.

If we examine the range of views about human sexuality held by
contemporary Protestants, we find a curious anomaly. Holding
ourselves to be guided primarily by the Bible, or by Jesus Christ as
revealed in the Bible, we Protestants have nevertheless, at various
times and places, been somewhat less than faithful to the primarily
positive (and Jewish) view of human sexuality set forth in the Old
Testament and also, in some surprising ways, in the New Testament. Thus, the reasoning may be different from that of the Vatican, but many of the conclusions about behavior may be the same.
A primary variation with regard to conduct is now the appraisal
of masturbation. About homosexuality the dominant position concerning conduct is almost the same. The clear variations in related
areas like contraception, abortion, and divorce are all of quite
recent origin and probably reflect more the greater permeability of
Protestantism by the prevailing culture than anything else, although
the greater readiness of Protestant theologians to reconsider previous positions ought not to be left out of account. On all such
points, however, recent reflection by particular Catholic theologians
is quite similar to that of Protestants.

THEOLOGICAL VIEWS OF SCIENTIFIC APPROACHES TO HUMAN SEXUALITY

Whatever the final verdict of future historians on the ambiguous
role that religious institutions of the West have played in the development of modern science and the institutions that have culti-
vated it, it seems clear that the churches' suspicions about the scientific enterprise have been directly proportional to the degree to

which either the subject of study or the method of study has been felt to threaten, at least potentially, what Gordon W. Allport called the *proprium* in an effort to find a more neutral term than *the responsible self* [8]. In most of these suspicions, as Freud noted, the culture as well as the churches has participated. His illustrations were Galileo, Darwin, and his own discoveries about the so-called unconscious [9]. It has always seemed to me no accident that the development of science has been, so far as the proprium is concerned, from the far toward the near. As an independent discipline, we know that psychology is less than a century old. And there is a sense in which those disciplines, such as the modern study of sexuality, that move back and forth between what is close to the proprium and what is at some distance, have had to develop after the proprium itself has been closely approached. A psychologically informed sexology usable by gynecologists, urologists, and marriage counselors could apparently appear only after there appeared both a Freud and a Kinsey.

With rare exceptions, the older types of quarrels of a general nature between the institutions or views of religion and of science have disappeared, along with the need to show them as not incompatible. We ought not, furthermore, to see the new quarrels—about ecology, human experimentation, and the like—as between religions on the one side and science and technology on the other, for the need to safeguard the uses made of scientific findings, or the ways in which such findings are explored with minimum detriment to human life and values, are as much a concern of responsible scientists as of theologians and other persons of ethical sensitivity.

In another place I have tried to trace the response of the churches, through their theologians and ethical leaders, to the work of Kinsey from the late 1940s until the 1970s [10]. Kinsey's actual findings about white American sexual behavior were in themselves no closer to the proprium than were Galileo's findings about the place of the earth in relation to the sun. With far too few exceptions, however, including Protestants and Jews, church leaders and thinkers were either negative or silent about even the most important of the findings. Most of the leaders who did speak made little or no effort to distinguish the actual Kinsey findings from the implications about attitude and conduct that Kinsey, at least half unwittingly, seemed to attach to them.

If any lesson can be learned from the reception of the Kinsey materials, it would seem to be: Take care about the context in which findings are presented. If a scientist or researcher wants his or her findings to be assimilated, it seems neither necessary nor desirable to conceal the implications the scientist as a person draws on the basis both of the findings and of other experiences with the subject matter; but it ought not to be too difficult to make a separation between the two. Nevertheless, the fact is that studies involving human sexuality, if they are honest and penetrating, are likely to find some predetermined enemies, in or out of the churches, if any of their findings run counter to underlying views and convictions.

In our day one of the principal indices of social attitudes toward particular areas of research is the relative availability of funding sources; and such sources increasingly involve tax funds. One of the recommendations of the Health, Education, and Welfare (HEW) Task Force on Homosexuality that worked in the late 1960s was for the creation of an Institute for the Study of Human Sexuality within the National Institutes of Health. So far as I know, that recommendation has never been formally considered. Over and above what the neglect suggests about cultural attitudes toward sex research, there have been, of course, complications of a political kind. My own view is that the attitude of the culture, as well as of the churches, toward creating such an institute would be considerably more favorable today than it was in 1970, although any Gallup-type poll today would show only a minority voting for it even if economic and political factors were set aside. I would attribute the gain to a recognition by a growing number of people that sex research might help alleviate sex problems that, even if acknowledged only privately, they believe they may have. Although church opinion may be as divided as that of the general population, I would see a growing number of theologians welcoming such moves.

SPECIFIC ISSUES IN SEX THERAPY AND RESEARCH FROM THEOLOGICAL PERSPECTIVES

When I examine the recent Vatican statement from the point of view of its implications for sex therapy and sex research in particular areas, I am surprised by how little it seems to ban, provided the therapists or researchers are competent and responsible and not out to shock some establishment. Studying the behavior and attitudes of homosexual persons would not seem to be barred so long as degrees of homosexual orientation are taken into account, orientation is not automatically related to behavior, and the personal convictions of the researcher about social attitudes toward homosexual persons and homosexual communities are separated from the findings even of studies focusing on just those areas. Barred would be any active bringing together of homosexual persons in sexual relationships for purposes of the study.

There could also be studies of sexual behavior before marriage in the sense of ceremony or law. If the study promoted or encouraged sex behavior that would otherwise not take place, it would be criticized, of course. That would also be the result if the findings were set against some superficial norm like "later marital happiness," if the latter were appraised only by question-and-answer confined to subjective feelings. It is even possible that significant studies might be done on masturbation without arousing Vatican ire, although this is less likely.

In my judgment, the principal event that has already altered many theological attitudes favorably and will alter many more in the future is the linkage of sex research with competent sex therapy. The idea that research leading to therapeutic procedures can alleviate or cure many types of sexual disorders and frustrations has a powerful appeal. It is probable that the exploitation of this appeal by incompetent and irresponsible people retards general public approval of sex research and therapy. Running in the other direction, however, is the recognition by a growing number of people that they have settled for too little in the realm of sex, and thus their consequent interest in receiving guidance and help.

To the best of my knowledge, no Western approach to ethics based on theology has asked whether ethical concern is involved in taking the specific measures needed to make sex life fulfilling, even in marriage. Particularly when marriage is addressed, however, the basic principles upon which that question may be answered affirmatively are present. Even the Vatican statement, for instance, talks of affection as well as love, something that would have been unthinkable a century ago. The concern of many churches for marriage counseling; preparation for marriage, including its sexual dimensions; and a constructive sex education for persons at various stages of development, all indicate not only that the churches need not be impeded by their own convictions from approving sex research and therapy, but also that at least some of them, in some ways, are likely to see positive ethical or moral merit in such research and therapy.

There is another level, however, at which sex therapy and research related to it require consideration. What are the criteria for appraising movement in a therapeutic direction? In medicine, including psychiatry, these standards take seriously the subjective experience of the person, but many other factors are also included. Not all subjective desires of the person may be met if therapeutic gain is to be realized. Putting together the complex factors required for a proper criterion is seldom easy, and it is plainly difficult in dealing with matters like sex. Especially when many of the problems have been accentuated by cultural attitudes of inhibition, even in marriage, there is a temptation to regard liberation or freedom as an automatic and unqualified good. Increase in freedom is indeed a good, but it is always accompanied, as Reinhold Niebuhr demonstrated, by an increased capacity for producing more bad as well as good results [11]. A therapist cannot prevent the person he has helped from robbing a bank or committing rape. But his therapy may properly include helping his patient to anticipate the consequences of his decisions in a state of greater liberation. Competent theologians are likely to be attentive to factors of this kind in the work of sex therapists of the present and future.

As to who deserves therapy, and what the therapy should consist of, competent therapists should, in my opinion, stick to their guns and give help wherever they believe it is needed. Only a little more than a generation ago, soon after the repeal of the Prohibition Amendment, large numbers of Protestants believed that therapy for alcoholics was a threat to their views on the use of alcoholic beverages. With minor exceptions, nearly all Protestant groups now support therapy for alcoholics. As to therapy for homosexual persons who seek it, for instance, even the Vatican statement is cautiously in favor of that, although qualifying it in a way that may not always accord with the facts about the development of some degree of homosexual orientation. In the longer run, responsible sex therapy is likely to win both public and church support, even though courage may be required in the interim period.

As the studies of Masters and Johnson have been reported, I have made only one public criticism of their past procedures, relating to their use for a time of a small number of surrogate partners. The grounds of my criticism were prudential rather than in terms of basic principle. I feared that the church and general public might react so negatively to this procedure that they would ignore everything else—a fear that has fortunately not materialized. As the therapeutic approach to human sexuality gains increasing public support, I predict that even this kind of procedure, when properly safeguarded, may be less criticized on moral grounds, although it is unlikely to receive approbation.

Some aspects of sex research and therapy are bound to elicit ambivalent social attitudes—for example, studies of the female orgasm. It should be noted, however, that there is similar ambivalence toward some aspects of what has become standard medical practice, an illustration of which would be the procedures taken to help a married woman become pregnant. In such cases, the moral conviction that such a woman should receive the help she desires takes precedence over any reservations that may be felt about some of the procedures used to that end; and what happens is that discussion of the latter gradually drops out of sight.

Up to this point I have discussed church attitudes as actual or potential antagonisms to sex research or therapy, and that dimension cannot be ignored in terms either of principle or of prudence. But it may be even more important to draw theologians into research and therapeutic endeavors, partly for their inherent potential contributions and partly because they can interpret procedures and findings to their constituencies as outsiders cannot do. There are now theologians in every one of our traditions who are equipped to engage in such collaboration. They should not, of course, be required to shed their ethical and theological values at the door of the laboratory or consulting room, and they should be chosen for their competence and not for their readiness to become captive to the projects of which they are a part. A few such persons can, I am convinced, do much to advance the cause of needed sex research and therapy.

REFERENCES

1. *The New York Times*, January 16, 1976 (translated by the Vatican from the original Latin).
2. Kinsey, A. C., Pomeroy, W. B., and Martin, C. E. *Sexual Behavior in the Human Male.* Philadelphia: Saunders, 1949.
3. Piper, O. *The Christian Interpretation of Sex.* New York: Scribner's Sons, 1941.
4. Bailey, D. S. *Homosexuality and the Western Christian Tradition.* New York: Longmans, Green, 1955.
5. Barth, K. *Church Dogmatics,* Vol. 3. Edinburgh, Scotland: T. and T. Clark, 1951. P. 4.
6. Brunner, E. *The Divine Imperative.* Philadelphia: Westminster Press, 1937.
7. Thielicke, H. *The Ethics of Sex.* New York: Harper & Row, 1964.
8. Allport, G. W. *Becoming.* New Haven: Yale University Press, 1955.
9. Freud, S. *A General Introduction to Psychoanalysis* (revised ed.). New York: Simon & Schuster, Pocket Books, 1969.
10. Hiltner, S. Kinsey and the church—after twenty years. *Journal of Sex Research* 8:194–206, 1972.
11. Niebuhr, R. *The Nature and Destiny of Man,* Vol. 1. New York: Scribner's Sons, 1941.

DESIGNATED DISCUSSION

ROBERT GORDIS

I am very sympathetic to Dr. Hiltner's hesitations with regard to utilizing natural law for dealing with the contemporary issues of sexual morality and sex research. As I have pointed out elsewhere [1], the natural-law doctrine has historically been utilized to support old ideas from the past rather than to stimulate new attitudes in the present. By and large, natural law has tended toward a static concept of human nature. This is due largely to the limited perspective of its proponents, due to their ignoring the Hebraic component in the emergence of natural law. If reinterpreted properly and understood, natural law might well prove to be a useful—indeed an indispensable—concept. In brief, I believe that natural law needs only to be rescued from its friends in order to win over its foes.

I am also grateful to Dr. Hiltner for his recognition of the dynamic versus the essentially static concept of human nature, of the Judaic as against the Hellenistic principle, both of which have entered into classic Christianity and have been struggling for mastery ever since. Several years ago, in a paper called "The Rejudaisation of Christianity," I pointed to the growing tendency in Roman Catholic, Protestant, and even Greek Orthodox thought to emphasize the Hebraic contribution to the Christian outlook in many areas of theological concern [2]. I regard Dr. Hiltner's stimulating paper today as part of the same process of rediscovery.

It is in no sectarian spirit that I plan to discuss some insights of the Jewish tradition. I believe that they can be useful to Christian thought as well as to the modern outlook in general. I share the widespread feeling that all is not perfectly well with the world today. The notion that in the social and ethical realms society is progressing steadily onward and upward has few defenders today. Since we can use light from any available source, there is interest and value in the Jewish tradition, which is the distillation of nearly four millennia of experience and reflection.

Obviously, some basic understanding of the nature of Judaism is essential. Judaism cannot be equated with the Old Testament, just as the society and government of the United States would be gravely misunderstood by someone who has read only the Constitution. The insights of Judaism go far beyond the Old Testament, which represents only the first stage—albeit a highly influential and creative one—in the rich development of the tradition. In fact, it may well be argued that contemporary Judaism is much closer to the Talmud than to the Bible, if only because the Talmud represents the growth of the tradition in its second great creative era. Now the Talmud is a mass of some three thousand folio pages that originated during a period of a thousand years with more than two thousand authorities in constant debate with one another. But not even the Talmud exhausts the full extent of the normative literature of Judaism! That complicates the task for the researcher and the student but, unfortunately, to simplify is to distort.

It is interesting to note that some precursors of Masters and Johnson are mentioned in the Talmud. The Talmud tells a story about a young disciple who hid under the bed of his master to see how he behaved in the privacy of his chamber. When finally discovered in his hiding place, the disciple said to the master, "This too is Divine Law, and I want to learn it" (Babylonian Talmud, Berakhot 62a). Thus, he was engaged in the same kind of observation several thousand years ago, though his methods were perhaps not quite as sophisticated as they have become since.

Jewish tradition, as correctly indicated by Dr. Hiltner, takes a very positive attitude toward the sexual component in human life. Sex was never regarded as inherently evil or as a concession to the lower impulses of man, permissible only for the purpose of procreation. While some Christian churches have only recently recognized the full biblical rationale for marriage, Judaism from its inception has always recognized two purposes in marriage, both spelled out in the opening pages of Scripture.

The first is the fulfillment of the first commandment: "Be fruitful and multiply" (Genesis 1:28). The procreation of children is a basic goal of marriage, but it is not the only one. It is noteworthy that in the Bible, Eve is created for Adam before procreation is contemplated, while they are still in the Garden of Eden. The second function of marriage is that of companionship. Actually, it is the only motive assigned in the creation of a helpmate for Adam: "It is not good for man to dwell alone; I will make a helpmate for him" (Genesis 2:18).

In the medieval mystical treatise *Iggeret Ha-kodesh*, attributed to Nahmanides, the classic Jewish attitude is clearly and vigorously expressed: "We who are the descendants of those who received the sacred Torah believe that God, blessed be He, created everything as His wisdom dictated, and He created nothing containing obscenity or ugliness (*genai o kiyyur*). For if we were to say that intercourse (*ha-hibbur*) is obscene, it would follow that the sexual organs are obscene. . . . And how could God, blessed be He, create something containing a blemish or obscenity, or a defect; for we would then find that His deeds are not perfect, though Moses, the greatest of the prophets, proclaims and says, 'The Rock, whose work is perfect' (Deuteronomy 32:4). However, the fact is, as it is said, that 'God is pure-eyed, so that He sees no evil' (Habakkuk 1:13). Before Him there is neither degradation nor obscenity; He created man and woman, fashioning all their organs and setting them in their proper function, with nothing obscene in them."

Perhaps I can bring this point home to you in an interesting theological observation. In the past, Christian theologians have been wont to point out that there are two words for "love" in Christian theology derived from the Greek (aside from *philia*, which means "friendship" or "affection"): *eros*, or "carnal love," and *agape*, meaning "spiritual nonphysical love." The Hebrew outlook, on the contrary, finds it entirely proper to apply the same root, *'ahabh*, to all aspects of love. The ideal relationship of man to God ("You shall love the Lord your God"), the love of one's fellow man ("You shall love your neighbor as yourself"), and the love of man and woman ("How fair and how pleasant you are, O love, with its delights!") are all expressed by the same Hebrew root. There is no dichotomy between the physical and the spiritual.

It is not simply that Judaism regards a human being as an animated body; it sees the human person as an inextricable organic interweaving of body and soul, which are complementary, not antagonistic, aspects of personality. Thus, the Talmud contains a passage that suggests how often sexual intercourse ought to take place according to the husband's occupation (Babylonian Talmud, Kethubot 62b). It is stated that scholars should have relations on Friday evening, which is the eve of the Sabbath. The commentators ask why that particular evening is chosen, and two answers are given. Rashi, a straightforward literalist, explains it on the grounds that the Sabbath is "for pleasure, rest, and physical enjoyment" and the Sabbath is a day of joy. Nahmanides, who is a mystic, declares that since the Sabbath is a sacred day and intercourse is a sacred activity, it should take place on Sabbath eve.

From its inception, Jewish tradition did not regard the procreation of children as the sole purpose and goal of marriage but recognized the importance of companionship and friendship as essential components. Hence Jewish law enjoins marriage not only on people who are vigorous, youthful, and fertile and who would be expected to produce children, but also on people who are old, ill, or sterile. In fact, according to Jewish law, the injunction to "be fruitful and multiply" is fulfilled as soon as the family has two children. In practice, for reasons rooted in the desperate battle for group survival to which the Jewish people have been exposed for millennia, this guideline has often been breached in favor of large families; but two children is what the law actually requires. The only question is whether two boys are necessary, as the school of Shammai insists, or one boy and one girl, as Hillel avers (Mishnah Yevamot 6:6 and the Codes).

Once we recognize the role of the physical component in personality, there are some very interesting consequences. Today there is a great disarray in the relations of men and women, quite aside from any dogmatic considerations. Let us consider, for example, the question of divorce. Unlike other traditions, Judaism does not regard divorce as a crime but recognizes it as a tragedy. Every divorce is a tombstone on hopes once shared by two people who entered into matrimony feeling that they could find happiness with one another. When we observe the rising tide of abortion, divorce, drug abuse, and venereal disease, is it so far afield to insist that the new morality is not necessarily an improvement over the old, any more than one can maintain that the old is invariably superior to the new in its contribution to human welfare and happiness?

Many factors—economic, sociological, and cultural—have united to create the sexual revolution today. Astonishing though it may seem at first glance, one of the sources of the "new morality" lies in classic Christianity itself. I regret that only a brief summary of this subject can be offered here. I have dealt with the subject in greater detail in *Sex and the Family in Jewish Tradition* and in a larger book now in the process of preparation. St. Paul's teaching derived from the Hellenistic component of early Christian thought that regarded the physical as low, transient, and corruptible. Hence classic Christianity adopted as axiomatic the principles that love does not require sex, and that the less sex is involved in love, the higher the love.

In secularized form, this doctrine produced the phenomenon of romantic love. If you consider the classic examples in both fact and fiction—Heloise and Abelard, Dante and Beatrice, Tristan and

Isolde, Romeo and Juliet—in every case you find unrequited or frustrated love. They are symbolic of the "purest" form of love.

What has happened to the modern world is simply that it has inverted the classic Christian view. Traditional Christian morality glorifies love and maintains that sex is, or should be, irrelevant and as unrelated to love as possible. The modern age glorifies sex and maintains that love is, or should be, irrelevant and unrelated to sex. Many modern men and women have therefore drawn the conclusion that sexual experience is desirable and permissible even where there is no love.

The same dichotomy between sex and love in the contemporary scene, I think, lies at the root of a good number of our difficulties.

I should like to add a few other brief observations on other frontier areas of contemporary concern. Although premarital sex is strongly opposed in Judaism, traditional Jewish law does not regard a child born out of wedlock as illegitimate. The tradition realistically took into account the proclivity for such contacts between engaged couples, and it took measures to minimize such occurrences. But above all, it did not develop the obsession with the subject that seems to prevail in some traditions.

It is true that very little is said on the subject of masturbation, but I believe this to be the case because, to a large degree, marriages took place at an early age. The Bible makes no mention of masturbation, the passage in Genesis 38:9 being a reference to coitus interruptus. While rabbinic law does take a negative attitude toward the practice, it does not regard it as a major sin worthy of the kind of opprobrium that it has often aroused in other religious systems.

The biblical teaching in regard to homosexuality is, as Dr. Hiltner has pointed out, strongly condemnatory (Leviticus 18:22; 20:13). Recent efforts, like that of Father O'Neill, to argue that the Bible regards homosexuality as a legitimate alternate life-style to heterosexuality may be well intentioned, but they are unconvincing. The tradition clearly stigmatizes homosexuality as an abomination. However, since the basic Hebrew term for "sin," *het*, means "missing the mark," the scriptural approach to homosexuality as sin may perhaps be reinterpreted as a form of abnormal, aberrant activity. As such, the phenomenon requires research analysis, sympathy, and therapy. The homosexual, as a suffering fellow human being, deserves compassion and understanding. There is no warrant to be found in the religious tradition—and this, I believe, is true of Christianity as well as of Judaism—for harassment and discrimination against homosexuals or their exclusion from the larger community.

Finally, Jewish tradition would favor sex research when it is motivated by a goal beyond the research itself. I was somewhat uncomfortable with some of the illustrations Paul Gebhard presented this morning because they raise questions with regard to the ultimate goal of the search for truth. Is the search for truth an end in itself, brooking no other goal? Is sex research really not expected to contribute to the advancement of human welfare? If it is true that religion is too important to be left entirely to religionists, I would suggest that science is too important to be left exclusively in the hands of scientists. What we need today is cooperative activity between ethicists, philosophers, religionists, and scientists, who will formulate principles of ethical judgment and norms of conduct that are needed to make the search for truth an instrument for the enhancement of human life.

REFERENCES

1. Gordis, R. *The Root and the Branch—Judaism and the Free Society.* Chicago: University of Chicago Press, 1962. Chap. 13.
2. Gordis, R. *A Faith for Moderns* (revised and augmented edition). New York: Bloch, 1971. Chap. 19.

DESIGNATED DISCUSSION

JEROME F. WILKERSON

At the outset I would like to note my resonance with Dr. Hiltner on his following four observations:

1. That Jewish, Protestant, and Catholic views of sexuality find a concurrence in their common appreciation of the seriousness of

sexuality both in the plan of the Creator and in the subsequent life of man.

2. That increased freedom is not an automatic and unqualified good, but that, as Niebuhr has demonstrated, it increases capacity for both good and bad consequences.

3. That the theological acceptability of sex research is heightened by its nexus with therapy, the scientific alleviation of sexual disorders and frustrations.

4. That there is little to be found in the recent Vatican declaration on sexual ethics [1] that is at variance with sex research and sex therapy as it is presently pursued by responsible professionals.*

Dr. Hiltner and I disagree principally on the intellectual viability of revised natural-law theory. I should perhaps also acknowledge some disappointment that his analysis of the Vatican declaration did not extend to some of its more positive foci, such as the document's accent on chastity as related to human dignity, mutual respect, and unselfish service. I do appreciate, however, that our limited time restricts us all to selected emphases.

In the following remarks I propose to direct your attention to some specifically Catholic theological perspectives on the subject at hand, the ethics of the scientific investigation and treatment of human sexuality.

By *theological*, I mean deductions from the data of revelation—in this case the Old and New Testaments and Christian tradition—as distinct from philosophical   perspectives, which have as their starting-point principles attainable by the light of human reason alone. Incidentally, this is the root of the Catholic distinction between "moral" and ethics, the former being a theological study, the latter a philosophical one. The interplay, however, of philosophy and theology was a great concern of medieval thinkers, and an understanding of it is especially important in the comprehension of traditional Catholic moral theology.

Thomas Aquinas in the thirteenth century saw philosophy and theology as mutual allies, differentiated basically by the source of their data [2–4]. He found them both ultimately of divine origin

---

* For example, the therapy teams at the Reproductive Biology Research Foundation are principally concerned with helping married couples to achieve normal sexual function.

and therefore incapable of contradicting one another. Judging Aristotle's dualism a more accurate mirror of reality than Plato's idealism, Aquinas built thereon his own philosophical speculations. Since then these speculations, known as Thomism and developed over the years by others, have held sway in the Catholic church—albeit with some ebb and flow—as the "philosophia perennis." For our purposes it suffices to focus on the concept therein of natural law, the philosophical conclusion, which is then guided and enlightened by theology.

Its continuing importance in Catholic thought is apparent in the recent Vatican declaration discussed by Dr. Hiltner. Repeated reference is made there to this concept of fixed natural law. The document states [1]:

There can be no true promotion of man's dignity unless the essential order of his nature is respected. . . . All evolution of morals and every type of life must be kept within the limits imposed by the immutable principles based upon every human person's constitutive elements and essential relations—elements and relations which transcend historical contingency.

Several paragraphs later the document continues [1]:

Since sexual ethics concern fundamental values of human and Christian life, this general teaching equally applies to sexual ethics. In this domain there exist principles and norms which the church has always unhesitatingly transmitted as part of her teaching, however much the opinions and morals of the world may have been opposed to them. These principles and norms in no way owe their origin to a certain type of culture, but rather to knowledge of the divine law and human nature.

Near the end of the same section, the document states that it is respect for the finality or purpose of the sexual act that ensures its moral goodness. This statement reflects the corollary of natural-law theory that the morality of actions is drawn from three sources: the act itself, its circumstances, and the special circumstance of its final end or purpose. In this view, however, a good purpose cannot redeem an act that is intrinsically evil. In other words, then, the final end does not justify the means.

I can, of course, hardly do justice to the concept of natural law in so short a time. And while I appreciate that you, my fellow conferees here at this meeting, are well familiar with it, I am also aware that it is a term that means different things to different people and that in recent years natural-law theory of whatever stripe has not enjoyed a good press. For that reason I would like to draw your attention to the section "Natural Law and Ethics" of Dr. Vernon J. Bourke's book *Ethics in Crisis* [5]. Acknowledging that the dominant ethical trends in the United States are not in the direction of natural-law theory, and expressing the hope that natural-law thinkers will make a greater effort to ground their speculation in the contemporary data of the social sciences, Bourke presents a brief though lucid explanation of natural-law theory. He concludes with an insightful response—as he says, "not in a spirit of rebuttal but of cooperative discussion"—of Kai Nielsen's "An Examination of the Thomistic Theory of Natural Moral Law" [6].

Before we leave this more philosophical aspect of our discussion of theological perspectives, I would like to make this point. I am pleased that among the participants in this conference there are at least two fellow philosophers, Dr. Ruth Macklin of Case Western Reserve University and Dr. Tristram Engelhardt of the University of Texas Medical Branch, from both of whom we will be hearing later in the conference. The disproportionately small representation here of philosophers is, I think, symptomatic of our time. Philosophy today has lost its centrality among intellectual disciplines.

Dr. Edmund D. Pellegrino, Board Chairman of the Yale University Medical Center, has written an excellent monograph, *Medicine and Philosophy*, for which one of our conference participants, Dr. Fritz Redlich, wrote the foreword [7]. In it Dr. Pellegrino sees philosophy's retreat from substantive questions as the culmination of a growing reaction over the past century to the speculative excesses of German idealist philosophy. He sees analytic philosophy, phenomenology, and existentialism as putting a limit on the pretensions of this idealist philosophy and turning in on itself in the process. As he states, "Philosophy, so construed, is unequal to the most urgent questions now besetting mankind." And he hopes that the time is ripening for philosophy to sit again at the side of medicine, to share its burden, to provide leadership in humanistic discussions such as this conference, to sensitize medicine, in his words, "to the intersections of values inherent in every medical art."

Returning from this philosophical digression to our theological perspectives, I feel I must address myself to some of the questions put to me informally last evening—questions for which I was not unprepared. How monolithic is contemporary Catholic moral theology? Who are the dissenting theologians within the church and what are they saying? What is the binding force for Catholics of this new Vatican document on sexual ethics?

To dispose of the last question first, let me state at the outset that this declaration on sexual ethics is not proposed as an infallible teaching of the church, nor even as an apostolic constitution of Pope Paul. Rather, it was issued by the Congregation for the Doctrine of the Faith, signed by its prefect Cardinal Seper, approved by Pope Paul, and consequently proposed to Catholics as what is called "an authoritative, noninfallible teaching." What assent to this type of pronouncement is owed by the Catholic faithful? The answer to this question is complex and the subject of controversy. Basically, however, Catholics are expected to approach such a pronouncement with great respect and concern and to have an appreciation of its importance in view of the teaching office from which it comes, even though it is "not a definition of faith" and is "to some extent provisional" [8]. Theological dissenters within the church, moreover, are expected to pose their opinions "with prudence born of intellectual grace and a Christian confidence" that the truth will prevail [9].

In answer to the first question—no, Catholic moral theology is presently anything but a monolith, as Dr. Hiltner has indicated. The titles crowding the moral theology shelves of Catholic bookstores attest to this. What, then, is being said in books by such Catholic moralists as Bernard Häring [10–13], Charles Curran [14–17], and Richard McCormick [18, 19]? Shortness of time prohibits going into their various approaches to the subject, which basically consist either of a revision of natural-law theory, as mentioned by Rabbi Gordis, or of its abandonment in favor of a more existential approach. The Vatican document has occasioned an expression of these often sharply divergent viewpoints [20–22]. Charles Curran has provided an instructive survey in his presidential address to the American Society of Christian Ethics entitled "Moral Theology: The Present State of the Discipline" [23]. In this connection I would also recommend the opening chapter, "Change of Focus," in Bernard Häring's recent book *Sin in the Secular Age* [12].

Besides dogmatic theology, which reflects on church doctrine, and moral theology, which applies this doctrine theoretically to human behavior, there is also pastoral theology, theology's application at last to the people of God. Just as clinical medicine at times is not considered as important or as instructive as medical research, so pastoral theology at times is not considered as important as the speculation of dogmatic theologians. But in another sense clinical medicine is the ultimate medicine and pastoral theology is the ultimate theology—grounded as they are in the crucible of reality, the true testing-ground, the flesh-and-blood people for whom, after all, medicine and theology exist.

For this reason I also hold important pastoral theological perspectives on the ethics of the scientific investigation and treatment of human sexuality. Medical and social scientists, moreover, are perhaps more at home with the inductive methodology of pastoral theology than with the deductive character of speculative theology. And, finally, this particular theological perspective should generally prove more intelligible and useful to those who recognize no theological orientation.

I think, moreover, that to start from the zero-point in endeavoring to formulate guidelines for sexual research and therapy would be a wasteful and dangerous procedure. As writer Dan Herr [24] states in a somewhat different context, "I would hope that in this particular revolution we can preserve the progress that we have achieved during the past decade without losing what has seemed worth preserving for almost 2,000 years."

Doctor Masters and Virginia Johnson in Chapter 8 of *The Pleasure Bond* also warn of a too-sanguine dismissal of the past, citing the importance of learning everything possible "about the physiological and psychological realities of human sexual experience" before recommending "changes in ethical standards" [25]. I thought of these words the other day when a resident psychiatrist complained to me about his inability to break down his young son's sexual modesty and reserve, a complaint much in the spirit of the naive, Rousseauistic concept of human sexuality expressed in the recently published sex book for children, *Show Me* [26]. I think these authors could have profited by the words of Jacob Bronowski with which Dr. Emily Mudd concluded her interesting presentation.

But to return to this application of pastoral theology, how could even this tack be intellectually feasible for those who reject natural-law theory? By working with these concepts—genuine theological concepts—as constructs, as working hypotheses to be carefully tested, and then retained or discarded in ongoing research. Teilhard de Chardin's close associate, the Bergsonian Edouard LeRoy, with whom I otherwise little identify, proposes such an "as if" use of theology [27]. In this case I think it has merit.

From my pastoral experience I can join Virginia Johnson when she says [25], "We see a lot of things that happen to people as a result of repression. Needless to say, we're not a cheering section for that." My experience also prompts me to concur in the caution she adds about idealizing specific reactions to repression and to reiterate that it is not the only enemy. Excesses, selfishness, exploitation—a point alluded to by Rabbi Gordis—are also to be feared. Human nature has its shortcomings, however one accounts for it theologically or verifies it empirically.

Virginia Johnson also says, in the passage cited earlier: "To learn—that's why we're here . . . to learn what works for you." I might comment parenthetically that I find this openness to learning from others characteristic of the Reproductive Biology Research Foundation; it figured, no doubt, in the convening of this conference.

"To learn what works"—I would like to offer my personal statement that these behavioral constructs from Christian tradition, to use our "as if" terminology and procedure, work for many people. This is not a superficial judgment. It is forged through a quarter-century of sharing in the confessional and counseling office, of struggling through the later psychosexual development of many young men and women, and of witnessing success in their often spirited striving toward integrated, effective Christian lives.

This affirmation hardly repudiates the need for sex research and therapy, for in this same pastoral experience are other youths who point up how inadequate is our knowledge and teaching in this area and how important our recent progress. Let me also cite the pastoral fulfillment, as father and brother, of being able to lift with the aid of solid data the clouds of self-doubt or anxiety from the brows of even my seemingly sophisticated medical students, of being able to serve their needs with effective caring and dignity, either in person or through responsible referral—in short, of having more than the scorpion (Luke 11:12) of vacuous generalities to offer them. Meeting these needs is sound pastoral theology.

How congruent to the compassion of Christ—alleviating suffering in an area so close to the core of self-identity and personhood. How congruent to the church's vision of Christian marriage—rendering viable and stable marital units in distress. I would say in closing that sexual research and therapy, far from having only theology's reluctant blessing, have rather, in the spirit of Rabbi Gordis' remarks, its mandate.

REFERENCES

1. Declaration on certain questions concerning sexual ethics. Translated by the National Catholic News Service. *Origins* 5(31):485–494, 1976.
2. Aquinas, T. *Summa Theologica*, Part 1, Question 1. Translated by the English Dominican Fathers. New York: Benzinger Brothers, 1947.
3. Aquinas, T. *Summa contra Gentiles*, Book 1, Chaps. 1–8. Translated by the English Dominican Fathers. New York: Benzinger Brothers, 1929.
4. Aquinas, T. *Commentary on the "De Trinitate" of Boethius*, Questions 1, 2. Translated by R. E. Brennan. London: B. Herder, 1946.
5. Bourke, V. J. *Ethics in Crisis*. Milwaukee: Bruce, 1966. Pp. 95–149.
6. Nielsen, K. An examination of the Thomistic theory of natural moral law. *Natural Law Forum* 4:44–71, 1959. (The *Natural Law Forum* is presently entitled the *American Journal of Jurisprudence*.)
7. Pellegrino, E. D. *Medicine and Philosophy*. Philadelphia: Society for Health and Human Values, 1974.
8. Rahner, K. Pastoral letter of the German bishops, September 22, 1967, "Disput um das kirchliche lehramt." *Stimmen der Zeit* 185: 73–81, 1970.

9. Pastoral letter of the American Bishops, November 15, 1968. *The Pope Speaks* 13(4): 377–405, 1969.

10. Häring, B. *Ethics of Manipulation*. New York: Seabury Press, 1975.

11. Häring, B. *Medical Ethics*. Notre Dame, Indiana: Fides, 1973.

12. Häring, B. *Sin in the Secular Age*. New York: Doubleday, 1974.

13. Häring, B. *The Law of Christ*. Translated by E. G. Kaiser. Westminster, Maryland: Newman Press, 1963.

14. Curran, C. E. *Absolutes in Moral Theology*. Washington: Corpus Books, 1968.

15. Curran, C. E. *Catholic Moral Theology in Dialogue*. Notre Dame, Indiana: Fides, 1972.

16. Curran, C. E. *Contemporary Problems in Moral Theology*. Notre Dame, Indiana: Fides, 1970.

17. Curran, C. E. *New Perspectives in Moral Theology*. Notre Dame, Indiana: Fides, 1974.

18. McCormick, R. A. Notes on moral theology. *Theological Studies* 37(1):70–119, 1976.

19. McCormick, R. A. The moral theology of Vatican II. *The Future of Ethics and Moral Theology*. Chicago: Argus Press, 1968.

20. Maguire, D. The Vatican on sex. *Commonweal* 103(5):137–140, 1976.

21. McCormick, R. A. Sexual ethics—an opinion. *National Catholic Reporter* 12(14):9, 1976.

22. Mugavero, F. J. The gift of sexuality. *Origins* 5(37):581–586, 1976.

23. Curran, C. E. Moral theology: The present state of the discipline. *Theological Studies* 34(3):446–467, 1973.

24. Herr, D. Stop pushing. *The Critic* 25(4):6, 1967.

25. Masters, W. H., and Johnson, V. E. *The Pleasure Bond*. Boston: Little, Brown, 1975.

26. Fleischhauer-Hardt, H., and McBride, W. *Show Me*. English adaptation by H. Davies. New York: St. Martin's Press, 1975.

27. LeRoy, E. *Dogme et critique*. Paris: Librairie Bloud et Cie, 1907.

GENERAL DISCUSSION

MARY S. CALDERONE: I am concerned that science should indeed be vocal within the framework of ethics. In 1971 the Sex Information and Education Council of the United States (SIECUS) sponsored a conference here in St. Louis on sexuality and human values, at which researchers discussed their findings with representatives of various religious faiths selected by the faiths themselves. That was probably the first time that religion became aware of the work of Lawrence Kohlberg and his associates at Harvard University School of Education relating to how human beings develop their moral values. Recently a statement has come from the Vatican—a pronouncement, actually—that in many respects either denies or refuses to recognize observations about human sexuality that are considered truths by a majority of prominent scientific researchers today.

Let us consider for a moment the ethics of masturbation. I really think masturbation is so nearly universal that it might be looked on as a state of being. Yet the Vatican statement calls it "a grave disorder, an intrinsically and seriously disordered act," with the implication, therefore, that a person of any age who masturbates is intrinsically and seriously disordered. Young men—and, as we realize today, women—are really in an almost perpetually erectile state, and masturbation could be considered the overflow, if you will, of that perpetual state. It is a fact that in our society more people masturbate than do not. It is also a fact, I believe, that it is rarely if ever chosen in preference to intercourse. Masters and Johnson have established that, even though women do find that their orgasms are sharper and more intense with masturbation, they still prefer intercourse. It cannot therefore interfere with procreation in any real sense, it cannot replace the procreative act, and it is looked on very widely today as not only acceptable but actually desirable in the sexual development and evolution of human beings. Let me read one of the ten position statements of SIECUS. "Sexual self-pleasuring, or masturbation, is a natural part of sexual behavior for individuals of all ages. It can help to develop a sense of the body as belonging to the self and an affirmative attitude toward the body as a legitimate source of enjoyment. It can also help in the release of tension in a way harmless to the self and to others, and provide an intense experience of the self in preparation for experiencing another. Masturbation and the fantasies that frequently accompany it, can be a subtle way of maintaining or restoring the image of one's self as a fully functioning human being." This is why I propose that its place as part of the sexual experience should be supported as having an ethical and positive role to play in human life.

HAROLD I. LIEF: In the last several years, a number of historians have written some excellent papers on the history of masturbation. Apparently, although masturbation was regarded as a sin by the Catholic church, it wasn't until the Protestant Reformation that it was seen as a very important part of human behavior. It seems that Daniel Defoe quite anonymously published a penny dreadful that sold in the streets of London for one penny, and in it he cited all the evil consequences of masturbation. Since this was the best-seller of its day, it was quickly picked up and became part of the general atmosphere. Then, in the nineteenth century, a Swiss physician published a book on the horrors and medical consequences of masturbation. Doctors picked this up and used it as an explanation for the various grave consequences of infectious disease. When large numbers of children were dying of infectious diseases, they cited masturbation as the cause of anything from scarlet fever to measles. This continued into the twentieth century. In the first decade of this century, at the Vanderbilt Clinic, a masturbation clinic existed where patients with such disorders as multiple sclerosis and various kinds of epilepsy were paraded in front of the clinicians as examples of the evil consequences of masturbation. At that time, the doctors felt that this was scientific truth and passed their beliefs on to their patients.

PEPPER SCHWARTZ: When I was in London in the summer of 1975 at a conference on venereal disease, the Bishop of Durham spoke and advised physicians and therapists to go back to moral and ethical values and to advise their patients of their moral and ethical responsibilities. At the time, I objected to this. It seemed to me that what we were trying to get away from was the individual therapist as an arbiter of right and wrong, moral and immoral, except in the most general terms, rather than the narrowest ones. I would certainly like some comments when we talk about religious ethics, not only as an issue when people go to some kind of church or synagogue, but also as it integrates with the day-to-day work of science and therapy.

SEWARD HILTNER: My own view is that scientists and therapists have to be completely true to their own consciences, scientific and otherwise. Don't take anybody, including us as theologians, more seriously than we deserve, even if we appear to criticize— as long as you as researchers or therapists have conscientious reasons for going ahead with what you're doing. I think some of the potential problems that sex therapy or research may have with broadly ethical issues may come not out of fundamental principle disagreement, but out of a lack of common sense or diplomacy, or what is generally called prudence.

ROBERT GORDIS: If I understood Dr. Schwartz's question properly, she was asking whether scientists in this area should pass value judgments in their work with patients. I would like to answer by saying that they cannot avoid offering value judgments. The vaunted position of "neutrality" is itself a value judgment. The only two safeguards I can suggest are, first, intellectual honesty in answering the question, in making clear where the practitioner stands; and, second, the recognition by the scientist that he has an obligation not to be content purely with the techniques of science but also to concern himself with its ultimate values and ends. The scientist, strange as it may seem, is a human being. In fact, he was human before he was a scientist. Whether he achieves a theistic, a nontheistic, or even an atheistic world-view, he must work at the task of developing a philosophy of values, for without it he cannot really do justice to his function in this area. In a word, value judgments by the scientist are both inescapable and essential.

JEROME F. WILKERSON: I would like to interject here a word of caution. I think it is important that the therapist not permit the client to thrust on him the responsibility of moral decision-making while in therapy. I agree with Rabbi Gordis when he speaks of honesty, of the therapist answering a direct question by stating and sharing what he thinks, where he is. But that's a different thing than falling into the trap of imposing one's belief on others.

CARL S. SHULTZ: I would like to reinforce Dr. Wilkerson's point. It seems to me that we have taken the wrong position, in part, in regard to the role of the therapist. It is as though the therapist were the seeking party. Instead, I think it is much more important that the therapist be sensitive to where the patient is and what the patient's needs are and not assume some type of doctrinaire position. It seems much more important to tailor the response to the patient's construct and try to develop from the dynamics of that interaction whatever response is necessary. If you are doctrinaire or authoritarian, what you're doing is imposing another requirement on the patient and on yourself.

VIRGINIA E. JOHNSON: I think we are getting to the core of the reason for the existence of this conference. We want to begin to realize that a major subtlety of working in this field is not only focusing on the needs of the patient or the needs, ethical or otherwise, of the research subject, but also being able to identify the difference in ourselves between our commitment to the field and our personal values. The statement, for instance, that "masturbation is rarely if ever chosen in preference to intercourse" is on the face of it reflective of a personal value judgment and, of course, untrue. When we assume a scientific role or commit ourselves to help someone else, we must be able to separate those things that are uniquely our own, representing our own beliefs and needs, from a set of ethics—openness and so on—that answers to the need of the other person. We can only listen objectively. I was very interested when Paul Gebhard introduced the thought that we possibly mislead subjects or the people we interrogate in order to keep them on our side. I happen to believe that you don't have to mislead them. Maybe it's never-never land, the Pollyanna attitude, that leads me to believe that you can be a scientist and separate yourself, showing neither approval or disapproval. You can imply compassion, openness, receptivity, and so on by the very nature of your being there, but I would hate to think I had to mislead them with a smile. We label ourselves and are perceived as scientists and as health-care professionals, and as such we should not use misleading directions in order to achieve our goal.

ROBERT L. STUBBLEFIELD: I would like to raise a question about listening objectively. Assume I am trying to treat a woman who says that her husband beats her and she wants a divorce. If I do not examine my own beliefs and convictions about that issue, I cannot listen very objectively. I must pay some attention to whether she is a Catholic, a Jew, a Protestant, a Christian Scientist, or a Buddhist if I am to be able to help her. I am suggesting that we want to listen objectively and intervene objectively, but that is a very difficult thing to do. I wanted to emphasize that we try our very best to minimize those unconscious and learned early kinds of experiences that dominate us in many ways. Most of us deal with them successfully, but they remain a major problem, as I see it.

CHARLES REMBAR: I am undoubtedly the most ignorant in this field of anybody you'll hear in these two days. I am reminded of an antiobscenity case in which a lower-court judge came out with a remarkable opinion: When a reporter asked him how much he really knew on the subject of sex, he said, "Only enough to get by." I feel that way in this group. Nevertheless, unless I misunderstood Rabbi Gordis, I think he said that the Bible said nothing about masturbation. Very deferentially, I want to cite the story of Onan.

ROBERT GORDIS: Onan's sin was his refusal to fulfill his obligation to his brother's wife by begetting a son to carry the dead man's name—the levirate rite. The story of Onan has to do with coitus interruptus, not with masturbation.

CHARLES REMBAR: No one knows, Rabbi, no one knows.

ROBERT GORDIS: If you take refuge in that kind of argument, you have it over the theologians.

3

ETHICAL REQUIREMENTS FOR SEX RESEARCH IN HUMANS: INFORMED CONSENT AND GENERAL PRINCIPLES

ROBERT C. KOLODNY

In approaching a discussion of ethical issues in sex research, the question "Is sex research different from other types of research?" must be addressed promptly. I have deliberately chosen this phraseology instead of the more speculative query raised by asking, "*Should* sex research be different from other types of research?" since I believe that these are two unique and separate topics. It is my belief that sex research *is* different from other types of research, not simply in its form and content (as research in physics differs from research in sociology) but also in terms of public, political, and professional attitudes—terms that cannot be ignored without missing the contemporary context of some of the very forces shaping the need for such research. If we are to discuss today the ethical issues interwoven with such investigative activities, we would be less than fully responsible if we were to dismiss current attitudes toward sex research—both positive and negative—in a search for timeless principles.

Let me plainly distinguish this approach from a plea for a framework of situational ethics, which it is not meant to be. Instead, it is a recognition of what I perceive to be the central dilemma of this discussion: how to enhance knowledge via systematic data collection and assimilation in a less than ideal reality. It is the divergence between the world of reality and how we wish things might be that prompts the need for a discussion of ethics in research.

A point that exemplifies the problem of real versus ideal is the noticeable absence of systematic training in ethical concerns in the curricula of graduate schools in a wide variety of scientific disciplines. The researcher as well as the clinician is expected to be conversant with ethical guidelines for the conduct of his or her work, but the researcher's training neglects, for the most part, any meaningful exploration of the broad spectrum of ethical concerns that a person may contend with in his or her career.

Traditional models of medical education have, unfortunately, typically minimized or omitted the formal teaching of ethics, presumably due to both time constraints and the assumption that ethics are absorbed, deus ex machina, by the time one graduates from school. In the everyday world of medical education, including internship and residency training, ethical issues often seem to be brought up primarily as they relate to possible litigation—hardly a means of encouraging developing physicians to assess objectively these issues of importance. Senior clinicians and senior researchers often appear arbitrary, defensive, and uncomfortable when pertinent ethical queries are raised by a student or house officer, leaving unanswered the nagging question of who will teach medical ethics. That medicine is not alone in its quandary is no surprise to the group gathered here today, for almost all of us first systematically approached the ethical issues of human experimentation following the completion of our training.

Despite this reality, both professional and public focus on ethical issues in human research has intensified tremendously in the past few years. Difficult questions have been argued concerning such areas as fetal research, psychosurgery, abortion, and population genetics. The Tuskegee experiment of the Public Health Service, the Edelin case, and the Harvard study in behavioral genetics have all been in the news in the past year. Along with opinions on and reactions to these cases, a dichotomy of sorts has arisen in the scientific community that questions whether this new concern with ethics is curse or blessing [1].

The eminent editor of the *New England Journal of Medicine*, Franz Ingelfinger, has warned of the calamitous effects on public opinion of what he terms the frenetic fringe of medical ethics. "In the name of ethics, anti-intellectualism and anti-science are encouraged, hostility to medicine is nourished, clinical investigation is compromised if not castrated, and paradoxically enough, the cause of probity itself is harmed" [2].

Willard Gaylin and Samuel Gorovitz have written, "To question what science should do and how science should do it is not to be against science. Such questioning is at the heart of scientific methodology. When it is simplistic and rhetorical, however, it serves neither science nor the public" [3].

How can we approach the ethical issues of human sex research in a manner commensurate with both human dignity and the facilitation of knowledge? Certainly there can be no rigid formula for such an approach, but it is my impression that issues of informed consent comprise the latter phases of such ethical deliberations by the would-be investigator. Ethical considerations begin in the design of the project and the professionalism of the investigators.

RESEARCH DESIGN

Planning investigations in the area of human sexuality is not different at the first conceptual level from other biological or behavioral research design. Current knowledge is assessed, hypotheses are formed to extend or verify this data base, and strategies are devised to test each hypothesis. The investigator is ethically constrained principally in the latter task: The appropriateness of the research strategies employed must be viewed in light of a complex set of variables that reflect legal, social, medical, and psychological concerns. Within the domain of these variables the researcher must select a population to study, being reasonably assured it is suitable for the hypothesis; he or she must determine what types of data will be obtained and how this information will be gathered; and plans must be made for analyzing the data to yield maximal information. Each of these steps necessarily entails many decision-points with a variety of ethical considerations; this presentation will only provide examples of some of the problems that may be encountered.

In selection of a study population, including designation of test and control groups, the researcher must recognize the inherent difficulties if he or she is involved in clinical investigation in which potential research subjects are all patients. The contention has been made that it may not be proper for the physician to request that his or her own patients participate in studies he or she is conducting, whether therapeutic or nontherapeutic clinical research, since such a situation may produce a division of loyalties between the therapeutic and investigative processes [4]. Although such separation of research from clinical care is impressive in its ostensible justice, examining the issue more closely leads me to the conclusion that this strategy is lacking in a variety of ways. From a practical viewpoint, the availability and interest of trained personnel are surprisingly limited, particularly in highly subspecialized areas such as study of sexual problems of persons with neurologic limitations. Furthermore, adding an independent researcher will in many instances of sex research decrease the degree of confidentiality that can be extended to the patient-subject, so that the risk of additional embarrassment or worry on the part of at least some subjects must be weighed against the purported gain in objectivity. Beyond the encroachment on personal privacy entailed by such a model, the independent investigator who is not clinically knowledgeable will, in certain situations, be unable to recognize or utilize the serendipity that is so frequently a consequential product of research endeavors. Since making maximal use of research findings is essential to translating research into tangible benefits beyond the expansion of knowledge alone, it appears less than fully ethical to neglect this aspect as well.

The individual working at the interface of clinical care and research in human sexuality must have an awareness of these difficulties in designating a potential study population; however, the initial issues of population selection may change as the details of the research protocol become more clearly developed. Thus, one may wish to evaluate two different types of intervention in the treatment of human sexual dysfunction: Selecting the specific interventions that may be made and deciding on the use of a "no-intervention" control group raises the question of allocation of study subjects to each of several groups. The first theoretical approach to this problem, which might have been random assignment to the test and control groups, may be both methodologically and ethically incomplete if, for example, one intervention involves couple therapy and the other involves individual psychotherapy. Random assignment is not possible in a situation defined in this manner, since individuals without partners cannot be assigned to couple treatment. Furthermore, what are the implications of placing a subject in the no-intervention control group? Will this subject be "rescued" from the control group and removed from the study if participation has adverse effects on his or her marriage, psyche, or well-being? How will such effects be monitored, and how will subsequent decisions be made? While I do not believe these are simple questions to answer, I raise them to illustrate the ethical dilemmas that may be faced by investigators far in advance of consideration of mechanisms of informed consent.

Similarly, the researcher who is not involved in the situation of clinical care has a responsibility to address ethical issues in the selection of a research population. Whatever the target population, the researcher must decide how to contact, and solicit research participation from, this designated group. This apparently simple act can create myriad problems. For example, the researcher who advertises in a campus newspaper may unwittingly create an erroneous impression of the nature of the research project due to the brevity of the initial announcement. This necessarily has repercussions for individuals who choose to participate and share with friends or family the fact of their participation, and for individuals who initially volunteer to participate without reasonable understanding of the subject that will be investigated. The person who agrees to discuss potential research participation with an investigator without knowledge that this discussion will involve material pertaining to sexual behavior and/or sexual attitudes may be upset on discovering the actual content of the interview. While I am not invoking a formalized "Consent to Consider Giving Informed Consent," it should be apparent that preliminary disclosure of the nature of a study and of what is involved in hearing a full description of the project may often be of value in preventing difficulty and resentment in subject recruitment.

While on the subject of selection of research populations, it is equally relevant to consider for a moment a further aspect of subject selection. In utilizing whatever screening criteria are necessary to select study participants, many researchers fail to comprehend that they have responsibilities to the people who volunteered but were not included in the study: Along with the obvious guarantee of confidentiality, these individuals should be notified of why they were not selected for research participation. Individuals not extended such information may react in a variety of ways, including loss of self-esteem or doubts about their sexual normality. This problem can also be minimized (but not eliminated) in the first exchange of information about the project, by specifically stating that only a portion of volunteers will be selected for participation, and explaining what criteria will be applied and how selection will be accomplished after initial screening.

Research conducted in areas such as adolescent or childhood sexuality, sex education, and psychosocial studies of the sexual behavior and attitudes of minority groups presents a different sort of problem that must be kept at the forefront of the responsible investigator's mind in planning such projects. The specific concerns for each of these areas are so complex that they cannot be discussed in this presentation. However, in such situations it is particularly important to recognize that the researcher must be an advocate of the rights of study subjects as much as an objective scientist.

This observation may provoke strong reactions from some, since the scientific impartiality of the researcher may be seen as precluding advocacy of subjects' rights. I do not believe that this is true. The investigator, in theory, can never provide a buffer as effective for protecting the dignity and comfort of subjects involved in human experimentation as can a third party not affiliated with the research. However, it *is* a prime responsibility of the researcher or research team to be concerned with, and productive in, the task of safeguarding subjects' rights. Failure to do so seriously diminishes the dignity of science as well as the dignity of man. Accepting this responsibility does not diminish scientific objectivity but enhances both public and professional opinions of research.

This emphasis on subjects' rights in sex research assumes a position of more practical consequences than in many other research fields. This is the case partly because there is a strong tendency to regard research that involves factors important to the quality of life as less worthy or less defensible than research that deals with disease and death. Both in past years and at the present time we contend not only with this attitude but with a view, strongly promulgated by some, that research in sexual functioning or sexuality violates an implicit moral code that precludes sex from the realm of investigation. There are, unfortunately, scientists, politicians, theologians, and educators who regard sex research as a bastardization of science and an unwarranted intrusion into the private lives of our citizenry. We can afford to be neither cavalier nor callous in the conduct of our work precisely because we are dealing with an area heretofore surrounded by so much ignorance and such strong taboos. This may serve to clarify my original point that sex research is different from other types of research.

The formulation of research hypotheses sets the stage for some of the methodological problems we have considered; yet remarkably little discussion has taken place in scientific meetings or professional journals addressing the ethical decisions inherent in this first step of research planning. Following publication of *Human Sexual Response* in 1966, some critics implied or stated that this work was an affront to human dignity because of its triviality—that is, because it was purely descriptive research. Had they fully understood the importance of the underlying hypotheses for these investigations, the relevance of basic physiological inquiry to frequently encountered clinical problems of sexual functioning might have allayed their concerns. Nevertheless, there are undoubtedly ethical limitations on certain areas of sex research, just as there are in other fields. The problem is to define these limitations. Research involving direct sexual activity between an adult and a minor is clearly unethical. What about research that entails sexual activity between consenting unmarried adults in violation of state or local laws? Use of placebo contraceptives is unequivocally unethical. Is the use of placebo antiandrogens different? These questions are raised to stimulate discussion, rather than to present final answers—and rational discussion can just be a beginning step toward the derivation of answers.

Data analysis can create ethical dilemmas for the scientist, and consideration must be given in the process of research design to each of several alternatives. Preliminary data analysis may indicate, in certain situations, that a working hypothesis is verified conclusively prior to the termination of a project. In this instance, the problem of whether to terminate the project or whether to release the findings, or both, may arise. In projects involving collaborative centers, one must decide whether one set of data suffices in some situations or whether independent replication is needed. Data analysis at the conclusion of a study is important in many ways. For the purpose of this presentation, only two of the ethical issues that may arise in this context will be mentioned. Should certain types of research data ever be suppressed? If so, for what reasons, and for how long? Such a question might arise if a substance known to be physically harmful was found to have major aphrodisiac effects. A similar dilemma might be presented by data that are dramatic but nongeneralizable, with strong potential for social or legal consequences. Second, in the field of sex research we must be particularly cognizant of the impact our research and clinical findings may have on the individual. Thus, delineations of "normality" or "abnormality" must be carefully considered, since many individuals will all too readily accept an external label as a sign of their own inadequacy, sometimes causing severe emotional anguish and economic repercussions. How many women have accepted the label *frigid* and entered long-term (and expensive) psychoanalysis when this label did not in fact apply? How many women have been trapped by the myth of clitoral versus vaginal orgasm into a pattern of diminished self-esteem and guilt? How many lives have been adversely affected by the label *latent homosexuality?* It is obvious that if we were speaking of types of lipid patterns, such far-reaching consequences would not apply.

REVIEW PROCEDURES

Thus far, the discussion has focused on the role of the sex researcher in making ethical decisions. Although this is the first necessary step in the sequence of safeguarding the rights and welfare of research subjects, it is only a beginning. There are formal and informal opportunities for review that have a special relevance to this problem. Peer review is a sometimes-neglected informal opportunity for both scientific and ethical evaluation of research proposals. Consultation with colleagues can be undertaken periodically during the evolution of a research project, when such input can be most easily integrated into the methodologies chosen, the minimization of risks, and the development of contingency plans. This consultation among scientists should not be restricted to one discipline alone, for it is particularly helpful in uncovering potential ethical pitfalls when a multidisciplinary group reviews the situation. The physician-investigator would be well advised to enlist the assistance of scientists and professionals outside the medical community in such critical review, just as the social scientist would frequently benefit from consultation with medical and legal researchers in planning investigations.

Formal review mechanisms, beginning with institutional committees on human experimentation, are, at a second level, a vital component of the system of checks and balances on the ethical conduct of research. Unfortunately, review by committee presents a variety of problems as well. Since much has been written about the structure and function of such committees, I will restrict my comments to a few of these problem areas.

In general terms, many researchers look at institutional review committees as hurdles to be jumped rather than allies in their research. From this perspective, the committee is seen as another bureaucratic edifice requiring time to fill out forms, outline a proposal, and await a decision. There is also a degree of futility in the review process, in the sense that few institutions provide an ongoing monitoring of research activities to ensure that promises made in the documentation submitted to the committee are actually implemented and adhered to during the study itself. Given this lack of continuity, it is no surprise to find projects approved by institutional review committees sometimes of questionable adequacy from an ethical viewpoint.

In addition, current regulations pertaining to institutional review committtees allow for little of what might be termed consumer representation. The danger implicit in this situation is that a committee of academically acclimated individuals will make decisions based more firmly on intellectual than experiential grounds. This may be an acceptable basis for decision-making, but it would appear healthier and more consistent with the intent of such a review process to integrate the intuitive and experiential input that such consumer representation might afford.

Despite such shortcomings, review procedures at present appear to be the most promising and effective mechanism for protecting the rights of human subjects. Unfortunately, many institutional review committees have no members with experience in the particular problems of sex research. Ideally, these committees would obtain consultative expertise to assess such research applications adequately; in instances of research protocols that have been turned down by an institutional review committee, it would appear mandatory to offer at least one channel of appeal. One of the major charges of human research committees is to ensure that an acceptable balance exists between the potential benefits of a research project, either to the individual participant or to society in general, and the risks assumed by the research subject. In making such judgments in the area of sex research, the committee will frequently be handicapped by lack of guidelines to follow. The assessment of such risks, which will be discussed in the following section, may be impossible in certain situations because no data are available to provide the answer. Should such a project be blocked because of speculation as to risks?

Sex research is, of course, sometimes simply an euphemism for trickery, quackery, or erotic exploitation. At other times, well meaning but scientifically and ethically naive people engage in studies about sex without adequate attention to methodological or ethical issues. There appears to be little that can be done to stop such abuses in this field, just as little can be done to eradicate the illegitimate purveyors of "sex therapy," but, clearly, public disclosure of discussions such as this can provide some awareness of the problem.

INFORMED CONSENT

The physician is familiar with the concept of *primum non nocere* —above all do no harm. The researcher, whether physician or not, also strives toward this ideal. In the real world of research, as in the real world of medicine, it is rarely possible to guarantee this benevolent state. Thus, the investigator is aware of possible risks inherent in research participation and assumes an awesome responsibility to convey an understanding of these risks to potential research subjects. Without adequate delineation of the risk potential, a subject cannot truly give informed consent.

Informed consent, of course, also requires that other conditions be met: (1) The individual must understand what procedures will be done during the study; (2) the individual must be free to choose whether to participate or not without any element of coercion, force, or deceit; and (3) the individual must be aware of his or her right to withdraw from the study at any time. Since there is a large scholarly literature on informed consent, I will restrict my further remarks to some specific aspects of relevance to sex research.

For all categories of research subjects, there are risk factors rather unique to sex research that are extremely difficult to evaluate. One of these is the possibility of the violation of confidentiality in any of a variety of ways. This may occur if a subject is a relative or social acquaintance of a member of the research team who has even limited access to data; it may occur if research records are stolen or tampered with; it may occur in less flagrant form if a questionnaire is found or read by a parent, spouse, friend, or colleague, or if one of these individuals simply takes a telephone call intended for the research participant (and directed to a number he or she designated). Any identification of an individual with participation in a research project about sex carries the potential risk of social stigma. Even when subjects are fully aware of this problem and are carefully protected by elaborate methodological steps to ensure anonymity, the subject himself or herself may break the confidentiality without realizing all of the possible sequelae. For example, in a study involving return of a daily record form identified only by a subject study number and containing only coded answers, one subject mailed the form to us with her name and address on the envelope and a notation on the form describing use of illicit drugs and participation in a type of sexual activity that is illegal in this state.

A second category of risk factors that cannot be fully described in the process of obtaining informed consent concerns the potential long-term consequences of study participation. For example, a subject who participates in research involving observation of sexual activity may experience no problems while the study is underway, but may discover years later that feelings of guilt have arisen concerning the study participation. This same subject might also find unexpected and unfortunate social consequences if a potential spouse refuses marriage when he or she learns of the person's earlier participation in a sex-research project. It is also possible, albeit unlikely, that remote legal consequences might occur as a result of participation in a sex-research project. An example might be the parent who is denied child custody in divorce proceedings partly on the basis of a judicial decision about moral character adversely affected by testimony from the other spouse that this person had participated in a sex-research project.

These types of risks are mentioned not to dampen enthusiasm for sex research but to extend the scope of our deliberations to areas where no real data exist. In these instances, the problem is the degree to which such risk-taking is modified by *any* consent process. Can a person truly consent to assuming unknown risks of unknown magnitude? I would suggest that this is common practice in our everyday lives, where we continually engage in risk-taking—both knowing and unknowing—with infrequent calculation of a risk-benefit ratio and even rarer knowledge of a scientifically acceptable data base. Choices of occupation, marriage, life-style, and friends are often empirical. A prudent person does not avoid any and all risks, but rather makes intuitive choices in the process of living. The prudent person whose values are not violated by a particular type of sex research may choose to assume certain risks, including unforeseeable possibilities, in his or her study participation. The reasons motivating such a choice may be simple or complex, but I do not believe that it is the responsibility of the research scientist to weigh and judge such motivations under ordinary circumstances.

The concept of informed consent represents an ideal toward which the community of researchers must strive. However, there must be recognition of the limitations on attainment of this ideal goal. It seems to me that we usually (and rightly) compromise, for the instrument required to present full disclosure of every risk, every contingency, and every methodological component of research would be so cumbersome that scientists would have no time for anything but its preparation, and potential research participants would either be frightened away or would consent without bothering to read or understand this tedious morass of detail.

Scientific observation and experimentation implies that "nothing can be detected or measured without affecting in some way the observed phenomena" [5]. To minimize this problem, it is sometimes necessary to utilize deliberate deception of study subjects as an inherent aspect of the scientific methodology. In some instances, subjects may be informed about such deception in advance, as in the use of double-blind drug-treatment programs with identically appearing placebos and active drugs. In other instances, particularly in behavioral studies, the experiment would be worthless if the subject were fully informed before study participation. This type of situation is fraught with ethical cross-currents that are not easily sorted out, but have been thoroughly addressed by the Ad Hoc Committee on Ethical Standards in Psychological Research recently [6]. In the realm of sex research, it appears particularly important to ascertain that deception of study subjects, whenever employed, entails no significant additional risk to study participation. Furthermore, such deception should be corrected as soon as possible by informing the participant, at the conclusion of the study, of the facts.

A different question arises when studies are conducted without obtaining consent from subjects at all. The spectrum of such studies may be quite wide: at one extreme, the use of blood or urine specimens obtained for routine clinical care for a different research purpose; perhaps at the other extreme, the type of study exemplified by concealed observation of sexual and social activity between clients and prostitutes [7]. Although the former example would appear to many to represent no infringement on individual rights and no additional risk assumed due to the research conducted, the latter poses a different question indeed. The same objective might have been attained by videotaping these encounters, using a concealed camera so that spontaneity would not be lost, and then obtaining consent from subjects to extract and analyze the data and destroy the tape.

An area of considerable controversy in the field of bioethics is the use of prisoners as an experimental group. The prisoner is necessarily influenced by his or her conditions and term of confinement; compensation offered may be a disproportionate induce-ment to research participation; influences on prisoners are not al-ways apparent to either the researcher or prison authorities; and the belief that research participation will lead to earlier parole or other advantageous action persists even if explicitly denied; these are all problems in such investigations. [8]. Nevertheless, although it seems true that the prisoner cannot give truly informed consent, the question we must really ask is, How different is the prisoner from a wide range of other potential subjects who are also unable to give free and informed consent in the utopian sense for which we would strive? In a recent provocative discussion of the question "Can convicts consent to castration?" Klerman [9] has stated his view that prisoners have the right and ability to make choices, specifically identifying an attitude that seems prevalent regarding such decisions:

We romantically believe that incarceration, even with its humiliations and restrictions, is less likely to impair our inner essence than psycho-active drugs or than procedures altering certain parts of the body. . . . I suspect that we have been overly influenced by accounts of rare in-dividuals who have maintained their sense of autonomy while incar-cerated, and tend to ignore the many thousands whose capacity for autonomy and freedom has been overwhelmed by the indignity of pro-longed incarceration.

I would argue that sex research on prisoners, although requiring careful advance review on a project-by-project basis, can and should be conducted when appropriate safeguards can be utilized to maxi-mize the opportunity for knowledgeable consent and to minimize the inherent risks.

Research in childhood or adolescent sexuality also highlights the dilemma of informed consent. A minor may or may not be capable of understanding a research project; unfortunately, obtaining pa-rental consent does not necessarily ensure that an intelligent de-cision will be made, while it does frequently skew the nature of the research population. Unfortunately, there have been instances in which minors agreed to participate in studies pertaining to sex because of parental insistence; without being aware of this pres-sured situation, the researchers collected data that the child deliberately falsified and had no knowledge of the discomfort of the child in answering such queries. I mention this not to argue against parental consent, which appears highly appropriate in research involving minors, but to point out that such a consent mechanism is no panacea.

CONCLUDING REMARKS: ATTITUDES AND VALUES IN SEX RESEARCH

I have examined some aspects of ethical issues in sex research in the preceding commentary from a viewpoint that is primarily theoretical. As I read and thought about these problems, it was painfully apparent that there is far too much theorizing and far too little actual data to assist us in reaching any conclusions. To begin correcting this situation, the Reproductive Biology Research Foundation has begun a research program to evaluate public attitudes toward sex research, to assess motivations for participation in sex research, and to determine the ethical concerns of potential research subjects themselves in varying types of research programs.

As illustrative of the information we are gathing, I would like to summarize some of our findings in a population of women aged 18 to 30 who had volunteered to participate in a study of correlations between hormonal patterns in the menstrual cycle, stress events, and sexual activity. One hundred and forty-five women who volunteered for this study during a single month subsequently completed a questionnaire describing attitudes toward a variety of research situations. A subsample of 20 women were then personally interviewed to obtain further details about their responses. Fifty-four percent of respondents indicated that the major reason they volunteered for study was financial compensation. Nineteen percent cited general curiosity as their major reason for volunteering; 18 percent wished primarily to find out about their hormone levels or reactions to stress; 9 percent indicated that their primary motivation was to advance scientific knowledge in general. Of this entire group, only 12 percent denied that financial considerations were among even the secondary reasons for volunteering for study.

Each person was queried about a series of hypothetical research situations and asked whether she would participate in such a study, whether she considered the project safe, and whether she would participate in the project without payment. The following points may be of interest:

1. Fifty-seven percent of these women stated that they would participate in the original project they had volunteered for without pay if they were shown the results of their hormone testing. An additional 22 percent said they might volunteer without pay.
2. Ninety-eight percent said that a study involving measurement of blood pressure, pulse, and temperature while viewing an erotic movie was safe; 2 percent were not sure of the safety of this project. Sixty-seven percent of respondents said they would participate in such a study without pay, while 84 percent would participate if ten dollars' payment was provided.
3. Twenty-six percent of the women said that they would ingest 200 mg of phenobarbitol to determine hormonal responses to barbiturates. Fewer than half the women who agreed to participate felt this was a safe project, however. On the other hand, 59 percent of the women queried stated that they would not participate in such a study. Many respondents commented that they would not ingest any pharmacologically active substance as part of a research protocol.
4. Eighty-eight percent of these women regarded a hypothetical project to monitor physiological changes during masturbation as safe; only one of the 145 women questioned regarded this study as unsafe. (Twelve percent of respondents were unsure of the project's safety.)
5. Twenty-eight percent of the women stated that they would participate in physiological monitoring of heterosexual activity with their husbands or boyfriends; an additional 22 percent indicated they might participate in such a project, depending on a variety of details of methodology.
6. Only 3 percent of the women regarded a hypothetical project involving use of a new chemical form of contraception of unknown safety as safe. (This is both reassuring and alarming—reassuring in that so many respondents recognized without difficulty the nature of the information given to them, but alarming

in that the 3 percent believed such a project to be safe when it was *labeled* unsafe.)

A full description of these studies will be presented elsewhere; however, I would like to conclude by mentioning several comments that were made by respondents. Remarkably, only one negative comment was received. "I question the necessity of some of these hypothetical projects. I also question the morality of this." However, most of the comments fit one of two general patterns: (1) "I think it is important that advances continue in the field of sex research. I would be very happy to participate in any projects that I feel emotionally comfortable with to help this work"; or (2) "Although I am afflicted by many values that come from years and years of biases of parental and cultural upbringing, I think that your research is very necessary to all of us. While I am too embarrassed to participate in any studies involving observation of sexual activity, I salute those people who can do this because it helps us all. I am very interested in participating in any other kind of sex research, and hope that I can discuss these results with you."

If we treat research participants as our co-investigators in the search for knowledge, we may be able to continue responsibly the progress that has been slowly begun but is gathering momentum.

REFERENCES

1. Callahan, D. The ethics backlash. *The Hastings Center Report* 5:18, 1975.
2. Ingelfinger, F. J. The unethical in medical ethics. *Annals of Internal Medicine* 83:264–269, 1975.
3. Gaylin, W., and Gorovitz, S. Academy forum: Science and its critics. *Science* 188:2186, 1975.
4. Spiro, H. M. Constraint and consent—on being a patient and a subject. *New England Journal of Medicine* 293:1134–1135, 1975.
5. *Scientific Freedom and Responsibility.* American Association for the Advancement of Science, Washington, D.C., 1975.
6. Ad Hoc Committee on Ethical Standards in Psychological Research, American Psychological Association. *Ethical Principles in the Conduct of Research with Human Participants.* Washington, D.C., 1973.

7. Stein, M. L. *Lovers, Friends, Slaves . . . The Nine Male Sexual Types.* New York: Berkley, 1974.
8. Committee on Human Research, University of California at San Francisco. *Guidelines*, January 1975.
9. Klerman, G. Can convicts consent to castration? *The Hastings Center Report* 5:17–18, 1975.

DESIGNATED DISCUSSION

RUTH MACKLIN

While I have little quarrel with most of what Dr. Kolodny has said, I remain somewhat unconvinced by his essential contention that sex research is different from other types of research. Most of the ethical problems that he cites as unique to sex research seem to occur as well in research or experimentation using human subjects in a wide range of biomedical and behavioral contexts. After commenting on a number of specific issues raised by Dr. Kolodny, I shall close by suggesting the appropriateness of a prominent moral principle for evaluating the ethics of sex research or, for that matter, any form of research using human subjects.

Before turning to ethical principles, however, let me first address some of the more specific issues that Dr. Kolodny has brought up. Among the ethical problems he notes in connection with research design, the most important seem to be the difficulties that arise in clinical investigation in which potential research subjects are all patients. The stated objection to this procedure is that it may set up conflicting loyalties within a physician whose goal includes both therapy for patients and contributions to medical knowledge. Dr. Kolodny offers several counter-arguments in support of his own contention that it is not an optimal solution to separate research from clinical care. The reasons he gives are the likelihood of a decrease in the degree of confidentiality that can be maintained when there are two investigators, a lack of trained personnel in the area of sex research, and the shortcomings of research by an independent investigator who is not clinically knowledgeable. Only the factor of confidentiality would seem to constitute a morally relevant reason, however, since the lack of trained personnel in this field will, it is hoped, be remedied with time, and it is always possible for a clinically knowledgeable investigator to work with a physician whose patients are being used as subjects. In any case, the consideration that Dr. Kolodny cites may be sufficient to override the objection that rests on the occurrence of conflicting loyalties when a physician conducts research on his own patients.

There is, however, a stronger objection to this practice, which Dr. Kolodny does not bring up here, and this is the objection that the special features of the doctor-patient relationship increase the difficulty of gaining informed consent without the intrusion of subtle coercive elements. Later in his paper, Dr. Kolodny explicitly notes some problems of lack of wholly free or uncoerced consent in the case of sex research on minors and on prisoners. Similar issues arise in the case of patients who are used as experimental subjects, since the patient role invests these people with a quality of dependency, and the trust they place in their own physicians may render patients especially vulnerable to unintended, but nonetheless genuine, coercion that may be brought to bear on them. While I think this consideration does not constitute an absolute barrier to the use of patients as subjects in sex research or other forms of human experimentation, special care must be taken to eliminate such pressures whenever possible. In my own view, there is a considerable moral difference between clinical research that stands to benefit the patient-subject and research that does not. Dr. Kolodny fails to distinguish between these two in arguing for his position, but it is a distinction that has some ethical import and needs to be addressed explicitly.

In his discussion of ethical limitations of some areas of sex research, Dr. Kolodny offers several examples for our consideration. He notes two clear cases of ethically unacceptable research: first, research involving direct sexual activity between an adult and a minor, and, second, the use of placebo contraceptives. Cases about which he is uncertain are research involving sexual activity between consenting unmarried adults that violates state or local law, and use of placebo antiandrogens. While my moral intuitions coincide with

Dr. Kolodny's in the cases of obviously unethical research, I fail to see how these ethical problems are unique to sex research. Many forms of research that are permissible on adults are morally proscribed for minors, and objections have often been raised to the use of placebos in clinical investigations where there is a drug known to be curative or even ameliorative for the condition in question. As for sex research that violates state or local laws, there are precedents at least in the area of research using narcotics, psychedelic drugs, and marijuana. So here, too, the ethical problems raised by sex research do not seem to be unique.

It is worth noting that state and local laws pertaining to sex remain archaic in many ways. One blatant example is an Ohio statute prohibiting all sexual acts except face-to-face intercourse between married partners. As in many circumstances, there is sometimes good reason to disobey the law. I do not mean to urge that researchers ignore legal considerations such as these but, since law and morality do not always coincide, it may sometimes be ethically permissible to violate the law. What is needed, quite independently of what the law says, is to articulate the moral principles that underlie the sorts of judgment on which most of us would agree, such as the ethical impermissibility of research involving direct sexual activity between an adult and a minor.

In his discussion of data analysis, Dr. Kolodny asks whether certain types of research data should ever be suppressed. The example he gives is that of a substance known to be physically harmful, but found to have major aphrodisiac effects. If time permitted, I would argue that the suppression of research findings in such cases would be an unwarranted exercise of paternalism on the part of researchers or the state. Other physically harmful substances, such as alcohol and tobacco, are not only known and readily available but are used without penalty. The question of the desirability of suppression of research data has been raised in other areas, such as research into the possible genetic determinants of antisocial and other forms of behavior or the connections between IQ and race. So there may be contexts in which such ethical dilemmas do exist in the area of sex research. Here, too, the moral problems do not seem peculiar to this field.

While I agree with Dr. Kolodny's claim that, in the field of sex

research, we must be particularly cognizant of the impact our research and clinical findings may have on the individual, I remain
unconvinced that the issue is peculiar to this field of inquiry. The
effects of labeling persons as abnormal are well known, and the
ethical implications of such labeling have been explored in some
depth in connection with mental illness and mental retardation.
Whether the labels are ones like *frigidity* and *latent homosexuality*
or, instead, terms such as *schizophrenia* and even *epilepsy*, the
stigmas of labeling may be present and likely to be harmful to those
to whom they are applied.

Dr. Kolodny also points up the problem of abuses in the field
of sex research, such as where well-meaning but scientifically or
ethically naive people engage in studies about sex without adequate attention to methodological or ethical issues. While I agree
with his observation that little can be done to stop such abuses in
this field, I do think that steps might be taken to ensure that the
public is better informed in this area. It is incumbent on those who
engage in sex research and who report the findings to the general
public to develop and state criteria for distinguishing the legitimate from the bogus. Here again, the issue seems no different in
principle from the problem of quackery in other therapeutic contexts, but perhaps it is made somewhat worse by the fact that sex
is a highly emotionally charged topic and therefore lends itself
more readily to various forms of exploitation.

When it comes to applying the doctrine of informed consent in
research and therapeutic contexts, it is worth noting explicitly that
there are two separate but related issues. While Dr. Kolodny refers
to both of these, he does not separate them sharply for analysis or
discussion. The first problem is that consent must be truly informed. The difficulties here are those of conveying information to
lay persons, ascertaining that they understand the information conveyed, and deciding how much and what specific sort of information are adequate for securing truly informed consent. The second
problem is that consent, even if truly informed, must be freely
granted. The difficulties of transmitting and processing relevant
information to patients or research subjects seem not to be different in this field from what they are elsewhere. But Dr. Kolodny
raises two problems concerning whether or not consent can be

wholly voluntary. The first is the case of proxy consent for minors, and the second concerns consent from prisoners. While the problem of how to obtain truly voluntary consent seems at first glance to be somewhat similar in the cases of minors and of prisoners, on closer reflection it is apparent that the issues are quite different. The problem with minors is largely one of the moral limits of third-party consent for someone else to serve as a research subject. If the dilemmas of informed consent in the area of sex research on minors are primarily those that Dr. Kolodny mentions, such as parental pressure, it would seem to be an appropriate solution to require consent of the child himself in addition to parental consent. Indeed, in the case of adolescents there would seem to be good reason to bring about changes generally in the existing procedures regarding informed consent, since it is likely that children over the age of 12 or so do possess the requisite competency for making many such decisions. With younger children the problems are more significant, but still it would seem that the presumption in favor of securing a minor's consent in addition to parental consent could go a long way toward preventing the kind of unfortunate situation Dr. Kolodny describes.

In the case of prisoners, a curious irony emerges concerning their participation in sex research. While the problem of prisoners' ability to make fully voluntary uncoerced choices is one that is not easily resolved, if we judge that at least some research with prisoners as subjects is morally permissible, then the difficulty is to decide what sorts of research may be done under what circumstances. In an article that is a companion piece to one cited in Dr. Kolodny's paper, one writer observes that the sexual opportunities open to prisoners are neither many nor attractive. Others have noted that the use of prisoners as volunteers in human experimentation may provide a chance for meaningful and even altruistic actions on the part of an incarcerated population whose routine is monotonous and whose choices are few. It would seem, then, that while precautions should certainly be taken to ensure that prisoners' consent is fully voluntary, there are no special ethical barriers to the use of prisoners as subjects in sex research. If it is ethically permissible to use prisoners in research generally—in the belief that, although their social freedom in prison is diminished, they are still capable of free choice—their ability to serve as subjects of sex research may even enhance an otherwise poor quality of life.

In the case of prisoners, as with any research subject, it would be well to heed an ethical principle that might perhaps deserve the epithet "timeless." This principle is one formulation of the categorical imperative put forth by the eighteenth-century German philosopher Immanuel Kant: "Always treat other persons as ends and never solely as means." Although this moral principle is rather general and therefore difficult to apply, the moral sentiment it expresses can nevertheless serve as a guide in a wide range of situations where the moral permissibility of research using human subjects may be open to question.

G E N E R A L   D I S C U S S I O N

R. CHRISTIAN JOHNSON: I would like to direct a question regarding the terms *morals* and *ethics* to Dr. Macklin. It seems to me that we use *ethics*, as when we speak of professional ethics, in a somewhat different sense than we use *morality*.

RUTH MACKLIN: Among secular philosophers, the terms *ethics* and *morals* are used interchangeably. The difference is only an etymological one: *ethics* derives from a Greek root, *morals* from a Latin one. What's known as professional ethics has lately come to be referred to by philosophers who engage in these fields as professional etiquette. Now, if there is a distinction in ordinary life between etiquette and ethics, then perhaps that distinction might also occur in a biomedical or behavioral context. While there may be nothing but an etymological difference between the terms as used by philosophers, others may use the terms differently. If we're discussing topics usually referred to as medical ethics, as opposed to professional ethics, there is little difference whether we refer to them as ethical problems or as moral problems in medicine.

H. TRISTRAM ENGELHARDT, JR.: There was a bit of tittering about *professional etiquette*. It is worth noting, though, that medical ethics was usually referred to as medical etiquette in the United

States until 1847, when the American Medical Association adopted its code of medical ethics. Moreover, rules of etiquette help professional groups to gain internal coherence and to integrate themselves within the larger society.

CHARLES REMBAR: I don't think the word *etiquette* is unnecessarily deprecatory. I think we can use a bit more of it.

HELEN S. KAPLAN: I really liked what Dr. Macklin said. I have the same attitude of responsibility toward the welfare of the research subject as I do toward the patient, and I think that was essentially what you were saying as being a sensible moral guideline.

RUTH MACKLIN: What you point out is that an ethical researcher ought to consider research subjects as he or she would consider patients. The problems that are inherent in the physician-patient relationship add special difficulties. Even when an investigator using patients as subjects has the best intentions and utilizes the most care, there may be something in the nature of the patient's view of the situation that might lead a patient to be more vulnerable to requests that he or she participate in experimentation. This is without impugning the researcher or the physician, but rather suggesting that there may be some kind of psychological limitations on anyone in that kind of situation.

HELEN S. KAPLAN: I didn't mean that I use my patients as research subjects, but I think having the same basic responsible attitude toward the research subject as toward the patient can guard against many of the abuses that can happen in the course of research. I do not think that such an attitude interferes with research; in fact, I think it creates special opportunities from which both the subject and the investigator can benefit.

ROBERT GORDIS: I wonder whether one might possibly build a bridge between the remarks of Dr. Kolodny and Dr. Macklin. I have the impression that Dr. Macklin's position is theoretically sound and that the distinction between sex research and other areas of research is essentially one of degree. On the practical level, however, Dr. Kolodny—who has been working in the field—is calling our attention to the fact that in the area of sex research there is a tremendous backlog of prejudice and withdrawal that makes the subject more vulnerable than it otherwise would be. While I believe Dr. Macklin is correct in saying that there is only a slight difference, a sufficient difference of degree is almost a difference in kind. What we have here, therefore, are the two faces of the same problem: one the practical problem, the other the theoretical base.

ALAN A. STONE: I wonder if Dr. Masters and Mrs. Johnson would comment on whether, had they been subjected to peer review and a committee on human subjects' rights, they would have been permitted to do their research; and, if not, what does that say about Dr. Kolodny's paper?

WILLIAM H. MASTERS: If we had been subjected to peer review the research would never have been instituted. However, I don't think this disagrees with the premise of Dr. Kolodny's paper because it simply reflects how deeply attitudes have changed over the last quarter of a century. Had we had peer review or been required to follow careful procedures of informed consent 25 years ago, we wouldn't have started—there would have been no way to do it.

In a sense, Rabbi Gordis' comment reflected exactly the way I feel about this. I agree totally with Dr. Macklin's theoretical position. I empathize completely with Dr. Kolodny's position because there *is* a difference in sex research using human subjects. It isn't so much the situation, it isn't so much the examination, it is the concern for public opinion. I have repeatedly said to those working with us that I don't think you can work in this field for a quarter of a century without developing a tendency to paranoia.

CHARLES REMBAR: Mrs. Johnson, what would you say about concern for the individual with whom you are working?

VIRGINIA E. JOHNSON: Respect for the dignity and privacy of each research subject is an absolute prerequisite to our work. If this had not been the case years ago, we could never have continued such studies. I am also pleased to have an opportunity to draw from the past in order to understand the present. We did not spring full grown, separate, and apart from the kind of changes and transitions that were occurring in the whole of society. We have always acknowledged that we exist because of the times, not in spite of them.

In a sense, we stepped into a flow of motion begun by Kinsey, who described the changing mores and needs of a nation and went on to produce facts and concepts based on science rather than myth and folklore. In so doing, we often asked each other if we were willing to commit professional suicide. In reaching out to supply the answers, we took the steps we needed at the time.

CARL S. SHULTZ: I'd like to confirm Dr. Macklin's point that we're really dealing with a spectrum, and not an inherent difference between sex research and other forms of research. But I'd like to get back to the question of informed consent. In the matter of relative risk, I feel the basic issue is that in various types of research the individual is exposed to different ratios of risk. One of the problems that we found in a project in genetic counseling was that the manner in which information is transmitted to patients makes a great difference to the way the information is interpreted. For example, if you say, "There is only one chance in four that the next child will be born with this condition," it is rather different than saying, "There is a 25 percent chance that the next child will be born with this condition." I think this typifies the problem of how information is transmitted in regard to a research project as well, and what the understanding of the respondent or the patient is in regard to the information transmitted. We are all aware that there is a marked degree of selective perception of such information.

ROBERT C. KOLODNY: Biases in making a potential research subject informed prior to obtaining his or her consent enter both from the selective perception you mention and from at least two other sources: the researcher's manner and the potential subject's interpretation of what he or she has been told. These important imperfections are a major factor in our discussion today.

HAROLD I. LIEF: We have been discussing in this session whether there are any significant differences between sex research and research in other areas of biomedical affairs and other health areas. I think Dr. Macklin has made a very firm case in demonstrating that the similarities are probably greater than the differences, yet I think some differences are definitely there. Dr. Masters has talked about the climate of public opinion. We also must mention the charged feelings of subjects which play into this and, of course, the attitudes of colleagues. I assume that, in talking about public opinion, you were including the attitudes of your colleagues—because you certainly went through that with your colleagues in obstetrics and gynecology during the early days of your research.

I think that Dr. Kolodny mentioned one important area that we haven't discussed. He mentioned an additional difference, that most research deals with life-support systems or research aimed at improving our life-support systems. In this instance he talked about the *quality* of life, noting that sex research deals not with life support, but perhaps the quality of life support. I think that I would like to ask Dr. Kolodny to come back to this point and elaborate on it because it may be a very significant difference.

Recently, at the University of Pennsylvania, I was asked by the Human Research Committee to comment on a project of the Monell Institute involving the possible presence of pheromones in women. This project entailed collection of vaginal secretions after masturbation to see whether these secretions contained substances acting as pheromones. Although this project was approved, there were feelings that this was different from the usual research dealing with life support and, consequently, more attention was paid to some of the ethical issues that we have been discussing.

ROBERT C. KOLODNY: Dr. Lief raises some very pertinent points. Perhaps I may use them as a means of addressing several aspects of this discussion. As I hear it, Dr. Macklin and I do not stand very far apart. Perhaps we're using different words to convey much the same thought processes. I don't see the ethical dilemmas involved in the field of sex research as different in kind from the ethical dilemmas involved in any other kind of research. I think, however, that there are some differences of detail, which Dr. Masters highlighted very well in terms of pinpointing the visibility to which Dr. Lief has just returned.

There would be no question of the ethics of a research project being presented to a university committee that involved obtaining a sperm specimen for biochemical analysis. This is a very routine piece of research. We are well aware that such research requires masturbation to produce the sperm specimen. However, when we introduce the other side of that coin and ask about the production of vaginal secretions by female masturbation, ethical concerns are raised. This seems to me to be a somewhat sad but true sign of the times.

If I may return to Dr. Mudd's opening remarks, I think I can elucidate my meaning. She described a context three or four decades ago of being asked not to use the word *sex* in a fund-raising activity. It may interest you to know that we were requested by a government official to drop the word *sex* from the title of this conference. This followed shortly on some testimony that Dr. Masters and I gave before the President's Panel of Biomedical and Behavioral Research in July, where we mentioned previous problems we had had being asked to remove the word *sex* from the titles of several grant applications. In other testimony, a government representative denied that such a request had ever been made. None of us are here to be political nitpickers, but I think most of us are aware of the fact that the field of sex research is evaluated by a different set of standards than many other kinds of research. If we were talking about lipid patterns, if we were talking about dermatological diseases, much of this discussion would make no sense.

I return now to Dr. Lief's question. I was not speaking of life-support research alone, because I think such research has its own distinctive features. Much of what we do does not deal with disease or illness as such. Of course, there are many kinds of research that deal with behavior that has no connection with disease at all. Research on adolescent self-esteem or group interactions are examples that come to mind quickly. However, we are beginning to focus on some of the particular issues that we are confronted with in the everyday work of sex research—namely, although the general principles of our research may be very similar to the general principles of all other kinds of research, we must exercise an extraordinary degree of care in not offending community or professional standards, since we are scrutinized more intensely than our scientific colleagues and are frequently faulted for anticipated transgressions. We will never be sure how much this public and professional accountability serves not simply to protect but, as Dr. Stone implied, also to obliterate responsible ethical innovation in research. I think those of us who have been in the field for the past few years are aware that, although this is becoming less problematic than it was perhaps two or three decades ago, it certainly hasn't ceased as yet.

Finally, returning to Dr. Stone's earlier query, I would like to ask Dr. Masters to explain a bit more fully the procedures he followed to get permission to begin his work.

WILLIAM H. MASTERS: As I said before, we did not have true peer review. But in order to work within a department, within a medical school, within a university, we needed academic support. To answer you a little further, had we gone to the executive faculty of the medical school, had we gone to the executive faculty of the university, I'm sure we would have been denied permission to do the research. What we did do was go to our professor, who said, "I think you ought to go to the dean." And then we went to the dean, who said, "I think you ought to talk to the chancellor," and the chancellor said, "I have to talk to the board of trustees, but I will be back to you." He actually gave us permission to do this work, although the authority came from the Board of Trustees of Washington University at the behest of the chancellor taking a position—a position not in support of sex research, but in support of academic freedom.

CHARLES REMBAR: It seems to me that if this conference is suffering from anything, it is suffering from a strong compulsion to agree. It sounded to me as though there was a rather deep difference between what Dr. Kolodny said and what Dr. Macklin said. We may label it a difference of degree, but differences of degree can have very important practical consequences.

JACK WIENER: I wonder if Dr. Kolodny would make clear whether the National Institute of Mental Health (NIMH) asked that sex be taken out of the title.

ROBERT C. KOLODNY: No, it was not the NIMH that made that request.

JOHN MONEY: I have an example of sex research that is taboo today. As I guess most people in this room know, I am particularly interested in development from infancy onward of psychosexual status and gender identity. I would very much like to know more about the sexual rehearsal play of children in late infancy and early childhood, since there is abundant evidence that it occurs in all primates and is probably necessary for proper and healthy differentiation and development of psychosexual status and general identity in a human being. At the present time, I would not even bother wasting my time writing out a grant proposal to send to the ethics committee, nor to submit to NIMH or any other granting agency, because it would be dismissed as a dirty old man wanting to watch children fucking. Likewise, I would not even write out a grant proposal for something else I deem very important, and that is the wisdom of sex education in the early prepuberty years by using pictorial material, possibly films—very well-selected ones—that show the act of copulation before the child is able to get too sexually aroused. That would also be a forbidden kind of research at the present time.

CHARLES REMBAR: Dr. Money, who would give the consent if you went forward with a program of this sort?

JOHN MONEY: Nobody.

CHARLES REMBAR: Dr. Money, perhaps you misunderstood my question. I meant if the program were sanctioned, how would you get the consent of the subjects?

JOHN MONEY: With children at the prepubertal age, I personally would like to get their own consent, although I would be willing to work in the initial stages with those families who were about to give consent, too, because in this particular instance I would prefer to work collaboratively with the parents on the sex-education project rather than in spite of them. With regard to young children from 12 to 18 months onward, I would not by any means need the infant's consent because the parents themselves would be the participant-observers. It would be their consent I would get.

ROBERT L. STUBBLEFIELD: If you substitute the word *aggression* for *sexuality*, would you not have the same problem today? I think one of the big issues is the gradual withdrawal of federal and private support for research about human behavior, except microscopic bits of human behavior. Some people have suggested that this reduction is related to the general attitude of the public in the postindustrial society. I have the notion that when you talk about resistance to research and support at the federal level, the public is interested in studies that deal with fatal illnesses (heart disease and cancer), which diminishes the chances for obtaining funds for the study of behavior. I would like to know whether a part of the resistance you now encounter around these human rights issues and other issues is not simply the reaction to a more general negative attitude about research inquiry into all human behavior, not just sexuality.

PEPPER SCHWARTZ: Peer review is a very important thing to the social sciences because the social sciences have very little tradition of training you in what to do about the mental health and future of your subject. In most social science research, you go in and observe, or administer questionnaires, or interview—then you say goodbye, with very little concern and no training about your moral or therapeutic relationship to those subjects. It was only recently in my own research that I first realized that people may be changed by the interview I give them or be influenced by things I say. Suddenly I realized that we were ill-prepared for this role, and I personally feel that one of the things peer review has done is made the social science researcher much more aware of this.

RICHARD GREEN: In the study of atypical sexuality, anthropology sometimes utilizes a research strategy that methodologically or euphemistically (I haven't decided which) is called "participant observation." In such a case, the scientist-observer is actively engaged in the behaviors being studied. This appears to be a two-edged sword. One is indeed able to obtain data that might not be available utilizing other research methodologies, but there may also be a compromise of the validity of the data so collected due to the lack of the distance scientific disciplines traditionally impose between themselves and the subject, during the intermediate process of data collection. I would be interested in comments on this issue.

CHARLES REMBAR: I'm afraid we won't have time for comments at this session. Let me close by suggesting something disagreeable that applies to all professions, including—perhaps especially—the legal profession, and that is that we all have a strong tendency to confuse what's good for society with what's good for ourselves. I think it's something we all must watch out for.

4

ETHICAL ISSUES AND REQUIREMENTS FOR SEX RESEARCH WITH HUMANS: CONFIDENTIALITY

MIRIAM F. KELTY

CONCEPTS OF PRIVACY AND CONFIDENTIALITY

The concept of confidentiality is related to the concept of privacy, that is, the common need of individuals and organizations for a degree of secrecy about themselves. *Webster's Third New International Dictionary* defines privacy as "the quality or state of being apart from the company or observation of others," and as "freedom from unauthorized oversight or observation." Confidentiality is defined as "known only to a limited few: not publicly disseminated." It is the quality or state of being confidential (private or secret), that is, not freely disclosed. A confidential relationship is one that is indicative of intimacy, mutual trust, or willingness to confide. Issues concerning confidentiality relate to delineation of the limited few who may have access to information, and to the specification of their responsibilities.

Our society recognizes that privacy is necessary to human dignity, and that it plays a role in the development of individuality as well as in the maintenance of the social, economic, and political well-being of the individual. Protection of privacy and confidentiality has been incorporated into the legal system. For example, the law provides testimonial privileges to protect the confidentiality of certain human relationships: communication between spouses, between lawyers and clients, between doctors and patients, between clergy and individuals. Further, confidentiality applies not only to individual human relationships and property, but also to organizations, including professional and social organizations, businesses, and government.

Although several writers have distinguished between privacy and confidentiality [1, 2], for the purposes of this paper the concepts will not be separated. Attorney General Levi, in his talk to the Association of the Bar of the city of New York, uses the two concepts interchangeably [3]. The legislation summarized in the following pages deals with privacy in some instances and with confidentiality in others, but they will be considered as functionally related.

WHY IS CONFIDENTIALITY AN ISSUE?

For the researcher, a high value is placed on the development of knowledge in his or her field. In fields in which research is conducted with humans, including the biomedical and behavioral social sciences, the topics of research may be such that research participants assume confidentiality or seek explicit assurance that any information they communicate is confidential. Confidentiality may serve various purposes, ranging from respect for privacy because of the personal sensitivity of information to the possibility of prosecution of the research participants if information about illegal activities were not held confidential.

The successful conduct of research in many areas, including sex research, depends on participation of volunteer and/or consenting persons. A reduction in the number of willing participants may occur if privacy is not respected and if the confidentiality of the data provided is not upheld. Aside from the development of negative attitudes in individuals, a lack of trust in research may grow to such proportions as to limit severely the amount of research that may be conducted in particular subject areas. The integrity and dignity of individual researchers and their subjects are at stake, as well as the public's attitude toward the human sciences.

In recent years confidentiality of both research sources and data have been challenged. The challenges have included the issuance of subpoenas to researchers to testify in courts and in grand jury investigations. The challenges to confidentiality of data have involved uses of data for purposes other than intended, and access to data by persons other than the principals concerned.

LEGAL BACKGROUND OF
RESEARCH CONFIDENTIALITY

In the United States, assuring confidentiality of research data stems from an 1840 statute against disclosure of census interview data [4]. The right of privacy was first discussed by Warren and Brandeis in a *Harvard Law Review* article in which they held that public disclosure of personal information is a wrong against the "inviolate personality" [5]. Although a right to privacy is not explicitly guaranteed in the U.S. Constitution, an implied right to privacy is based on interpretation of the Bill of Rights amendments. The First Amendment guarantees freedom of expression (and the liberty of silence) and serves to protect confidentiality of thoughts and beliefs. The Fourth Amendment safeguards against unwarranted search of person and property, and has been interpreted as guaranteeing confidentiality of the person and his property and as a recognition that an important aspect of individuality would be lost if all aspects of a person's life were disclosed to the public. The Fifth Amendment's mandate for due process and against self-incrimination implies confidentiality. The Fourteenth Amendment's due process clause also protects against unwarranted intrusion into matters of personal privacy.

In *Katz* v. *United States* (1967), the Court held that the Fourth Amendment protects not only the privacy of the person, but also the confidentiality of his or her communications [3]. The legal principle that confidentiality applies to groups as well as to individuals was established with the Supreme Court decision in *NAACP* v. *Alabama,* when the Court held that disclosure of NAACP membership rosters might result in public reaction such as to "condition their freedom of association upon their payment of an intolerable price" [3]. The Supreme Court explicitly recognized the right to privacy in *Griswold* v. *Connecticut* (1965), a case in which a state attempted, by statute, to prevent the use of contraceptive devices. The Court explicitly found a right to privacy arising from specific guarantees provided for in at least the First, Third, Fourth, Fifth, and Ninth Amendments, which taken together "have penumbras, formed by emanations from those guarantees that help give them life and substance . . . various guarantees create zones of privacy" (p. 484). That decision also held that ". . . the State may not, consistent with the spirit of the First Amendment, contract the spectrum of available knowledge. The right of freedom of speech and press includes not only the right to utter or to print, but the right to distribute, the right to receive, the right to read . . . and freedom of inquiry, freedom of thought, and freedom to teach . . . indeed the freedom of the entire university community . . . without these peripheral rights would be less secure" (pp. 482–483). It is notable that, despite this broad language and enumeration of types of freedoms of privacy, privacy itself is not defined. However, subsequent Court decisions have held that freedom of personal choice in matters of marriage and family life are included among the liberties protected by the due process clause of the Fourteenth Amendment. Thus, *Eisenstadt* v. *Baird* (1972) recognized that married or single individuals have the right to be protected from unwarranted governmental intrusion into matters affecting a person, specifically the individual's decision whether to have a child. Similarly, the more recent abortion decision, *Roe* v. *Wade* (1973), was decided to be within the purview of personal liberty protected by the due process clause.

REPORTERS' RIGHTS TO PROTECT NEWS SOURCES

Another series of cases, in the area of newsmen's privilege, has resulted in further explication of the right to confidentiality. The news media have maintained that they need a privilege to protect the confidentiality of their sources. Freedom of expression, including the rights to free press, speech, assembly, and petition, has been advanced by Nejelski and Peyser to support an argument for

First Amendment protection of confidential research data [6]. Nejelski holds that freedom of expression implies freedom to gather information. A number of court cases have recently been decided dealing with maintenance of confidential sources of information provided to newsmen.

In *Branzburg* v. *Hayes* (1972), a reporter who wrote an article about the manufacture, use, and sale of illegal drugs was subpoenaed by a grand jury and asked to identify persons whom he had observed engaging in illegal activities. Branzburg claimed protection from such disclosure of confidential sources by the First Amendment. In a second case, Pappas, a television newsman, gained entry to Black Panther headquarters prior to an anticipated police raid. No raid occurred and no story ensued. However, Pappas was subpoenaed by a grand jury to testify about what occurred during the time he was present in the Panthers' headquarters. Pappas argued that the subpoena, as well as the questions he was asked by the grand jury, violated his First Amendment rights. A third case involved Caldwell, a *New York Times* reporter who gained the confidence of Panther party members, was subpoenaed by a federal grand jury, but claimed that his appearance would destroy the confidence he had gained with Panther members [7]. The three cases were heard by the U.S. Supreme Court at the same time, since all raised the issue of whether the requirement that newsmen appear and testify before state or federal grand juries abridges the freedom of speech and press guaranteed by the First Amendment. The Court decided that the newsmen were not protected by the First Amendment and ordered them to testify to the respective grand juries. However, the Court implied that there might be a limited privilege when it decided that there is no First Amendment privilege to refuse to answer the relevant and material questions asked during a good-faith investigation. Thus, the limited privilege protects newsmen against irrelevant questions or attempts at harassment that might be considered to be in bad faith. Justice Powell, who cast the deciding vote in the five-to-four majority decision, held that the newsmen could ask the trial court to dismiss the subpoena when: (1) the newsman is called on to give information bearing only a remote and tenuous relationship to the subject of the investigation; or (2) he has some other reason to believe that his testimony implicates confidential sources without serving a legitimate need of law enforcement. The minority held that ". . . when a reporter is asked to appear before a grand jury and reveal confidences, . . . the government must (1) show that there is a probable cause to believe that the newsman has information which is clearly relevant to a specific probable violation of law; (2) demonstrate that the information sought cannot be obtained by alternative means less destructive of First Amendment rights; and (3) demonstrate a compelling and overriding interest in the information." Justice Douglas, dissenting, advocated an absolute privilege for newsmen as essential to a free press.

Nejelski and Peyser point out that, in the *Branzburg* decision, *press* was construed broadly: "Freedom of press . . . is not confined to newspapers and periodicals . . . but includes pamphlets and leaflets and comprehends every sort of publication which affords a vehicle of information . . . The information function assured by representatives of the organized press in the present cases is also performed by lecturers, political pollsters, novelists, academic researchers, and dramatists . . ." [6]

Since the *Branzburg* decision, several cases have arisen in which arguments have been advanced that the courts should balance competing interests, and that they might distinguish protection of the confidentiality of individual relationships from the revelation of information to protect the public interest. Such arguments are based on the U.S. Supreme Court's suggestion that violation of the First Amendment may, in some situations, be justified.

Thus, there have been several attempts to distinguish civil and libel cases from criminal cases. For example, in the civil case *Democratic National Committee* v. *McCord* (1973), concerning the break-in at the Democratic National Committee's Watergate headquarters, subpoenas for papers and photos were quashed; thus, newsmen were granted a limited privilege. On the other hand, in *United States* v. *Liddy* (1972), a criminal case involving the Watergate break-in and bugging, reporters were defeated in their attempts to quash subpoenas and were ordered to make tapes available to the defense. *Res Ipsa Loquitur, Georgetown Review of Law and Public Interest* [8, 9] summarizes a number of cases, differentiating libel, civil, and criminal cases that have been heard since the newsmen's cases, as does the National Academy of Sciences Report, *Protecting Individual Privacy in Evaluation Research* [6, 10, 11]. In most of the recent cases since *Branzburg*, freedom of the press is balanced against the responsibility of all citizens to provide relevant testimony with regard to criminal behavior and the public's need to know.

Although the cases dealing with confidentiality of newsmen's sources form one kind of argument for researcher privilege, the judicial decisions have been somewhat inconsistent and the existence of even a limited privilege is far from certain. However, there are a number of state and federal statutes that do protect specific kinds of research activities, data, researchers, and subjects.

INFORMATION RETRIEVAL SYSTEMS

The area that has probably generated most public concern about issues of privacy and confidentiality is the development of computerized information systems and data banks. This concern has led to congressional hearings, a study by the National Academy of Sciences, and both federal and state legislation. An example of state legislation to protect research data is described below.

In 1967 the National Institute of Mental Health awarded a grant to the Research Foundation for Mental Hygiene, Inc., to develop the Multi-State Information System (MSIS), a computer-based clinical and administrative data system for psychiatric programs. Participating programs and facilities may use on-site computer terminals and/or independent computers. Data-collection instruments are designed to collect (1) demographic information (including name of patient, in most instances); (2) administrative data (referral source, ward or clinic assignment, transfers, legal status, income information); (3) patient problems and progress information; (4) treatment and service data (medications, direct clinical services, and laboratory test data); and (5) other service information (indirect services performed by psychiatric facilities, such as community consultation and information). The computer prepares regular standardized reports from the information received and permits users to retrieve other information to meet specific needs. Additionally, statistical information is aggregated for the use of cooperating health-delivery systems to aid in administrative management of the participating facilities. Research is facilitated by the availability of large amounts of data.

An elaborate data-protection system was developed to assure ethical and legal confidentiality of the MSIS data files, "secret" passwords are required for input and output, and guards secure the MSIS main computer facility. Nonetheless, concern was expressed by participating organizations about the security of the system and the possible breach of confidentiality if persons of questionable integrity should acquire administrative control.

Following legal consultation and consideration of alternative safeguards, it was decided to seek a special statute from the New York Legislature declaring the system and all its records confidential. A bill submitted and subsequently passed by the legislature provides that the information in the data files is neither public nor the property of the New York State Department of Mental Hygiene, that the records stored in the system are not open to inspection by any agency or individual other than the facility submitting them, and that they are not subject to subpoena by any court or administrative agency. The immunity of these records from subpoena was justified on the basis that they are not primary information but, in all instances, secondary sources of data submitted by the participating jurisdictions. Auditors and investigators are also denied access to the MSIS data files. A single public official is given the responsibility of assuring proper operation of the system. The bill also gives MSIS authority to release aggregate data for research and planning purposes, provided identifying information is removed. The bill was passed by the New York Legislature in 1972 and is an example of a state statute that provides for protection of specific data, in this case, that contained within the data files of the Multi-State Information System for psychiatric facilities.

The MSIS commissioned a study and analysis of the laws concerning security and confidentiality of patient records. The development of the system and the legal analysis are described by Curran, Laska, Kaplan, and Bank [12].

The state of Maryland also has such a law, which pertains to confidentiality of records obtained by the State Board of Health and Mental Hygiene for the Maryland Commission to Study Problems of Drug Addiction. Agents of the commission and board have immunity from subpoena to disclose information. However, the law, like the New York statute, pertains only to specific data and specific agencies or facilities. Both are too narrow to protect researchers and research data in general.

FEDERAL PROTECTION OF RESEARCH CONFIDENTIALITY: NEW DEVELOPMENTS

Only one month ago a proposed amendment to the Code of Federal Regulations (Chapter 1, Title 42 CFR) was published that establishes procedures under which persons conducting mental-health research, including research on the use and effects of alcohol and other psychoactive drugs, may apply for an authorization to protect the privacy of research subjects by withholding the names and other identifying characteristics of the research subjects from all persons not connected with the research.

Any persons engaged in such study would apply to the relevant Alcohol, Drug Abuse, and Mental Health Administration (ADAMHA) agency for a confidentiality certificate. Exemptions are specified for research involving investigation of new drugs and for research related to law-enforcement activities.

The certificate of confidentiality is project-specific, so a researcher would have to apply separately for each project conducted. A statement of compliance with human subjects requirements must accompany the application if the research is federally funded. Persons who receive authorizations of confidentiality would not be required to identify research subjects in courts or in administrative or legislative proceedings, except when (1) the subjects consent to disclosure of information; (2) failure to disclose information would threaten the research subjects' medical welfare; and (3) the Federal Food, Drug and Cosmetic Act requires release of the information. Procedures for termination of confidentiality certificates are specified and include notifying subjects that the certificates of confidentiality have run out.

Although the proposed regulations extend to all mental-health-related research, and as such might represent a broadened scope of protection, they are project-specific. Obtaining a certificate of confidentiality is optional for the researcher, and it is possible that the option will not be known to many researchers or utilized by them.

The U.S. Congress has enacted some legislation that protects the confidentiality of research data; researchers themselves have, in some instances, been granted a testimonial privilege. The Comprehensive Drug Abuse Prevention and Control Act of 1970 provides that the Attorney General may grant a testimonial privilege to those conducting research on the use and effects of drugs. The researcher must specifically apply to the Secretary of Health, Education, and Welfare (HEW) and to the U.S. Attorney General for a grant of confidentiality. Administrative provisions are such that the researcher's security procedures must be approved. A similar provision for confidentiality and testimonial privilege is granted in the Comprehensive Alcohol and Alcoholism Prevention, Treatment, and Rehabilitation Act of 1970 for those engaged in research or treatment of alcohol abuse and alcoholism. As in the drug-prevention legislation, the confidentiality granted is delegated to the discretion of the Secretary of HEW. The Drug Abuse Office and Treatment Act of 1972 provides for confidentiality of patient records maintained by treatment organizations. These acts, though broader than the New York and Maryland statutes, grant privilege for researchers conducting particular types of research. They are still narrow in that they relate only to drug treatment and research programs, although they are not confined to particular projects [6].

Other federal legislation provides limited privilege to researchers. For example, the government has legislated against disclosure of census information and records of the Social Security Administration. However, the privilege extends only to researchers employed by these agencies.

INDIVIDUAL PRIVACY:
COMPUTERS WITHOUT CONSCIENCE

Somewhat different in focus from the legislation that deals directly with confidentiality and privilege is legislation that empha-

sizes the need for protection of individual privacy in an era of
rapid development of surveillance capability. The nature of such
concern was summarized by Senator Sam Ervin: "With the advent
of computers, the government is able to increase by geometric proportions the amount of information it can collect on individuals"
[13]. Professor Arthur Miller [14] of the Harvard Law School, in
his book *The Assault on Privacy*, suggests that it will soon be technically feasible to store a 20-page dossier on every single American:
"At the same time, the new technology permits the Government
to reduce to microseconds the amount of time necessary to get
access to the information . . ."

The power of computerized data systems to impinge on the
present and future privacy of individuals has led to several attempts
to limit the uses to which such information may be put, and to
provide for correction of erroneous data in the system. For example,
the Crime Control Act of 1973 prohibits agencies that receive funds
from the Law Enforcement Assistance Administration to disclose
identifiable research data or statistical information without explicit authorization from the individual who furnished the data.
Consent is required if any data are to be utilized as evidence in
judicial or administrative proceedings. Without such consent, the
individual provider of the data is immune from legal process. Provisions are also included to correct erroneous data by permitting
access by individuals on whom criminal records are maintained
and disseminated [8].

PRIVACY, PRIVILEGE, AND SCHOOLS: STUDENTS' RIGHTS

In the area of education, concern with privacy issues is reflected
in the Family Educational Rights and Privacy Act of 1974. This
act permits inspection of all official school records, files, and data
on students by students or nonstudents over 18 years of age, and
by parents of elementary- and secondary-school children. In addition, files and school records may not be released to any individual,
agency, or organization without written consent of parents or college students. An exception is granted for release of information

within the school system, to schools in which the student intends to enroll, to U.S. officials or administrative heads of educational agencies, and in connection with students' applications for or receipt of financial aid. Information may be released to additional persons with written consent. No consent is required if the information is furnished to comply with a judicial order or subpoena, but the student or parents must be notified of such intended release in advance. Regulations subsequently issued provide that students do not have access to the financial records of their parents or to confidential letters of recommendation placed in educational files prior to January 1, 1975.

PRIVACY AND FEDERAL AGENCIES

Privacy of statistical information was assured by passage of the Privacy Act of 1974, a complex piece of legislation to provide safeguards against invasion of personal privacy by requiring federal agencies to: (1) permit an individual to determine what records pertaining to him or her are collected, maintained, used, or disseminated by such agencies; (2) prevent dissemination of records without consent of the individual; (3) be subject to civil suit for any damages resulting from violation of the act; (4) permit individuals to have a copy made of all or portions of records and to correct or amend records; (5) collect, maintain, use, or disseminate any record of identifiable personal information in a manner that assures that such action is for a necessary and lawful purpose, that the information is current and accurate for its intended use, and that adequate safeguards are provided to prevent misuse of such information; and (6) permit exemptions from the requirements with respect to records provided for in the act only in those instances in which there is an important public-policy need for such an exemption as determined by a specific statutory authority.

A *record* or *system of records* is defined as a group of records from which information is retrieved by the name of the individual or some identifying symbol. Agencies may not disclose records that are personally identifiable without written consent of the individual involved unless the disclosure is (1) for intra-agency disclosure to employees with a need to know, (2) required by the Freedom of Information Act, (3) for routine use as specified by the agency in the *Federal Register*, (4) to the Bureau of the Census, (5) for statistical research or reporting purposes and transferred in a non-personally identifiable format, (6) to the National Archives, (7) for criminal or civil law-enforcement activity, (8) for reasons involving the health or safety of an individual, (9) to Congress, (10) to the Comptroller General, or (11) to comply with a court order.

Additionally, the individual to whom the record pertains may, on request, be given access to the information in his or her record; allowed to make corrections and receive explanations; and given a right to appeal if requested corrections are not made. The individual may take civil action against an agency to correct his or her records and to recover costs for damages if such corrections are not made.

An agency is required to (1) maintain in a record system only information that is necessary to accomplish the purposes of the agency as required by statute or executive order; (2) collect information, to the greatest extent practicable, directly from the individual involved when the information may result in an adverse determination about the individual; (3) inform each individual from whom it requests information about its authority for collecting the information, whether response is mandatory or voluntary, the principal purpose for which the information is intended to be used, routine uses that may be made of the information, and the effects on the individual of not providing the information.

Agencies are further required to publish in the *Federal Register*, at least annually, notice of the existence and character of the system of records it maintains, including name and location of the system and the responsible agency official; categories of records, data subjects, and sources of records; routine uses, policies, and practices regarding storage and retrievability (access control, retention and disposal of records); and procedures by which a data subject may determine whether or not he or she is included in the records. Agencies must also establish rules of disclosure and rules of conduct, train employees, establish safeguards to ensure security and confidentiality, and publish in the *Federal Register* a notice of new uses of information maintained in records. The provisions of the act extend to government contractors, who are, for purposes of the act, considered employees of the agency and subject to the same penalties for violation as are other agency employees. A Privacy Protection Study Commission, with a two-year life span, was also established and given authority to study related issues and to recommend legislation in the area of records and privacy.

The Privacy Act of 1974 has some major limitations as far as research is concerned. As indicated above, the act does not protect research data from subpoena for law-enforcement purposes. Also, it fails to impose restrictions on nonresearch uses of research data but imposes certain restrictions on the use of data for research purposes.

FREEDOM OF INFORMATION: THE RIGHT TO KNOW

Despite the intended protections afforded to researchers and research participants by the Privacy Act of 1974, other federal legislation fosters citizens' need to know about the nature of the information maintained by the government, including design of research and collection of data. The Freedom of Information Act, passed in 1966, requires that the government publish in the *Federal Register* information concerning policies, staff manuals, and specified activities. Agencies are permitted to delete identifying data in order to protect the privacy of individuals. However, exceptions are made in the act for various records, including records that may protect national security or foreign policy; records exempted from disclosure by particular statutes; records of a personal and private nature, such as welfare, personnel, and medical files; records whose financial, commercial, or professional value requires an assurance of confidentiality; and certain other records, including investigatory or law-enforcement information except to the extent that it is available by law to private parties. Information may not be withheld from Congress. The exceptions to the Freedom of Information Act are not mandatory. Agency administrators may override them, and courts may issue orders for disclosure of information. In some instances the courts have not favored the interests of confidentiality over the need to know. Under the provisions of the act, researchers may not be able to resist demands for disclosure of information and may be ordered to release information in support of accountability.

The Federal Reports Act (1970), designed to facilitate transfer of information among federal agencies and to avoid duplication of effort, authorizes the Office of Management and Budget to require that an agency share information with another on request if the information is in the form of statistical summaries, if it is not confidential when the transfer is requested, if consent is provided by the individual who supplied the data, and if the agency requesting the information has authority to obtain it. Research participants should be aware of these acts and their implications for the potential release of data to other agencies.

PROPOSED SOLUTIONS

The above examples of legislation have been described to convey to researchers the types of precedents that exist to justify legislation that would protect the confidentiality of research data and personnel, and to indicate the kinds of arguments that might underlie an attempt to enact legislation to protect the broad researcher community. Other legislation has been described that supports the public's need to know and that may conflict with protection of confidentiality and privacy. To help overcome policy inconsistencies and the problems they generate, a number of solutions have been proposed to reduce the risk of inappropriate access to data and to protect from subpoena information provided to researchers in confidence. The merits of federal legislation in this area have been compared with the advantages of methodological safeguards by Boruch; his work will be discussed below [15].

METHODOLOGICAL CONSIDERATIONS

Confidentiality of data can be protected legally, technologically, and methodologically. Campbell, Boruch, Schwartz, and Steinberg describe strategies to assure the confidentiality of data without unduly restricting the researcher's freedom to conduct investigations of socially sensitive problems [11]. Such design and technological protections of confidential data make it unlikely that particular data will be linked to identifiable individuals. Thus, regardless of the legal provisions in a given jurisdiction, the researcher cannot breach confidentiality because he or she cannot link the data files.

Boruch discusses statistical and procedural strategies for fostering confidentiality of data without unduly compromising research objectives [15]. Procedural strategies involve methods that may correspond to classic research designs, such as cross-sectional studies, longitudinal studies, and studies that compare experimental and control groups. They may also be used to protect confidentiality when linkage of multiple data sources is desired. The procedural technologies include (1) the use of anonymous questionnaires (both truly anonymous responses, which may be inappropriate to some studies, and self-selected aliases); (2) the use of subject-supplied data, which is matched with archival data by various encoding and decoding methods; and (3) variations on the broker mechanism, in which each of several brokers has partial information, but no single individual can link data files. Such procedural strategies are designed to avoid the need to obtain identifiable information about a research participant but may restrict research design and data analyses.

Statistical strategies include (1) contamination methods, such as inoculation of random errors into subjects' responses; (2) randomized response methods; (3) balanced incomplete blocks methods, in which a combination of key questions is asked of less than the entire population; and (4) microaggregation methods suitable for mail surveys and other impersonal methods of data collection. Such strategies prevent direct linkage of identifiable individuals' responses but may constrain research design, increase costs of data collection and analysis, and render some types of data analysis impossible. These statistical strategies and their technological advantages and constraints are extensively described in a paper [15] available from Robert F. Boruch of Northwestern University, and will not be dealt with in detail here.

Although the major concerns of Campbell, Boruch, Schwartz, and Steinberg [10] are in the area of evaluation research and provision of data for social policy formulation, the solutions they propose may be generally useful. The relevance of Boruch's proposals to sex research and to sex therapy may be linked to accountability of practice and to the responsibility of both researchers and therapists to the entire community. Campbell has noted that the concepts of privacy and confidentiality have, on occasion, been misused to avoid program evaluation and individual accountability [16]. Boruch and Campbell demonstrate procedures that permit maintenance of confidentiality and also foster accountability. It is clear that if a researcher does not adhere to a promise of confidentiality, the privacy of the individual is seriously violated.

On the whole, their proposed solutions represent much greater sophistication than characterizes the MSIS protection strategy in that they protect against misuse by researchers themselves, as well as implying protection against legal demands for research information. In addition, the statistical and procedural strategies have implications for the law-related problems of (1) provision of testimony under subpoena, (2) development of support for a testimonial privilege for researchers, (3) the content of such a statutory privilege, (4) use and operation of restricted access data archives, and (5) confidentiality of research records on organization [15].

LEGAL CONSIDERATIONS

Nejelski and Lerman have published a paper entitled "What to do before the subpoena arrives" [17] which describes some of the legal problems of researchers and suggests the need for a statutory privilege. The more recent paper by Boruch advocates the use of methodological safeguards, which he claims will prevent effective subpoenas from being issued [15]. However, if prosecutors do not recognize that individual responses are not identifiable, data may be misused to make judgments about individuals. Misunderstanding of the methodology employed by researchers is not without precedent, as in some of the cases involving the validity concepts utilized in the development and use of psychological tests. Boruch also points out that probabilistic information may eventually be permitted as evidence [15], a development that would seriously challenge the protection afforded by the methods he advocates.

Alternative means of protecting research confidentiality have been advanced. For example, many of the professions have developed codes of ethics to which members must adhere. Although society's respect for professional behavior may carry over to the courts, so that researchers and practitioners may not be held in contempt if they refuse to testify on the basis of the ethical codes of their profession, one may expect that consistent decisions will not ensue.

Researchers would be well advised to think seriously of collecting empirical data on the relative protection afforded by the different solutions to protection of confidentiality of data. In a subject such as sex research, conducted in states having different laws and characterized by relatively little collaborative research on a national basis, one might begin systematically and collaboratively to design experiments to test different methods of protection for both researchers and research participants.

FUTURE CONCERNS

Although I support a privilege for researchers, their subjects, and research data, one must consider the advantages and limitations of such a privilege, whether relative or absolute, for society in general. We are all aware that testimonial privilege can be misused, so that it must be considered within the context of the public's need to know and within the context of public accountability. In 1966 the Office of Science and Technology appointed a panel to examine privacy issues in behavioral research. The report issued by that panel advocates continuing attention to maintenance of a balance between the interests of society, research, and private personality [1]. The panel report further discusses the obligations of researchers, including protection of privacy and confidentiality as well as the production of knowledge, and points out that such obligations are of the utmost importance if the right to collect information is to be maintained.

The concern about privacy and confidentiality in the conduct of research and surrounding data storage and retrieval reflects our society's conflict of values. A policy that protects confidentiality of researchers and of human research participants conflicts with our national policy of freedom of information. This conflict may be particularly germane for the scientific community as research and, increasingly, therapy are publicly financed. Some accommodation between the competing values of confidentiality and freedom of information is necessary.

It is reasonable to expect that future policy formulation with respect to researcher privilege will reflect the value policy-makers and society-at-large place on research. Arguments for the positive value of research may be the strongest arguments for the continued support of policies that foster research confidentiality. The value of research, so long assumed by our society, has been seriously questioned by certain members of Congress—particularly basic research in the behavioral-social sciences; in some instances sex research has been singled out for special scrutiny. It is incumbent on researchers themselves to communicate to policy-makers and to the general public the policy implications of gaining further understanding of, and knowledge about, such things as sexual behavior. Researchers must demonstrate the efficacy of the processes and procedures they have developed to enforce adherence to their professional codes of ethics, to legislation, and to regulations relating to ethical practices in the conduct of research. They must also demonstrate to their subjects that they are able to comply with guarantees of confidentiality.

This review of legislation, judicial decisions, and regulations concerning privacy and confidentiality has not dealt specifically with sex research, sex therapy, or sexual behavior. The major foci of activity in the areas of privacy and confidentiality have been issues involving protection of individuals from governmental access to information stored in computer data banks, and issues of constitutional rights. However, this information is relevant to sex research and to sex therapy, broadly construed, for it summarizes judicial and legislative precedents.

To the extent that research in sexual behavior is related to doctor-patient privilege, the general rules of privilege may be considered to apply. Privilege exists if four conditions are present [18]: (1) Communications arise in confidence under contract of trust terms; (2) it is vital to the relationship to protect the confidence; (3) the relationship is to be fostered for the social good; and (4) disclosure is more injurious to the patient than beneficial to society.

However, researchers must decide which line of argument is most likely to accomplish the desired objective of protecting the confidentiality of sources, subjects, and data. To the extent that research is engaged in by all behavioral and social scientists and their staffs, it may be less than desirable to seek protection in the context of medical treatment. This argument is particularly germane to those for whom personal growth is paramount in sex research and sex therapy. Nonetheless, privilege has been extended to behavioral–social science professionals in some instances.

Sex researchers and therapists must determine whether it is to their advantage to seek protection for a particular type of research, such as sex research, or to depart from the precedent of protection for one class of research apart from research in general. As an individual concerned with science policy, I personally would prefer to see progress in the more general direction than in still more specific areas. However, it is the community of sex researchers and therapists who must ultimately decide. Opting for specific rather than general decisions would mean that innovative research areas would always require new policy formulation to effect specific protection. This has been the situation in a number of areas, such as evaluation research and drug research.

Social changes imply changes in the boundaries and domains of privacy. For example, if welfare becomes a "right" rather than a privilege, an investigation of the potential client may be construed as an invasion of privacy. The years since the publication of the Kinsey reports have been characterized by an evolution in attitudes toward sexuality, sexual behavior, and sex roles. It is possible that, in future generations, discomfort surrounding sexual behavior may diminish to the extent that it is no longer singled out as a sensitive topic. If such changes in societal attitudes do occur, new issues may emerge that challenge today's notions about the importance of confidentiality of information relating to sexual behavior. For example, protection of the community from malpractice may be considered to justify invasion of privacy. It is likely that in the medium-range future, society's concept of privacy will evolve so that some behaviors that are considered private today will be less private as more information becomes available and they are more openly discussed by the general public.

REFERENCES

1. Ruebhausen, O. M., and Brim, O. G., Jr. Privacy and behavioral research. *American Psychologist* 21:423–437, 1966.

2. Duncan, J. W. Confidentiality and the future of the U.S. statistical system. Paper read at Annual Meeting of the Social Statistics Section, American Statistical Association, August 25, 1975, in Atlanta, Georgia.

3. Levi, E. H. Address to the Association of the Bar of the City of New York, April 28, 1975.

4. Eckler, A. R. *The Bureau of the Census.* New York: Praeger, 1974.

5. Warren, S., and Brandeis, L. D. The right to privacy. *Harvard Law Review* 4:193–220, 1890. Reprinted in Hofstadter, S. H., and Horowitz, G. *The Right of Privacy.* New York: Central Book, 1964.

6. Nejelski, P., and Peyser, H. A researcher's shield statute guarding against the compulsory disclosure of research data. In *Protecting Individual Privacy in Evaluation Research.* Washington, D.C.: National Academy of Sciences, 1975.

7. Nejelski, P., and Finsterbusch, K. The prosecutor and the researcher: Present and prospective variations on the Supreme Court's Branzburg decision. *Social Problems* 21:1, 1973.

8. Symns, S., and Hawks, P. The threads of privacy. *Res Ipsa Loquitur: Georgetown Review of Law and Public Interest* 27:1, 1975.

9. Goodbody, T. Newsman's privilege. *Res Ipsa Loquitur: Georgetown Review of Law and Public Interest* 27:1, 1975.

10. Campbell, D. T., Boruch, R. F., Schwartz, R. D., and Steinberg, J. Confidentiality-preserving modes of access to files and to interfile exchange for useful statical analysis. In *Protecting Individual Privacy in Evaluation Research.* Washington, D.C.: National Academy of Sciences, 1975.

11. Committee on Federal Agency Evaluation Research. *Protecting Individual Privacy in Evaluation Research.* Washington, D.C.: National Academy of Sciences, 1975.

12. Curran, W. J., Laska, E. M., Kaplan, H., and Bank, R. Protection of privacy and confidentiality. *Science* 182:797–802, 1973.

13. Ervin, S. *Congressional Record.* February 5, 1974.

14. Miller, A. R. *The Assault on Privacy.* Ann Arbor, Mich.: University of Michigan Press, 1971.

15. Boruch, R. F. Costs, benefits and legal implications of methods for assuring confidentiality in social research. Paper read at International Conference on Law in Conflict with Social Research, August, 1974, in Bielefield, West Germany.

16. Campbell, D. T. Reforms as experiments. *American Psychologist* 24:409–429, 1969.

17. Nejelski, P., and Lerman, N. M. A researcher-subject testimonial privilege: What to do before the subpoena arrives. *Wisconsin Law Review*, 1971. Pp. 1085–1148.

18. Wigmore, J. H. *Evidence at Trials at Common Law*, Vol. 8. Boston: Little, Brown, 1961.

CASES

Branzburg v. *Hayes*, 408 U.S. 665 (1972).

Caldwell v. *United States*, 434 F. 2d 1081 (9 Cir. 1970).

Democratic National Committee v. *McCord*, 356 F. Supp. 1394 (D.C. Cir. 1973).

Eisenstadt v. *Baird*, 405 U.S. 438 (1972).

Griswold v. *Connecticut*, 381 U.S. 479 (1965).

Katz v. *United States*, 389 U.S. 347 (1967).

Roe v. *Wade*, 410 U.S. 113 (1973).

United States v. *Liddy*, 345 F. Supp. 208 (D.C. Cir. 1972.)

STATUTES

Comprehensive Alcohol and Alcoholism Prevention and Control Act of 1970, P.L. 91-616; 84 Stat. 1848 (1970).

Comprehensive Drug Abuse Prevention and Control Act of 1970, P.L. 91-513; 84 Stat. 1236 (1970).

Crime Control Act of 1973.

Drug Abuse Office and Treatment Act of 1972.

Federal Reports Act, 44 U.S.C. 3501 (1970).

Freedom of Information Act, 5 U.S.C. 552 (1970).

Family Educational Rights and Privacy Act of 1974, P.L. 93-380, Sect 513, Title 20. U.S.C. 1232g to General Education Provisions Act; P.L. 90-247, as amended (1974).

Md. Code Ann., Art. 35, Sect. 101 (1971).
N.Y. Civil Rights Law, 79-j (McKinney Supp. 1972).
The Privacy Act of 1974, P.L. 93-579; 5 U.S.C. 552a (1974).

DESIGNATED DISCUSSION

RICHARD GREEN

Dr. Kelty's paper addresses one of the more compelling dilemmas of contemporary human-subject research. Before commenting on that issue, I must take note of the elegant research designs Dr. Kelty proposes for maintaining confidentiality. As a member of an NIMH study section that reviews research grant proposals, I am impressed that current methodologies for maintaining confidentiality of collected data are far more sophisticated than methodologies for *collecting* the data. That this is the case is a welcome signal that attention is being drawn to a need previously underattended to, but may also be symptomatic of a climate that will militate against research of benefit to the public. The climate is not entirely dissimilar from that enveloping the question of what constitutes informed consent. Indeed, the issues relate.

During this brief discussion I will ask rhetorical questions that I hope will elicit group discussion, and will focus on two contemporary research projects that engage the issues addressed by these questions.

The American public was recently "slapped in the face" with the issue of patient confidentiality. While Beverly Hills, California, typically has a high burglary rate, invasions are usually limited to wealthy residences and not psychiatrists' offices where patient files are kept. However, Dr. Lewis Fielding, Daniel Ellsberg's psychoanalyst, confounded Nixonian efforts to inspect confidential psychiatric records by utilizing a nonalphabetical, numbered filing system. This system is not very elaborate, but the Watergate gang did not distinguish itself with methodological brilliance. Rather, in the tradition of classic theatre, they played their supporting role, permitting the fatal personality flaw of the play's protagonist to unfold. The informed public was justifiably enraged.

At the interface of sex research and confidentiality, two research projects come to mind: transsexual surgery follow-up and sex-chromosome abnormalities.

TRANSSEXUALITY AND CONFIDENTIALITY

I will first cite an example in which inability to retrieve patients and collate data has significantly limited clinical advancement. During the past decade, hundreds of persons have undergone surgical procedures to modify primary and secondary sex characteristics so as to live in the sex role alternate to that in which they were born. The polemical question of the 1950s and 1960s—*Should* patients be granted their request for sex-change surgery?—has been replaced by the research question of the 1970s—*Which* patients should be granted surgery?

Controversy exists as to the best candidates for transsexual procedures. Three clinically distinct subgroups request surgery. Some candidates (anatomically male or female) assert that "as far back as they can remember" they felt they should have been born as a person of the opposite sex; that they have never effectively functioned socially or sexually in the sex role to which they were born; that dressing in clothes of the other sex has given them a peaceful, relaxed feeling, not accompanied by genital excitement; and that they abhor the thought of a sexual relationship with a person of the same anatomic sex.

Another group (males only) recalls childhood as more androgynous, found cross-dressing genitally arousing during adolescence, may have married and fathered children, and continued cross-dressing at an accelerating rate. Their self-image of femininity increased, the degree of genital excitement accompanying cross-dressing decreased, and they ultimately came to envision better adjustment living full-time as women.

A third group of anatomical males and females recalls a moderate degree of cross-gender behavior during preteen years, became aware of a strong same-sexed sex-partner orientation during adolescence, extensively engaged in same-sex partner contact, but became alienated from the "gay world." They found themselves attracted primarily to heterosexual persons of the same sex, and their self-image of femininity (for males) and masculinity (for females) increased.

Depending on the criteria for patient selection of a given medical-surgical facility, candidates representing each of these subgroups are undergoing sex-reassignment procedures. It has been argued by some that only patients in the first group are suitable. These persons have a lifelong core identity of belonging to the other sex, have not functioned socially or sexually in their anatomic sex role, and have not derived genital pleasure from cross-dressing (interpreted in the psychodynamic sense as a defense *against* castration).

Yet, because of the theoretical nature of this assumption and the insistence of *all* candidates for surgery, those who have been sex-reassigned have quite disparate sexual autobiographies. Follow-up is essential. The clinical-research test is time. We must be able to predict for whom these irreversible procedures yield tragedy.

But many patients refuse follow-up. They have obtained from their physicians what they wanted—psychiatric endorsement of sex-reassignment procedures, contrasexed hormones, and surgery. They have no further use for medical contact. They wish to forget their past life-style , characterized by grave conflict, and wish to experience their surgical rebirth unfettered by any past history. They desire to blend into a new community at a great distance, emotionally and geographically, from their former locale.

Physicians, too, are responsible for poor follow-up. In some instances they have focused on two matters: perfecting the technical aspects of the sex conversion and fee collection.

If we are ultimately to best serve future applicants, we must know how patients who have applied for sex reassignment—those whose sex-change request is denied as well as those for whom it is granted—are functioning in the subsequent years. Thus, those responsible for the follow-up evaluation must know where these patients are and must have a means of effecting periodic reassessment.

I have previously proposed what might be a solution to the

problem of patients being lost to follow-up. I have suggested that the $5,000 typically exchanged between the transsexual and the physician and hospital accounting office be placed in an interest-bearing, escrow follow-up account in the patient's name. This would be a 10-year escrow account from which, on a biennial schedule, the patient who returns for follow-up would receive $1,000 plus interest. This is coercive. But is it unethical?

If the patient has requested and received extensive, usually expensive, medical treatment, should he or she be expected to return the service? Health care is a right, not a privilege. But is the right coupled with responsibility? Is there a responsibility to those patients, similarly motivated, who will follow in the patient's footsteps in the decades ahead, a responsibility sufficient to justify the coercion?

Is it unfair to the physician or hospital? Should a physician's responsibility when conducting an experimental treatment procedure be toward advancing understanding of the efficacy of that procedure at the cost of economic gain?

Can we maintain the needed privacy of the postoperative patient whose adjustment may be sabotaged by knowledge of his or her prior life-style on the part of spouse, children, neighbor, or employer? The elaborate proposals in Dr. Kelty's paper for national data-bank systems could be adapted to establish a national file on transsexuals, those granted surgery and those not. The file could be available to a research board charged with the responsibility of follow-up evaluations, available to no one else, and cross-referenced to no other retrieval system.

Should a patient who has received tax-supported medical-research counsel of any type be free to withhold subsequent data that may determine the efficacy of the intervention? Are the rights of future patients who might benefit from this knowledge compromised by such a refusal?

A patient, physician, and medical institution may enter into a contract for the service to be provided to the patient and the service to medical science and, ultimately, the public. Is this coercive? Is paying income tax and driving at a speed under 56 miles per hour coercive? Can the individual demand for freedom from such constraint —in this case, total medical privacy—compromise the rights of others whose welfare may require such information? Can a delicate balance be struck between the individual's right to be left alone and the collective individuals' right to know?

Continue to consider longitudinal research. Consider a long-term study of psychological development in children who display typical or atypical early-life behaviors. If the research has value, someone has to know how to find these people later. Is it these persons' responsibility to remain available in the manner in which they remain available to pay taxes? Is that a civic responsibility? Should these people be permitted to "withdraw from the study at any time"? When public funds have been invested and service provided, is there a "payback" obligation? Should a child participating in longitudinal research be able, on attaining majority status, not only to rescind prior parental approval to participate but also to demand that all prior research records be destroyed?

CHROMOSOMES AND CONFIDENTIALITY

Another example that has engaged sex researchers is "stigmatization." A study in point is neonatal karyotyping to identify a population of sex-chromosome atypical males—those with XXY and XYY. The clinical and research literature, and the popular press, have ascribed varying behavioral features, typically less than socially desirable, to persons with such aneuploidy.

A methodological problem in evaluating a causal association between the chromosomal pattern and the behavior is the nonrandom patient sampling of most published research. Sampling tall prisoners or transsexual surgical candidates is hardly adequate for a condition characteristic of one of every 350 males.

One research strategy to circumvent these methodologic pitfalls, karyotyping consecutive male neonates in a large hospital complex, was instituted by Stanley Walzer in Boston. This approach could provide, in a few years' time, a large representative population of males with sex-chromosome aneuploidy who could be available for longitudinal evaluation and, if warranted, psychological counseling. With monitoring of psychological and physiological developmental parameters, parental attributes, parent-child interaction, and chromosomally normal siblings, the significance, if any, of an atypical sex-chromosome pattern on behavior at varying stages of the life cycle might be assessed.

This research strategy raised many issues. What information regarding the nature of the study should be provided to parents and children? What is the effect on the research design of providing such information? How does one maintain continuing contact with subjects over the extended period of time required for project completion? How is confidentiality of the atypical chromosomal pattern to be maintained, so that possible public misconceptions of its significance do not intrude into the lives of the families under study?

The study was stopped by public and professional pressure. The investigator and his family were physically threatened by persons asserting their desire to safeguard the rights of others.

Can such a study be conducted without significant risk to subjects or with this risk outweighed by potential benefit to the subjects and the general public?

One approach, admittedly imperfect, suggested for discussion, is the following: Parents may be told their child has an atypical chromosome pattern, that the study examines a variety of atypical chromosome patterns (which it would), and that research is being done because of the mystery of the significance of the atypical chromosomes. They can be told that some families report problems with learning, behavior tantrums, and the like, but that these are problems with many children; thus the need for study. If a parent asks whether or not the chromosomal variant is associated with atypical sexuality, the truthful answer is given: Probably not. The longitudinal evaluation can be part of the annual medical evaluation that all children should have.

Should the families be denied knowledge of the karyotype? Fertility and potency problems may accompany these chromosomal patterns. Should this be kept secret, allowing for no patient preparation for the subsequent surprise? Does the school need to know? Do neighbors need to know? A scramble system, as described by Dr. Kelty, can maintain subject identity secrecy.

The public continues to equate XYY and XXY karyotypes with

aggressivity and sexual abnormality. Will it continue to do so in the absence of disconfirming data? Who was helped by disruption of the Boston study?

CONFIDENTIALITY, CONFIDENCE, AND CONSTRAINT

These two types of studies suggest the potential need for patient registries. Such proposals have met with serious opposition for obvious and well-taken reasons. However, without registries, how would females whose mothers received diethylstilbestrol decades ago during pregnancy be retrievable for potentially life-saving periodic pelvic examinations?

If it is subsequently discovered that male children born of women who received "X" contraceptive pill within one year of conception run a significantly higher risk of testicular malignancy during their third decade, how will such persons be effectively contacted without a data bank on contraceptive practices and patient and progeny location?

What is much of the substance of what we as sex researchers hold sacred and demanding of privilege and confidentiality? Facts such as that the person has masturbated at a frequency of two to four times per week since age 13? The person prefers oral-genital stimulation as a source of orgasmic response? The male reaches orgasm earlier during coitus than he and his partner would prefer? The person has engaged in an extramarital affair? Is the public genuinely interested in such information unless the person under scrutiny is a former president?

Do the hordes of readers who bought *Human Sexual Response* and *Human Sexual Inadequacy* care to know the names of those who comprise the aggregate-column statistics of the racy reading of William Masters and Virginia Johnson, or the equally racy prose of Alfred C. Kinsey and his staff of accountants?

The right to be left alone is sacred. However, we sometimes act as though we all have something horrible to hide. Few of us are foreign spies. Publication of our names will not invariably lead to assassination in Athens.

Dr. Kelty notes changing standards of acceptable sexual conduct. What *can* set people free to feel left alone is the conviction that they have nothing to hide. Recently, with the stroke of the pen, Governor Edmund G. Brown, Jr., made 10 million California potential felons free from "needing" to hide the fact that they had experienced oral copulation or sodomy, a crime previously carrying a ten-year prison sentence.

Indeed, a cogent argument raised by ousted homosexual government officials with security clearance is that they are not blackmailable once they publicly announce their terrible secret, the secret that in prior times was "not fit to be mentioned among Christians."

Dr. Kelty also referred to the Freedom of Information Act. Will some research be compromised by this act, which commands that the contents of publicly supported research projects be made available to any citizen? Consider a project designed to assess psychosocial-psychoendocrine input to circa-menstrual behavioral features in human females. The methodology might call for an element of deception, in that subjects may be misinformed that prior research suggests one or another time of the monthly cycle (in which the subject falls) to be positively or negatively associated with task performance. (Subjects would be debriefed at the end of the test situation.) Publishing the protocol in the newspaper of the campus where the study is undertaken would blow the cover off this project with hurricane force and eradicate any research potential.

Confidentiality implies confidence. The practices of governmental personnel and governmental policy have undermined public confidence and contribute to current anxiety. Will a public aware of testimony that a president issued an order to a subordinate agency to destroy germ warfare chemicals and that the order was not carried out, and a public aware that its government reads citizens' private mail, believe in current legislation designed to ensure confidentiality? Perhaps the researchers who promise to destroy audio tapes after coding and identifying face sheets of questionnaires maintain files equivalent to those "long-ago destroyed" germ warfare containers.

I close with a point that has significance for the conduct of all sex research. Recently at Harvard, Professor Gerald Davison, on fellowship leave from the State University of New York at Stony Brook, proposed a sex-research project involving human subjects. A university review committee, as required under HEW guidelines, studied such issues as informed consent, risk-benefit ratio to subjects, and maintenance of confidentiality. The committee approved the project. An associate dean then vetoed it.

The precedent concerns us all. In light of this, coupled with the controversy over the sex-research project at Southern Illinois University, which is under cross-fire from several agencies, we may be reentering an era of academic fascism like the one that so significantly affected Alfred Kinsey's research in America's not-too-distant past, the era known by the eponym *McCarthyism*.

All of us have a responsibility to protect the prospects for responsible sex research from sabotage by capricious, self-serving, unilateral, disruptive actions of a single person or group, whether it be a university dean, a United States senator, or a state or federal governmental agency.

GENERAL DISCUSSION

PEPPER SCHWARTZ: There are a number of important questions suggested by the topic of confidentiality. For example, there may be different ethical considerations as well as legal facts that depend on the discipline of the researcher or practitioner—theologians, physicians, or behavioral scientists. Although we must explore our responsibilities to protect the rights of our research subjects, we also should explore the implications of the lack of legal protection of the researcher who does not maintain confidentiality for reasons that are highly ethical. There are also intricate questions of confidentiality within the research situation itself, such as confidentiality between two spouses or between child and parent. These are difficult problems that need to be faced by all of us.

ALAN A. STONE: I would like to point out that, in reference to the doctor-patient situation of privilege, very few doctors realize that it is the patient who has the privilege, not the doctor. This is in contrast to the privilege of a reporter protecting the freedom of speech, where the privilege is vested in the reporter, not the news source. If researchers can analogize themselves to reporters, rather than rely on their therapeutic role, they may successfully extend the protection of confidentiality to themselves. The fact that the privilege resides in the patient tells us something about what confidentiality should mean.

Probably the greatest practical problem of confidentiality is caused by too much talking—researchers talking about their subjects, psychiatrists talking about their patients. I have confronted this matter in recent months, in dealing with psychiatrists who have gone on television to talk about their patients, or psychiatrists who have written books about patients and published them over the patients' objections.

CHARLES REMBAR: It's not only the patient who has the sole privilege in the doctor-patient situation, but the client in the lawyer-client situation, the penitent in the confessional situation. It's never the person to whom the confidence was given. It's rather important to keep that in mind. The so-called reporter's privilege is based entirely on the First Amendment, the theory being that in order to inform the public and to express himself, the reporter has to be able to keep his sources private. There's a social policy in each of these instances. The idea, where the lawyer and client are concerned, is that if the client cannot insist on the lawyer's not repeating what he is told, people won't go to lawyers with their problems. The same thing applies to medicine and to the confessional. In each case, we have to consider the social policy separately. While I agree with Dr. Kelty that confidentiality and privacy are functionally related, they are different things.

Privacy itself is a cluster of different things. We are most concerned, in some of the cases that were cited, with privacy in the sense of forbidding governmental intrusion into our lives. The kind of privacy that Warren and Brandeis were talking about is something quite different. That's the general feeling that people should be left alone. It's not that they want to keep things secret, necessarily. They tell their friends, but they just don't want it to be made a matter of wide public scrutiny. There are still other types of privacy that are involved.

The most recent ruling on the subject of what a psychoanalyst can publish is against the psychoanalyst, in a case recently decided in New York. There—and it's rather a new notion in the law—we find the idea that you can sue for breach of confidentiality, that there is an implied contractual condition between doctor and patient that the doctor will not disclose a thing. This despite the argument that there was a violation of prior restraint (which is, to my mind, a somewhat overrated concept in our thought about First Amendment freedom in any event).

ALAN A. STONE: I would like to make a response to the question of sex-change surgery raised by Dr. Green. One of the great problems in medicine is, When is something an accepted procedure and when is it an experiment? For a long time, it was quite clear that a doctor should not charge for an experimental procedure. (The way surgeons decide what is experimental research or clinical research would tax even the Jesuits.) Many of the problems that we face, in terms of the retrieval research that Dr. Green mentioned, are simply due to the profession's willingness to accept a procedure and charge for it and abandon ethical responsibilities.

HAROLD I. LIEF: Dr. Green brought up several instances in which research was stopped by coercion. I would like to point out that the decision *not* to conduct a particular piece of research may also be an ethical decision. John Money gave us several examples earlier today of research projects he would like to pursue that could not be approved. The decision not to conduct that research has ethical implications.

A parallel and practical example exists in the area of fetal research. There is currently an attack on fetal research, yet it is through such research that the mortality of neonates with respiratory distress has been significantly reduced. Without fetal research, this could not have been accomplished. This illustrates some of the ethical issues that plague us.

ROBERT C. KOLODNY: I would like to go back to a point raised earlier by Dr. Gebhard in speaking about confidentiality. He and his colleagues apparently decided early in their work that they would never violate the confidentiality of research-derived material under any terms at all. Mr. Rembar observed that there are situations in any relationships implying or guaranteeing confidentiality where an obligation might exist to take some action that would violate the confidentiality. In the particular case that Dr. Gebhard mentioned, there was a happy ending because it turned out to be a test of the researcher's intent rather than an actual attempt at violence.

While I think most of us understand the implications of our responsibilities to both patients and research subjects in the realm of confidentiality, are there instances where those responsibilities should be knowingly and willingly subordinated to some higher purpose? If so, how do we approach such decisions?

ALAN A. STONE: I have looked very carefully through the medical canons of ethics on this particular subject and, unfortunately, there is no good direction there; that is, the medical canons of ethics tell the doctor that, when there is some social need, he has the obligation to break the confidentiality. But no examples are spelled out to explain when that need arises. This became a matter of crucial significance recently in a case in California in which, essentially, the court tried to argue that it was a *duty* of a psychiatrist, not just his *right*, to break confidentiality. I think it's very important for us to recognize in this area of confidentiality that there are pulls and stretches in all directions. On the one hand, we have legislatures passing overlapping bills protecting confidentiality; then we have courts reaching decisions interfering with confidentiality. We have all sorts of notions of access, and now every time we have a conference on confidentiality, the hidden agenda is access and accountability, and we really are in a quagmire. I think the only way out is going to be to remember what the basic meaning of confidentiality is for the individual professional.

MARY S. CALDERONE: It occurs to me that, as Dr. Gebhard described it, the decision was to protect the welfare of the researchers, not the welfare of the prisoners. They were fortunate to guess right. Isn't that a different kind of ethical decision?

JACK WIENER: On the certificate of confidentiality for which the proposed rules were just issued last month, confidentiality shall not be provided when the medical welfare of the subject would be threatened by failure to reveal such information.

5

ISSUES AND ATTITUDES IN RESEARCH AND TREATMENT OF VARIANT FORMS OF HUMAN SEXUAL BEHAVIOR

JOHN MONEY

It was formerly part of the faith of scientists that they were seekers of pure truth, insulated from the moral and political concerns of how the findings of their pure truth might be applied or misapplied. Ethics was the specialty of philosophers and theologians. Hiroshima destroyed all that. Scientists have been rudely awakened to a sense of moral responsibility for the principles they are discovering and the technology to which they are applying them.

In medicine a quarter of a century ago, ethics was pretty much a fossilized discipline, embedded in the Hippocratic oath. The good patient, like the good child, was to be seen and not heard. His records were inaccessible to him, and his prescriptions, more than likely, were written in incomprehensible, abbreviated Latin. No more! Today the ethics of informed consent is the new "in" thing.

The practice of medicine is affected by informed consent insofar as a patient has increased ease of access to his record. It is the conduct of medical research, however, that is most affected by the new ethics of informed consent. In some instances the very existence and continuance of clinical investigation among human beings is threatened.

RESEARCH DESIGN

In clinical investigative design, the randomly selected group is a major casualty of the new concern with the ethics of informed consent. It is now absolutely impossible to get a genuinely random sample of human beings for any type of medical study, whether it be blood chemistry or sexuality. Informed consent implies the right of either refusal or cooperation. Cooperation is voluntary. Thus, under the new rules of informed consent, volunteer bias is universal in both treatment and control groups.

Occasionally one will be able to obtain a sample for investigative study that constitutes a complete census of a diagnostic group. An alternative in research design is to resort to the method of matched comparison or contrast groups. To illustrate, a group of 47, XXY men might be matched and compared with a group of 47, XYY men. Each group constitutes an experiment of nature and is homogeneous relative to the criterion by which it is identified. The composition of each group is equally subject to volunteer bias. Other possible biases, such as the secondary effects of being hospitalized or being followed in a clinic, are shared by both groups. That is to say, between groups, the uncontrolled variables are either sufficiently constant or sufficiently random as to permit consistent differences to show up. In the example noted, the independent variable is the chromosomal status. The dependent variable—the one being studied—may be fertility, serum testosterone level, IQ, behavioral pathology, and so on.

To circumvent volunteer bias, one may also have recourse to that research design in which volunteers act as their own controls in a before-and-after investigative strategy.

IDEOLOGICAL CONSTRAINT

The constraint imposed on human clinical investigation by the volunteer bias of informed consent may be irksome, but it is imperative in order to protect human beings from being treated amorally as experimental animals. Another form of constraint is far more insidious and dangerous. It masquerades as ethical, whereas in actuality it is ideological. It abrogates, by edict, the right of some human beings to have informed consent and the right of investigators to conduct their clinical studies. It also restricts the topics of clinical investigation. Its prime victims, at present, are children and prisoners; and its most vetoed topics are sex research and fetal research. This ideological form of constraint operates by way of legal threat, legal action, suing for malpractice, disapproving research protocols, and promulgating decrees and regulations pertaining to funding and the withdrawal of funds for research. On occasion it operates by way of terrorism.

The paradox and tragedy of this ideological constraint on human clinical investigation is that its proponents believe themselves to be protecting the welfare of research subjects. In fact, they have allowed the protective pendulum to swing too far. They are now depriving subjects, especially prisoners and children, of their right of informed consent; and they are depriving themselves and all mankind of the right to the benefits of clinical research.

CASE EXAMPLE: XYY SYNDROME

Recently there was a much-publicized attack on the Harvard study of the incidence of anomalies of chromosomal karyotype in the newborn [1]. Though the study was endorsed by the Harvard faculty, its principal investigator eventually discontinued it because his wife and children were subjected to continual harassment and intimidation [2].

The attack appears to have been instigated by a militant political action group, with support from a legally oriented group. Both groups may have been seeking public exposure quite apart from their social philosophy of protecting the public against science. They focused their attack only on the ascertainment of the 47, XYY anomaly. They used the rationale of the self-fulfilling prophecy, namely, that parents who knew they had an XYY baby would rear him to become a violent criminal, since the media had publicized the extra Y chromosome as the crime chromosome. No matter that the media were wrong!

There is already evidence to contradict the sensationalization of the supernumerary Y—the evidence that there are XYY citizens who do not get into trouble with the law. There is also evidence that the parents of XYY babies are profoundly grateful for whatever counseling they receive in rearing an XYY child, which is, by and large, an exceptionally difficult task. XYY boys are at risk for a high degree of impulsiveness. Their response to punishment is impulsive and destructive. They do far better on a program of incentive training than on punishment training.

According to the evidence available, it is an asset rather than a liability for a baby with a cytogenetic anomaly to have parents who know about it [3]. From now on the chances are that American children will be deprived of this asset, for their chromosomal status will either be unascertained or undisclosed—which is as foolish as suppressing a diagnosis of meningitis in the false belief that knowledge of the diagnosis itself will cause death.

CASE EXAMPLE: THERAPY FOR SEX OFFENDERS

Nonviolent sex offenders—exhibitionists, for example—who are arrested and found guilty frequently get inordinately severe and lengthy sentences. Studies begun in 1966 show that sex offenders may gain in self-regulation of sexual behavior if given a period of treatment with antiandrogen, preferably accompanied by counseling [4, 5]. In Germany the newly discovered antiandrogen cyproterone acetate was used. Its use is still prohibited in the United States by the Federal Drug Administration; medroxyprogesterone acetate (Depo-Provera) is used instead. The first trials with Depo-Provera were conducted at Johns Hopkins in the era prior to the requirement of approval by a clinical investigations committee.

By 1972 it was necessary to have committee approval, which was given with the proviso that no prisoners or men under arrest be treated. The committee was responding to the implications of federal policy regarding the rights of informed consent. In effect, it was saying that by being under arrest or in jail, a man forfeits his right to informed consent, for he is likely to sign anything that promises a lighter sentence or an earlier parole. That is a specious, if not a vindictive, argument, for being in jail is a fact of life for a prisoner just as being in a hospital is for a patient. The facts of our lives shape all of our judgments, including those of informed consent.

Being arrested or in jail is a trauma that allows the sex offender to seek treatment. Ordinarily, sex offenders do not feel any more hurt or disabled because of their sex lives than do nonoffenders. They know their behavior is socially stigmatized and punishable, but the threat of punishment is not traumatic enough to induce them to seek treatment. Thus, to fail to provide treatment at the time of arrest or imprisonment is, in most instances, to fail forever.

The precedent for resolving the foregoing dilemma was established by a sex offender serving concurrent life sentences for rape and attempted rape. Recently he took his case to federal court and obtained an agreement from the prison authorities that they would make him available for treatment if he was accepted into the Johns Hopkins antiandrogen program. Then he received from the same judge a ruling that his consent to treatment was indeed informed consent: A physician and a psychologist informed him in the courtroom of the pros and cons of treatment. He has since been treated on a weekly basis in jail.

POWER OF DECISION-MAKING

The foregoing illustrations exemplify an erosion of the power of medical people to make their own decisions. The law has long imposed certain constraints on doctors, for example, regarding abortion and euthanasia. But here we have two dangerous precedents. In one case a research decision was made not by experts, with all the data at their fingertips, but by militant dilettantes. In the other case, a therapeutic decision was taken out of the hands of experts who had researched the new form of therapy and was made by a judge who took a courtroom course on the treatment of sex offenders with antiandrogen. It goes without saying that a lone judge is no more and no less error-free than a lone doctor. One does not guarantee the rights of prisoners by handing over the guardianship of those rights to a judge instead of a doctor. It is a jury that is needed, and preferably a jury of one's expertly informed peers.

There is no ready explanation for why medical people are being robbed of, and are giving up, their rights of informed decision-making. Yes, it does reflect the antiscientism of our era, and antiscience may itself represent a backlash against the immense influence of scientific research on our daily existence. Despite the problems still unsolved, medicine has a life-and-death power undreamed of at the onset of this century.

Wherever power lies, there also lies someone to usurp it. Medical personnel and other people engaged in sexological research and therapy do not seem very alert in this respect. Those who should be natural allies snipe at one another in rivalry. The enemy rejoices. Meanwhile, our combined forces are not yet strong enough to have given rise to a single department of sexology in an American medical school.

MORAL STANDARDS

The current debate on the ethics of informed consent is a reminder that there are no absolute moral standards of right and wrong—only a series of approximations as new data, new events, new artifacts, and new people require the updating of old standards.

Intellectual obedience, studious self-discipline, and ethical conformity are prerequisites to beating the competition in order to enter and be successful in medicine and the allied professions. There are notable exceptions, but, as a group, medical professionals are more likely to endorse the ethical status quo than to question it. Once in a while a paroxysmal change occurs: Witness recent upheavals in the definition of mental illness and normality and in the reclassification of homosexuality as an erotic alternative rather than a pathology.

Such changes have major implications for priorities in research and therapy. For example, an exhibitionist is an inconsequential person in a nudist camp or a society unperturbed by nudity, whereas in hospitals and courtrooms such behavior is always regarded as pathological. Similarly, during and prior to the eighteenth century in Europe, adults who fondled infants' genitals were pacifying them, whereas today they would be jailed for pedophilia or incest, or both.

It is quite possible that medical attention today is too much focused on research and therapy of individual sexual and erotic pathology, as defined by today's criteria. We might well spend more time in medical anthropology. We might then discover that, like our relatives and neighbors, we are all overzealous in applying the sexual prejudices and taboos specific to our heritage. Without them, we may be able to make our heritage preventative; that is, the children of future generations might grow up free from the complaints to which we today so assiduously address ourselves.

PROFESSIONAL NONJUDGMENTALISM

Variant forms and expressions of human sexuality are among those human conditions and syndromes that absolutely demand a professionally nonjudgmental attitude on the part of the person who investigates or treats them. Neither you nor I would like to be morally chastised by a physician to whom we took a case of VD for treatment. If that happened, we would probably seek treatment from someone else.

Professional nonjudgmentalism does not require that the venereologist expose himself to VD. I make this point because I have found that medical students, when I lecture them on human sexuality, have difficulty differentiating the principle of professional nonjudgmentalism from the principle of personal moral responsibility. Sex therapists and investigators may have the same difficulty.

ETHICS OF TOLERANCE
AND THE INTOLERABLE

Among those variant forms of human sexuality that constitute the paraphilias, some are harmless and others are harmful to the partner or the self. Harmless forms are often defined as crimes in today's law. Even so, they do not pose as great an ethical challenge to the therapist or the researcher as do the harmful paraphilias that constitute crimes with victims, such as lust murder, brutal rape, sadomasochist homicide or suicide, and erotic self-strangulation. In my own practice and teaching, I draw an ethical dividing-line between harmless and harmful paraphilias on the basis not simply of the criterion of partner consent—for one can encounter cases such as that of a masochist who consents to, and indeed stage-manages, his own murder. Harmful sexual practices are those that invade the personal inviolacy of one or both partners and bring about severe and injurious personal abuse, up to and including death. Like child abuse, these are intolerable practices that demand some degree of obligative, nonelective intervention and help with a view to bringing about change.

ETHICS AND HOMOSEXUALITY

Many, if not most physicians, both clinical and investigative, are deeply enough imbued with our culture's sexual traditions that they are unable to accept as ethical the idea of treating a heterosexual person so as to bring about a homosexual response, even briefly and reversibly. There are cultures, however, in which homosexuality as one component of a tradition of developmental bisexuality is the ideological norm [6]. In such a culture, young males experience only homosexual erotic activities in the early years of their maturity, formally changing to heterosexuality after negotiating a bride-price and getting married in young adulthood. They are subsequently able to resume homosexual activity when working away from home, but such episodes are transient and do not impair the sexual relationship of marriage.

There is no absolute criterion by which to evaluate a bisexual cultural tradition as either superior or inferior to a monosexual one. The very existence and cultural viability of a bisexual society does, however, require that we in our society do not set up exclusive heterosexuality as an absolute norm. An exclusively heterosexual society is neither superior nor inferior to a bisexual one. Thus, it is purely rhetorical to ask whether or not heterosexual persons could be so treated as to become homosexual for a time. Nonetheless, the rhetorical question is a valuable exercise in both logic and ethics, for its obverse and precise counterpart is the question of whether homosexuals should be treated to become heterosexual (or bisexual) and whether such treatment should be enforced by edict.

Until the advent of modern sexology in the nineteenth century, homosexuality was classified in Western Christian culture as belonging with heresy and treason; there was no better way to dispose of a political enemy than to accuse him of homosexuality, for he was then eligible to be accused of heresy and treason as well. The sanctions and punishments were ruthless. In the Victorian era, some of the old ruthlessness remained and was even enforced legislatively while it was simultaneously being replaced by the new view of science and medicine—the same new view that had earlier removed the mentally ill from dungeons (where they were punished for having allowed themselves to be devil-possessed) and placed them in asylums or hospitals, ostensibly for treatment. Homosexuals became reclassified as sick people, their sickness being that they did not conform to the ideological norm. They were to be pitied instead of punished, and offered whatever treatment was in fashion for their supposed cure.

It goes without saying that medicine has throughout its history taken on more conditions than it can cure, more indeed than it can even ameliorate. In addition, medicine has also been indiscriminate as to what it defines as a condition needing cure; it has had no systematic philosophy, set of principles, or criteria as to what constitutes health or disease. The very etymology of the latter term tells the story: dis-ease. Traditionally, it has pretty much been left up to the patient to decide whether he or she was suffering or at ease, that is, in need of a cure or to be left to his or her own devices.

Germ theory in the nineteenth century changed all that, for it brought to medicine the first genuine theory of etiology and the first genuine possibility not only of cure but also of prevention. The theory of prevention became the basis of public health, notably with respect to preventing the spread of contagion. Prevention raised a new ethical issue: the right of society to enforce treatment on unwilling patients who were not yet diseased and who did not appreciate the risk of becoming diseased with sufficient urgency to accept preventive treatment.

The ethics of prevention, of the right to enforce treatment, is still a matter of unsettled debate and controversy; witness the controversies over fluoridization of water and over population growth, both of which arouse intense religious and political passions.

As a result of controversy over individual rights and the ethics of prevention, special subgroups within the population at large have become increasingly attentive to their ethical rights with respect to enforced treatment and with respect to being classified as diseased and in need of treatment. The issue is especially sensitive in the case of those conditions or diseases for which the etiology is still so imperfectly understood that there is no guaranteed method of either prevention or cure.

Sexuality is one of these conditions. Theory as to the origins and development of a person's sexuality—whether it be bisexual, heterosexual, or homosexual—still has virtually zero predictive power regarding either prevention or cure. Inchoately at first, homosexual people have in the last two decades formulated a revision of the concept of whether they should be considered diseased or simply representatives of an unorthodox, atypical, variant form of sexuality that could exist unobtrusively and unthreateningly in society, in much the same way as left-handedness and redheadedness exist amongst a majority who are different.

Homosexual men and women formulated this new view of themselves as they organized into a liberation movement contemporaneous with the women's liberation movement, in the era of widespread social change regarding acceptance of sexuality that goes under the name of the sexual revolution. Militant homosexual activists made direct attacks on the medical profession, especially its psychiatric representatives, and helped to bring about, despite a rear-guard defensive action, the declassification of homosexuality as a disease in America.

The ethical issue here is not denial of psychiatry or counseling to any men or women whose homosexual responses distress them. Rather, the issue is stigmatization—labeling people as in need of treatment when they consider that they can function satisfactorily. The result of the stigmatization process itself is impairment in a person's abilities. Historically, the wheel has turned from sin to sickness to social acceptability. That does not mean that research into the origins of sexuality will cease. It does mean that researchers will come to realize that their true interest lies in the origins of sexuality in general, not just homosexuality in particular. Eventually, when enough is known predictively to permit effective prevention and cure, in the authentic sense of cure, it will be time to engage in ethical debate as to whether our society, with its own special history and culture, will be improved or impoverished by providing a place for homosexuals and bisexuals as well as hetero-sexuals. Without the homosexuals who have contributed to the growth of Western civilization, its science, its art, and its literature, we would be sadly deprived; but there is, as of the present, no im-plementable research design for deciding the verdict one way or the other.

ETHICS AND SEX REASSIGNMENT OF TRANSSEXUALS

In the mid-1960s, I had a personal part to play in the history of the ethics of sex reassignment when the procedure for the rehabili-tation of transsexuals first became accepted in the United States. I shall tell the story autobiographically.

In the 1950s and early 1960s, I became acquainted with cases of sex reassignment in hermaphroditism, and also with some cases of reassignment of nonhermaphroditic transsexuals whose surgery had been performed overseas. Following surgery at the well-known clinic in Casablanca, two patients of Harry Benjamin in New York came to Baltimore in order to be examined surgically by the gyne-cologist Howard W. Jones, Jr., and psychologically by me. Jones and I had worked together for years on cases of hermaphroditism. We had also shared cases of nonhermaphroditic transsexuals, many of whom in those days had self-diagnosed themselves as herma-phroditic in an attempt to justify the necessity of reassignment surgery.

Convinced by the evidence that sex reassignment, in appropriate cases, could be rehabilitative, Jones and I were confronted with the ethical and legal issues involved in legitimizing this controversial procedure.

Jones held the opinion that some decisions in medicine, ethical as well as empirical, are the responsibility of the specialists involved. Only they are fully informed of all the facts of the case. Only they have the full range of information on which to base a decision.

Some years earlier, I had heard the same philosophy expressed by Lawson Wilkins, the founder of pediatric endocrinology and a specialist in neonatal and juvenile hermaphroditism. He was dismayed that a local judge of his acquaintance refused to cosponsor a seminar on legal and medical issues in the sex assignment and treatment of hermaphroditic babies, focusing especially on the legal status of therapeutic castration, which is necessary in some cases. Wilkins' verdict was that his past decisions involving castration might, on a technicality, have gotten him jailed but that, had he waited on the law to make a decision for him, he would have made no progress in the treatment and rehabilitation of hermaphroditic children.

Here was an instance of medicine's needing to lead the law rather than calling on the law for a decision that it was, through lack of precedent, powerless to give. The law would function later, should the physician's action be contested. In the meantime, the doctor had to put himself and his career on the line, so to speak, ready to face the consequences even if they were negative. In no other way could change be brought about.

The situation was the same with respect to sex-reassignment surgery for transsexuals. Approval of the first case of male-to-female reassignment surgery was, in the last analysis, made by Howard Jones and me. Administrative approval was subsequently institutionalized. A year later public approval was institutionalized in the wake of a press release strategically timed and designed to circumvent gossip and to inform and educate the public. The press release on November 21, 1966, was successful in mobilizing public support and stilling criticism [7].

The lesson from transsexualism is that professionals must sometimes assume the burden and responsibility of the ethics of a decision for which no custom or precedent exists. They must then assume the further responsibility of educating their colleagues and the general public about the rationale for and outcome of their decision. Left to chance, the professional and public response may too easily become negative. A positive strategy positively influences public opinion and policy in favor of the ethics of the new decision.

In the case of transsexualism, the public attitude toward a variant form of sexuality became more open-minded. Prospectively, that change in public attitude was as important to me in planning (and risking) the first transsexual operation at Johns Hopkins as was the improvement in well-being of the individual patient.

Today, as compared with 1965, I am not sure that transsexual surgery could be introduced for the first time at Johns Hopkins. Here is yet another example of how, under the pressure and encroachment of bureaucratic regulations regarding ethics of informed consent, medical researchers and physicians have all too readily surrendered their own rights of informed consent with respect to innovative and investigative procedures and treatments. It is time to call a halt.

CLINICAL RESEARCH PLUS SERVICE

For me it has long been an imperative that, when human beings are the subjects, clinical investigation must be combined with clinical service. The service may be as simple as reporting on and interpreting findings or as complex as providing a continuous referral-and-treatment program, which is of particular importance in longitudinal study, for example, of anomalies of gender-identity differentiation.

Provision of service builds in a guarantee that any untoward side effects, somatic or psychological, will not be missed and will be subject to remediation. It thus meets one of the needs of informed consent, namely, that concerned with possible risks. Moreover, it helps build a positive reciprocal relationship between investigator and subject (doctor and patient) and guards against attrition of patients during follow-up.

Provision of service extends beyond the specifics of a particular piece of research. It deals with the well-being of the subject in toto. In other words, one treats not only the lab results, nor the single organ system, but the person as an entirety. This means, in some instances, extension from the person to his or her relationship with a sexual partner, or a child or parent. Herein lies a potential advantage for research: In the case of an exhibitionist, sadist, or other paraphilia, for example, a subtle degree of collusion exists between the sex offender and his partner. Contact with the partner is necessary if all the facts are to be known and if attempted treatment is to be effective. For example, an abused and martyred wife in collusion with her sadistically paraphiliac husband, together with the therapist, can take steps to prevent her brutal injury and his imprisonment as a consequence. Thus, by working with both partners, one can circumvent ethical problems that might otherwise arise, for one is able to discharge one's ethical responsibilities jointly to each member of the partnership without betraying confidentiality.

REFERENCES

1. Culliton, B. J.   Patients' rights: Harvard is site of battle over X and Y chromosomes. *Science* 186:715–717, 1974.
2. Culliton, B. J.   XYY: Harvard researcher under fire stops newborn screening. *Science* 188:1284–1285, 1975.
3. Franzke, A.   Telling parents about XYY sons. *New England Journal of Medicine* 293:100–101, 1975.
4. Laschet, U.   Antiandrogen in the treatment of sex offenders: Mode of action and therapeutic outcome. In J. Zubin and J. Money (Eds.), *Contemporary Sexual Behavior: Critical Issues in the 1970's.* Baltimore: Johns Hopkins University Press, 1973.
5. Money, J., Wiedeking, C., Walker, P., Migeon, C., Meyer, W., and Borgaonkar, D.   47, XYY and 46, XY males with antisocial and/or sex-offending behavior. Antiandrogen therapy plus counseling. *Psychoneuroendocrinology* 1:165–178, 1975.
6. Money, J., and Ehrhardt, A. A.   *Man and Woman, Boy and Girl: The Differentiation and Dimorphism of Gender Identity from Conception to Maturity.* Baltimore: Johns Hopkins University Press, 1972.
7. Money, J., and Schwartz, F.   Public opinion and social issues in transsexualism: A case study in medical sociology. In R. Green and J. Money (Eds.), *Transsexualism and Sex Reassignment.* Baltimore: Johns Hopkins University Press, 1969. Chap. 17.

DESIGNATED DISCUSSION

H. TRISTRAM ENGELHARDT, JR.

Dr. Money has provided a rich paper that raises a number of intriguing issues, many of which have already been addressed quite well by Professor Macklin. I will select only two of these issues for comment here, and I will treat them together while also adding some tangential remarks.

First, when Dr. Money raises issues concerning the ethics of sex research, he addresses, for the most part, very general issues such as the right to free and informed consent and the right of prisoners to be free from coercion. These are basic moral issues concerning ethical conduct in general: One does not lie to others or use force to gain their consent.

Second, when he talks about what might appear to be ethical issues specific to human sexuality (involving, for example, homosexuality or the sex reassignment of transsexuals), he is in fact focusing more on issues concerning the cultural milieu or the law. But, whatever the status of legal questions, they cannot be equated with the questions we usually place under the rubric of ethics. After all, we speak of good and bad laws, of moral and immoral laws, presupposing that we have an ethical viewpoint that stands outside any particular set of laws. As to the acceptability of sexual behavior within a particular cultural context, the same observation may be made. There really is no such thing as sexual ethics in the sense of moral rules for conduct to which all rational persons should agree, and which apply uniquely to sexual behavior apart from the considerations of ethics generally. Since Dr. Macklin has already addressed this point, I will not dwell on it except to say that ethics concerning research about human sexuality must presuppose general moral considerations, such as protecting confidentiality, enabling free and informed consent, and the like.

But if research concerning human sexuality involves only general moral considerations bearing on respect for persons, where did the suspicion arise that sexuality involves unique moral considerations? As Rabbi Gordis indicated, such ideas are at least partially Greek in origin, derived from a view of the universe in which all things have their place and goal. The sun naturally goes around the earth in a perfect circle: Circular motion is the motion of celestial bodies. Action on an object that diverts it from its natural course is an example of violent motion. Drawing on such a world-view, St. Thomas said that natural law is what "nature has taught to all animals" [1].

Many of our attitudes toward sexuality are drawn from medieval thinkers who elaborated such concepts with regard to sexual conduct. For example, Gregory the Great, who was pope from 590 to 604, set the tone for medieval views of sexuality in teaching that if a

married couple derived pleasure from intercourse, "they trans-
gressed the law of marriage" and had "befouled their intercourse
with pleasure" [2]. To borrow a phrase from John Noonan, that is
something like asking someone to stick his hand in fire but not get
burned. By the twelfth century this position had led to rather involved teachings about the evils of sexual pleasure in marriage.
Pope Innocent III stated, for example, "Who does not know that
conjugal intercourse is never committed without itching of the
flesh . . . whence the conceived seeds are befouled and corrupted"
[3]. One also ran the risk of a mortal sin if one had intercourse
"too frequently, with inordinate affection or with dissipation of
one's strength" [4].

It is worth stressing that sex with inordinate affection was considered evil. Why? The grounds lie in the notion of the life of a
rational person as one in which reason should never be obtunded,
not even—or especially—by pleasure. Peter Lombard stated, for
example, that "in the union of man and wife, a loss of reason occurs . . . because reason is absorbed by the vehemence of delight,
so that it cannot understand anything during this delight" [5].
Thus, human sexuality was perceived as having very particular
dangers associated with it: loss of one's rational faculties during
moments of pleasure, as well as the diversion of sexuality from the
primary goal to which it was by nature ordained—procreation.

Similar attitudes still existed in St. Louis approximately one
hundred years ago at the beginning of its history of research concerning human sexuality. *The Medical Record* of 1872 gave this
critique [6]:

The following is a case in point. An article appears in the *St. Louis
Medical and Surgical Journal* in answer to the query, how do spermatozoa enter the cavity of the uterus? After reviewing the scanty literature
on the subject, the writer treats the medical public with the details of
a personal observation. The result of this observation is a conclusion
that "the act of coition arouses some special nervous action in the uterus
which causes the *os uteri* to open with successive gasps; when the crisis
arrives, the external *os* is drawn into the cervix each time powerfully,
and at the same time becomes quite soft to the touch." After the orgasm
passes away, the *os* closes and the cervix hardens, as before . . . [The
performance is likened to the motions of the mouth of a species of fish
known as the sucker; although this is a homely illustration, there is no

other in nature which answers so well.] However important it may be to demonstrate whether or not the *os uteri* opens or shuts during coition, we contend that in this case, even on scientific grounds, the end does not justify the means. It may be allowable to make experiments of this sort among lower animals, but ordinary propriety forbids it in the human female, between whom and her physician respectful relations should be maintained as between daughter and parent.

The objections to such a method of establishing scientific knowledge were, to the author of the editorial, so obvious they hardly deserved mentioning. They appear to be based on a supposition that sexual physiology, unlike respiratory physiology, should not be the subject of scientific research, because human sexuality has a proper purpose that does not include its examination in the service of increasing human knowledge. Thus, the editorial concluded [6]:

At least our female patients are not so much interested in furthering scientific research as to be ready to palpitate in the convulsive throes of an orgasm, merely to prove whether or not the *os uteri* opens or not. In view of all this, the question comes up, are we not presuming a little too much for science? Are we not drifting into an indifference to ordinary decency, which, as a learned and dignified profession, we should take every pain to prevent?

Natural-law arguments presuppose that one can decide the purpose of natural processes and that such purposes should not be thwarted. In this case, the argument is something like this: (1) The natural purpose of the genitals is procreation, and (2) one ought not employ anything in nature in a way not directed to its natural purpose.

Therefore, one ought not use one's (or another's) genitals except for procreation. This argument presupposes that organs such as the genitals have special and essential functions. But the fact that human females are potentially inclined to sexual intercourse at all times (that is, there is no human estrus) has been taken to be one of the bases of human society. Humans could form pair bonds in which sexual activity played a social role [7]. Further, the natural-law argument presupposes that there is something wrong in thwarting the designs of nature—an argument usually relying on some form of natural theology.

If one does not argue from the nature of human sexuality to

special moral duties, what is the alternative? One is left with the general canons of ethics and no more. To ask whether it would be unethical to perform operations that we have good reason to believe would be successful in the sexual reassignment of consenting, informed, and uncoerced transsexuals is to ask the wrong question. Perhaps the appropriate question concerns the efficacy of such treatment, or the liability of the investigator, or the likely success of the individual in assuming a new sexual identity. But to ask about its moral status is to confuse a question of ethics with a question of prudence or esthetics.

The final point I want to make is that our appreciation of sexuality and sexual mores is undergoing change. Our view of the conceptual geography separating the reproductive and social aspects of sexuality has been made clearer by the threat of overpopulation, the advent of effective contraception, and the collapse of a belief in a special teleology for human sexuality. Once the significance of this shift in the appreciation of sexuality is fully assimilated, vast cultural implications follow. First and foremost, we will have broken free from an instrumentalist view of sex in which sex is seen primarily as a means of procreation. Second, we will be confronted, as a consequence, with the need to reassess the significance of alternative sexual identities and sexual life-styles. The availability of the medical means to change sexual phenotypes will in particular emphasize the fact that sexual identities are not basic to personal identities. One person can be at one time a male and a father, and later a woman. Moreover, medical judgments with regard to homosexuality have also changed. It may turn out that no particular sexual life-style is best—which is what Dr. Money suggests—any more than expressionist painting is essentially better than impressionist painting. They may simply turn out to be alternative styles with different values, no moral reasons counting for one life-style and against another.

REFERENCES

1. Aquinas, T. *Summa Theologiae* I–II, 94,2. In Anton C. Pegis (Ed.), *Basic Writings of St. Thomas Aquinas*, Vol. 2. New York: Random House, 1945. P. 775.

2. Pope Gregory the Great. *Pastoral Rule* 3.27 (Migne, *Patrologia latina* 77:102).

3. Pope Innocent III. *On the Seven Penitential Psalms* 4 (Migne, *Patrologia latina* 217:1058–1059); cited in John T. Noonan, Jr., *Contraception.* Cambridge: Harvard University Press, 1966. P. 197.

4. Bernadine of Siena. *Seraphic Sermons* 19.3; cited in Noonan, *Contraception.* P. 250.

5. Lombard, P. *On the Sentences* 4.31.1.1; cited in Noonan, *Contraception.* P. 253.

6. Our relations to our female patients (editorial). *The Medical Record* 7:469–470, 1872.

7. Wilson, E. O. *Sociobiology.* Cambridge: Harvard University Press, 1975. P. 553f.

GENERAL DISCUSSION

ALAN A. STONE: I think we can all have a sense of humility when we hear the writings of 1872 and imagine another doctor from Texas 100 years from now reading the minutes of this meeting with the same amount of glee.

Dr. Money spoke eloquently, in what was obviously a *cri de coeur.* I wish I could agree with more of what he said. Dr. Beckwith, who is the protagonist in the XYY battle, believed that he was standing up to be counted. I have not heard from Dr. Money how I can tell whether Dr. Money, who is also standing up to be counted, is on the side of the angels or Dr. Beckwith. This relates to a distinction he made in his paper between ideology and ethics, which is an interesting one, but I'm not sure what that meant.

I have the feeling that the medical profession has not been giving up its decision-making power. It is being taken away from us and we are kicking and squirming. As members of the public learn about the Tuskegee study, research in psychosurgery, or the infamous Jewish Memorial cancer research, they become interested in usurping our power. To a certain extent, we are paying the price for our predecessors' casual approach to these ethical decisions. I think we have to remember that we are not guiltless.

R. CHRISTIAN JOHNSON: Dr. Money stated it would be an advantage to the parents of XYY children to know of this specific condition, and I was attempting to understand why this is so. Presumably, whatever services were necessary to both the control group and the group of XYY children would be available as the need arose; it's difficult for me to see how, unless one were to presume the question with which one began to study, how one would be in a position to advise the parents in any particular way about the effects of an XYY condition. I wonder if Dr. Money might elaborate on this.

JOHN MONEY: I was referring to the prospective aspects of what could be given to parents in terms of advice and counsel *if* they run into difficulty. I underscore *if* because it's already known today that there are some XYY babies who don't have major difficulties in development, whereas others have colossal difficulties. In these matters we already have a large backlog of knowledge, which is still growing and will continue to grow. This knowledge turns out to be very useful in helping parents who have difficult XYY children. If they don't know they have such a child, they are still today grossly mishandled by the guiding professions because the general principle supplied to them, usually quite covertly, is that "everything your child is, is something that you induced in the child yourself." These parents suffer agony because of self-blame that is not fully justified because they are dealing with a different kind of child who requires unusual expertise on the part of the parent. I can give one brief summation of what the difference can mean. In my experience, all XYY children who are given punishment training become absolutely crazy from punishment and retaliate in a most violent fashion. But if a parent gets educated—and in a way it's very difficult for parents to become educated, since they also are products of our society—in the techniques of reward training and the minimization of punishment training, they get much more satisfactory results in the rearing of their child, because they don't precipitate violent crises.

ROBERT C. KOLODNY: I would like to thank Dr. Money and Dr. Engelhardt for crystallizing many of the issues we are focusing on in this particular conference. They've come at it from two very different directions, but as I listened to both presentations and as I think about it, it seems that there is one point of centrality that I would like to offer: that there are differences in the field of sex research inherent in its visibility and apparent in the emotional reactions to the subject matter at hand. Are these ethical principles, then, universal or situational constructs?

VIRGINIA E. JOHNSON: I share Dr. Kolodny's curiosity and his desire for a consensus on this question. There seems to be a request for a different set of ethics in sex research, or at least a different degree of scrutiny involving the same moral principles. I hear a very fine but very real line of distinction. As we are in the process of actually doing research, we must continually be aware of the fact that the emotional component is always present both in the scrutiny of our work and in the reaction the impact of our work produces. We are not actually looking for a special set of ethics, but we are trying to deal with reality.

ALAN A. STONE: That sex research or therapy seems no different than any other problem when analyzed by philosophers does not convince me that this is the case. They may have only proved something about their philosophical tools. My own feeling is that sex therapy and sex research touch on questions of human identity that we all feel very strongly about *because* they touch on human identity. I feel that there is something there that the philosophical discussion, despite its rigor, has not yet managed to dissolve.

H. TRISTRAM ENGELHARDT, JR.: It is worth recalling that there are other areas, such as psychosurgery, that cause a similar sense of concern because they influence how we realize our particular personalities.

ROBERT GORDIS: Obviously the physician is far better equipped to pass judgment on a particular medical or surgical procedure than the judge. If so, why should the judge be given the right to decide rather than the physician? Now you, Dr. Stone, have suggested a possible answer in the variety of cases in which the medical profession may not have been sufficiently sensitive to the ethical issues involved. I think this historical answer to be perfectly true, but I should also like to suggest that it isn't necessary for the judge to know every detail of the techniques and all the mathematical probabilities involved in a particular operation. What I'm getting at is that this is a kind of parallel to the problem of "technocracy," which the graybeards among us may remember. Some decades ago, it was felt that the engineers in society, as its best-trained members, could answer the question of the ultimate goals of society. Of course, the weakness of this view resides in the fact that the technocrat too had certain vested interests and that, therefore, the ultimate goal had to be decided by someone who was not a technocrat. May I suggest that perhaps members of the medical profession act as technocrats in this area, on whom society calls when it wishes to have their expertise. But the ultimate moral decision must lie not with the technical expert, but rather with society embodied in whatever constituted authority it creates. In brief, I am merely suggesting that perhaps the decision to let the judge decide is not as completely irrational as it would seem at first blush, since the physician too has vested interests in his research.

HAROLD I. LIEF: I'd like to discuss the allocation of limited resources. Over and over again, society has to make decisions about which areas will receive support. When the government puts a lot of money into dialysis, it could also put that money into other aspects of health care and the delivery of health care. This is an ethical decision by virtue of the fact that we don't have enough money and resources to go around. It's a matter of robbing Peter to pay Paul. The same thing is true with the issue of sex research and sex therapy. Society at this point does not regard this whole area as being as important as other areas. At this conference, we are of the opinion that it is a highly important area of human behavior and human happiness and should be supported. I don't think that these views are shared by the vast majority of lay people, government officials, or even our medical brethren. I question if this is a moral or ethical issue or simply a question of values.

ROBERT L. STUBBLEFIELD: I want to ask if there is an ethical system emerging that is concerned about groups rather than individuals. If our world is going to have 10 billion people instead of 7 billion 25 years from now, will that not have some impact on what we do in research? I thought of this when Dr. Money spoke of the fact that the medical profession and the sciences really did not face the ethical problems raised by their research until after Hiroshima. However, "research" was done on a particular racial and ethnic group in Germany, which we found out in 1945. I think there are many decisions that involve ethics in some way and that deal with groups of people and not the rights of individuals. I am uncomfortable about our limited discussions and concepts about individual versus group ethical issues.

JAY KATZ: I agree that we need other decision-makers besides medical and scientific decision-makers. There are many social-policy issues involved in medical research, and scientists are not the best people to make such social-policy decisions alone. The real problem, and here I would very much disagree with Dr. Money when he said it's largely a nonjudgmental decision, is that there are no nonjudgmental decisions. In the distinctions Dr. Money introduced about "harmful" and "harmless," all kinds of value judgments are contained as to what is harmless and what is harmful. We physicians and scientists have to begin to undertake the task of sorting out the value conflicts inherent in the various decisions we are making. We must begin to develop policy and analytical frame works for deciding which values we want to maximize and why, and which values we wish to neglect.

ALAN A. STONE: There is a dialectic here that is very important and that I have had on my mind since we started. Because of where we are and instances I alluded to earlier of prior research abuses, there is (and I'm sure this is partly what is in Dr. Money's mind) in this world of ours a caving-in, erecting walls around not just the potential for such abuses but also the possibility of innovation that will bring good to a large number of human beings. That tension is extraordinary.

HELEN DARRAGH: Being representative of a large number of agencies and a tremendous number of clinically trained social workers dealing with marriage counseling, the Family Service Association of America, I was delighted by the discussions of the education and ethics of prevention. I stress the need for early intervention and preventive kinds of measures for the people that we all work with, and in a variety of ways.

MARY S. CALDERONE: I've been getting very uncomfortable sitting here mulling over the fact that physicians and researchers have it in their power to point a finger at a person and say, "This person is free of cancer or TB," but we have no criteria that allow us to point the finger at anyone and say, "This person is sexually healthy." Furthermore, there is no one involved in making such judgments who can say, "I am sexually healthy and free of sexual bias." This is a unique field of health in this respect, for it involves absolutely everyone.

6

THE ETHICS OF
SEX THERAPY

FRITZ REDLICH

This discussion of the ethics of sex therapy will confine itself mostly, though not exclusively, to the model that Masters and Johnson developed [1]. This type of therapy is a particular model of psychotherapy that falls within the boundary of medicine. One might place sexual dysfunction in the category of psychosomatic diseases, and the therapy, which is primarily a communications therapy, in the category of psychotherapy. This paper will center on values and rules of good or bad, desirable or undesirable, professional behavior. Following the advice of my philosophy teacher, Moritz Schlick, a logical positivist, I will be descriptive and explanatory rather than prescriptive [2]; this protects one from becoming a moralist.

Although there is a large literature on sex values, there is only one scientific paper dealing with the ethics of sex therapy; the authors conclude that the most ethical sex therapy is the one that works most efficiently and rapidly and costs the least [3]. Neither insight therapy nor direct sexual relations with the client satisfies this formula; hence, the authors imply that both are unethical. I am committed to a utilitarian point of view, but this conclusion is odd. It wrongly equates technological and moral objections. Or would we consider a surgeon who treats a patient ineptly to be as reprehensible as a surgeon who deliberately hurts him?

To do justice to the ethics of sex therapy, I would like to discuss it within the broader framework of medical and psychotherapeutic role models and to describe as well the historical events leading to the development of role models and the traditions fixing these role models.

ANTECEDENT ROLE MODELS

Modern psychiatry is a child of medicine. In the second half of the nineteenth century, psychiatry began to detach itself as a dependent specialty. The patients were psychotic. Psychiatry's rather low level of technology was a mixture of biological medicine and psychology. Then, under the influence of Freud, Charcot, Janet, and others, psychoneurosis became a legitimate diagnosis and such patients began to receive—mostly because of the impact of psychoanalysis—complex forms of psychotherapy. Soon disorders called character disorders were treated; since everybody has some characterological defects (otherwise we would be saints), the distinction between normal and abnormal became blurred and the psychotherapeutic approach clearly moved out of the medical orbit. Increasing numbers of neurotic patients have been treated by medical and nonmedical personnel. This brief sketch is the historical backdrop for a discussion of the different roles and models. Much of my thinking is based on and has been stimulated by the work of Parsons [4] and the interesting publication of Siegler and Osmond [5].

I will be brief and schematic about the sick role. One should really distinguish between an acute and a chronic sick role, but for the sake of simplicity I will not make this distinction here. According to Parsons, the person in the sick role is excused from social obligations, is not blamed for his condition or considered responsible for it (I am aware that there are exceptions to all these roles), and is obligated to seek medical help and cooperate with the physician to recover or improve. The physician, for his part, will accept such a person under certain conditions that delineate the physician's role. The symptoms, signs, etiology, and treatment must be primarily of an organic nature. Psychosocial considerations play a secondary role and are, unfortunately, all too often absent in practice as well as in medical education. The expectation of both physician and patient is restoration to adequate function.

The moral rules governing the physician's clinical work are ancient. Since the days of Hippocrates, the physician has been expected to perform competently in his field of technology: to help and, above all, not to harm; not to cause trouble through a breach of confidentiality; to receive fair monetary compensation for his service; and to derive no other social or sexual advantages. Parsons also specified collectivity orientation, rather than self-orientation, and universal availability. Both of the latter ideals are only approximated in varying degrees in the reality of practice. The relationship, until recently at least, has been characterized by the patient's trust in the physician, who has occupied a position of strong authority. Recent events have weakened this fiduciary-authoritarian relationship; a new contractual relationship, or—as I prefer to call it—working alliance, is developing. The key concept emerging in the new relationship is informed consent. The key value is health.

In the psychoneurotic model the patient is not at all, or at best only grudgingly, excused from social obligations; in varying degrees he usually blames himself or is blamed and held responsible for his troubles by others. It is his choice to seek help; more often than in biological medicine he is, for socioeconomic and cultural reasons, unable to obtain such help even if he wishes it. The professional helper may be a physician (psychiatrist) or may work in one of a variety of other mental-health fields such as psychology, social work, nursing, pastoral counseling, or newly emerging occupations. The ethical codes governing these professions, insofar as they exist, are similar to the Hippocratic oath—though usually stated in turgid prose quite unlike the powerful poetry of the oath. The signs and symptoms, etiology, and treatment can be characterized as primarily psychosocial. As far as the treatment is concerned, no simple unitary statement can be made; two extremes, however, may be distinguished. One of these might be called a directive-anaclitic model, in which the acquisition of insight is not of primary importance. The professional is authoritarian; he addresses himself to definite needs of the patient for gratification, interpersonal competence, self-esteem, and esteem by others. Under his direction the patient or client will move toward a specified and usually minimal goal of recovery. The persuasive techniques and the behavior therapies fall into this category.

At the other extreme we find the nondirective-analytic approach. In this model, insight is of prime importance. Freud [6] stated, and in an early paper [7] I echoed his view, that psychoanalysis is concerned only with the value of truth. Later this position was modified; autonomy is the goal specified by Szasz [8], Breggin [9], and Engelhardt [10]. Actually, Freud made different statements at different times. He spoke of the restoration to love and work, and many psychoanalysts have postulated very definite values as desirable goals of treatment [11, 12]. The goal, however, is open-ended and might be considered self-actualization, or increase of autonomy, rather than recovery from a disorder. Access depends on voluntary participation, but socioeconomic conditions impose harsh limitations. The methods of this approach are definitely educational. Freud used the term *adult education;* Szasz spoke of *metaeducation.* Even Szasz does not take the final step from treatment to education, nor does he speak of teachers and students rather than therapists and patients or clients.

ROLE MODELS AND VALUES IN SEX THERAPY

Where do patients with sexual disorders stand in the scheme? The sex-therapy patient role is a compromise between the classic medical sick role and the psychoneurotic role. The therapist's role is close, but not identical, to the physician's and directive-anaclitic psychotherapist's role. The patient is exempted from social (in this case, sexual) obligations. He is not blamed for his defects or considered responsible for them. There is no absolute obligation to seek treatment, but the stance of increasingly large segments of American society encourages it. Since the new treatments are relatively inexpensive and effective, such attitudes are of practical significance. Symptomatology, etiology, and therapy have both psychological and organic components, although psychological components dominate. Yet, it is of some interest that in Masters and Johnson's sex therapy a physical examination is obligatory, while in analytic psychotherapy the therapist is strongly cautioned against carrying out such an examination, even if he is a physician. Masters and Johnson's approach is directive; exercises are prescribed, and definite values and doctrines are postulated and conveyed to the patient. These values are (1) sex is a natural function; (2) therapy consists less of learning procedures than of removing culturally and psychologically acquired obstacles; and (3) treatment is directed at the dysfunction of the *couple*, not of the individuals. The partners are further expected to disregard past mutual accusations and objections. There is at least an implicit assumption of the equality of the sexes. Without acceptance of these values, treatment cannot proceed.

I am stating unequivocally that acceptance of such conditions is essential to sex therapy as described by Masters and Johnson. The therapist must know where he stands and not fudge the values, and the patient must know the therapist's values. What about other values? There can be little doubt that sexual attitudes in American society and in many other industrial societies have changed considerably in recent decades, but the extent of this change has not been extensively investigated. It is difficult, of course, to explore what people do, what they say, and what they think—which, as we know, are not the same. For our purposes, however, it is sufficient to assume—and I think we can—that values and attitudes concerning such subjects as the equal rights of the sexes, premarital intercourse, masturbation, homosexuality, and other issues have undergone considerable changes, at least in certain segments of the population [13]. What was once condemned and punished is to a certain extent accepted today. It may be expected that sex therapists and sex researchers hold rather liberal views on such topics, although considerable variability exists here too. Should sex therapists influence their patients to change their values beyond the prerequisites for therapy? I strongly believe they should not. The therapeutic contract does not call for it. If, of course, the patient wishes to change or is ready to change, this is another matter.

Another aspect of the problem of values in sex therapy, and indeed in all psychotherapies, is that the values of therapists and patients must be reasonably similar. Hollingshead and Redlich, in research on social class and psychotherapy, clearly established that psychotherapy is difficult and perhaps impossible unless certain cultural and subcultural values are shared by therapist and patient

[14]. If the value gap is too wide, the psychotherapeutic "spark" cannot fly.

Since sex education is a challenging and important endeavor, many sex therapists are engaged in educational pursuits; they lecture and offer courses on sexual behavior. They are as free as any other lecturers to express their convictions, which may be quite different from those of their audiences. Some sex therapists also hold educational and remedial workshops in which a change in sexual behavior is the desired goal; a type that has become popular is the preorgasmic workshop for women, always presided over by a woman instructor—or shall we call her a therapist? The difference between education and therapy may be tenuous, but it is important nevertheless. If the purpose of therapy (or education?) is to change troublesome behavior (for instance, difficulty or anticipated difficulty having an orgasmic experience), and the instructor tries to bring about change by teaching her students (or shall we call them clients or patients?) to masturbate with enjoyment, my thoughts about the necessity of value congruence between teacher-therapist and student-client hold. In my opinion it is not appropriate, and actually not feasible, to attempt to work with student-clients who are not ready for such treatment. It may be difficult to decide whether we are teachers or therapists, but in any case we are not missionaries.

Another question of values concerns the stance therapists should assume when they encourage activities that violate the criminal code. Because laws concerning sexual behavior in many American states and elsewhere in the world are archaic, hypocritical (because sporadically enforced), and inegalitarian, therapists can be hindered in the treatment of certain couples, such as homosexuals. There is a difference between prudence and morality. In order to help certain persons, the therapist may have to disregard prudence, act courageously, and take risks; this is probably truer in sex therapy than in other sectors. When to do this is, of course, a very personal decision. I would like to draw attention here to an important check on conveyance of the therapist's values to the patient: the dual sex-therapy team. The dual team is, as Masters and Johnson put it, not only a potential built-in peer review but also, because the values of the two therapists will never be identical, a device to protect the patient from undesirable indoctrination [15].

SEX BETWEEN THERAPISTS
AND PATIENTS

Let us turn to the sensitive topic of sexual relationships between therapists and their patients. Although I am concerned only with psychotherapists, and sex therapists in particular, sexual relations between clients and many types of professionals, both within and outside medicine and psychotherapy (educators, lawyers, ministers, all types of employers) are frequent. The essence of this particular immorality is a form of exploitation and abuse of human beings. I also believe that education and repair of damages would be a more effective approach to such unethical behavior than criminal lia-bility. We are dealing with an emotionally charged topic; mere acknowledgment of the existence of such relationships between professional persons and patients or clients makes some profes-sionals angry and defensive. I can detect some anger—possibly justified—on the part of Masters when he demands that therapists who have sexual relations with patients be charged with rape [15]. Because rape is defined as sexual intercourse with a nonconsenting partner other than one's spouse by force or threat of force, the charge does not quite hold; the act would be better compared with statutory rape of a minor or dependent person.

The taboos against sexual relations between therapists and patient-clients are strong. The Hippocratic oath specifically states, "I will abstain from . . . the seduction of females or males or freemen or slaves." (It is interesting that in the modern version formulated by the World Health Association in Geneva in 1948 the reference to sexual activity between therapists and patients has disappeared.) Freud was concerned. He clearly stated that conven-tional morality and professional dignity make a love relationship of an illicit character unacceptable. Without further comment, Freud mentioned that a few analyses terminate when the analyst marries the patient. At another point Freud stated that any love relation-ship destroys the influence of analytic therapy. When a sexual relationship occurs, it is not the therapist's personal qualities that account for the "conquest"; it is attributable instead to transference of unconscious feelings toward parental figures in the patient's past onto the therapist. In discussing this topic, interestingly enough, Freud mentions only male therapists and female patients. Psychoanalysts have taken his warnings seriously by stressing the taboo on sexual relations; in a draft of an ethical code by the American Psychoanalytic Association, the temptation is clearly recognized and the act clearly condemned. Any analyst involved in such a relation is required to terminate analysis with the patient in question, to refer the patient (if feasible) to another analyst, and to seek further analysis for himself pending disciplinary action by his peers.

The strength of the taboo is justified by the temptation and by the frequency of actual transgressions. Kardener and colleagues [16] report on an anonymous mail survey of physicians in the Los Angeles area; 7.2 percent of the respondents engaged in sexual intercourse with patients, most only rarely. Such relations occurred more frequently in general practice than in any of the specialties. In a clinical paper Shor and Sanville analyze erotic dalliances between therapists and patients and point to the importance of pregenital provocations [17], which makes sense in the light of what we know about transference. From this report it is quite evident that such provocations and dalliances lead to the evaporation of trust and the end of therapy. The same point is conveyed by Martin Shepard's book *The Love Treatment* [18]. The hubris of this book really amazed me: Shepard recommends "mature" sexual relationships with patients, but every case in the book (verbatim accounts of patients' sexual relationships with other therapists) testifies to the breakdown of trust and regard and to the hostility and disappointment that follow the sexual involvement. The book also illustrates the psychopathological motivations of therapists who become thus involved. Such behavior satisfies the needs of the therapist, which are incompatible with good therapy, and not the legitimate needs of patients. The Lowrys [3] ask why therapists who want to help clients with intercourse do not seek out the old, the ugly, and the crippled.

Learning from colleagues and patients about past sexual relationships in a therapeutic setting, I have been able to discern two types. In the first, the patient is infantile, passive, dependent, and often depressed, with marked feelings of inadequacy. The seduction of such a patient is indeed comparable to statutory rape. The result is termination of therapy and, on the part of the patient, further disappointment and increased inability to form social and sexual relationships. The patient is clearly damaged by the experience. The second type is characterized by the aggressive patient who seduces the therapist. Once the therapist succumbs, he is finished as a helping person whom the patient can respect and trust. In the literature this situation is dramatically and beautifully portrayed in Somerset Maugham's "Rain" [19]. Sadie Thompson, a wild and lusty prostitute, is almost converted by the Reverend Davidson, a missionary, when he loses control and succumbs to her seductiveness. With disappointment, anger, and cynicism she returns to her former life; he commits suicide.

There may be situations in which a mature partner (perhaps a mature prostitute, not easily found) will help a less mature partner achieve sexual gratification and personal fulfillment. Such an outcome is possible in a free and open relationship, but many of the affairs between so-called helpers and sexual partners in need of assistance are relationships of bondage, as described in Heinlein's *Stranger in a Strange Land* [20]. This book, incidentally, influenced Charles Manson, who also felt that he "helped" members of his "family" who desired it. None of these relationships, however, should be considered therapeutic, nor have they a place in professional therapy. I am also convinced that in such relationships the profound disturbances customarily seen in professional sex therapy are not touched on.

AFFECTIONATE BEHAVIOR BETWEEN THERAPISTS AND PATIENTS

While sexual relations with patients are clearly condemned by all practitioners except an irresponsible fringe, the problem of nonsexual affectionate behavior is more complicated and controversial. What Kardener and colleagues define as nonerotic behavior (such as kissing, hugging, and affectionate touching of patients) is more commonplace than sexual intercourse. Fifty-nine percent of the surveyed physicians engage in such practices: 33 percent rarely, 20 percent occasionally, and 6 percent frequently or always [16]. Of the psychiatrists, 56 percent engage in such behavior: 41 percent rarely, 14 percent occasionally, and only 1 percent frequently or always. In the course of their professional education, medical students and physicians in training are taught by word and example what Parsons calls affective neutrality—rational, logical, deliberate, cool, and unemotional behavior [4]. Such behavior is expected of many types of technologists to ensure good interaction with others. A surgeon cannot let tears fall in a patient's wound, nor is a general expected to weep when strategy requires that some of his soldiers die. But I believe that in medical education we overdo it; the result is often not affective neutrality but coldness, cynicism, and detachment. To resort to detachment under conditions of temptation such as occur in psychoanalytic treatment and sex therapy would be understandable, and certainly preferable to yielding to temptation. However, stiffness and defensiveness under the guise of a "super-correct" attitude may be therapeutically inappropriate as well. Where is the boundary between affectionate and erotic-sexual behavior? This is a judgment that undoubtedly requires mature and subtle thinking, and more humanity than we are taught in our medical or psychotherapeutic training. And patients, of course, may see this issue differently than professional therapists do. One can err in either direction.

The reason for the strong taboo is that the temptation to become sexually involved is considerable in a medical situation. Goethe knew this when he had Mephisto, dressed as Faust, describe to a student the joys of the medical profession:

> Besonders lernt die Weiber führen;
> Es ist ihr ewig Weh und Ach
> So tausendfach
> Aus einem Punkte zu kurieren,
> Und wenn Ihr halbweg ehrbar tut,
> Dann habt Ihr sie all unterm Hut.
> Ein Titel muss sie erst vertraulich machen,
> Dass Eure Kunst viel Künste übersteigt;
> Zum Willkomm tappt Ihr dann nach allen Siebensachen,

Um die ein andrer viele Jahre streicht,
Versteht das Pülslein wohl zu drücken
Und fasset sie, mit feurig schlauen Blicken,
Wohl um die schlanke Hüfte frei,
Zu sehn, wie fest geschnürt sie sei.*

In sex therapy both the content of the patient's history and the obligatory physical examination intensify the problem of temptation. It is well known that, even without the slightest intent of provocation by the physician, male and female patients frequently become aroused during an examination of their genitalia. Physicians wisely protect themselves against misunderstanding and awkward interaction by employing the ritual of the examining room and chaperones. In Masters and Johnson's technique, the dual-sex team provides an effective form of protection.

OTHER ETHICAL PROBLEMS
IN SEX THERAPY

One question that has been raised is whether actual observation of sexual relations is justified. The answer for therapy, in contrast to research, is clearly no. This answer is given on moral and technical grounds. On moral grounds, the need for privacy is greater for sexual behavior than for any other somatic function and should be set aside only for very sound reasons. (In human sex research such reasons exist, but not in therapy.) If a therapist insists on actual observations, the suspicion that he does so for his own ulterior reasons is more than justified. Such motivation is not, of course, compatible with therapeutic motivations. The same reasoning applies to other odd, unconventional, and often offensive practices—usually by untrained and inferior persons who call themselves therapists—such as the treatment of male patients by nude sex therapists or the demonstration of intercourse and masturbation. The nude mara-

* And give the women special care;/Their everlasting sighs and groans/In thousand tones/Are cured at *one* point everywhere./And if you seem halfway discreet,/They will be lying at your feet./First your degree inspires trust,/As if your art had scarcely any peers;/Right at the start, remove her clothes and touch her bust,/Things for which others wait for years and years./Learn well the little pulse to squeeze,/And with a knowing, fiery glance you seize/Her freely round her slender waist/To see how tightly she is laced.

thon may enhance human intimacy. Scandinavians and Japanese have incorporated such practices into their bathing cultures, but they disturb and do not enhance sex therapy. There is no trace of a therapeutic rationale for such practices in professional sex therapy.

A rather specific question has arisen with the use of so-called surrogate partners in sex therapy. Masters and Johnson provided partners for male patients with sexual disorders who had been unable to find partners. After a program of instruction and careful screening for desirable characteristics, the surrogate partners performed such service. Any "personal" involvement beyond the period of therapy was forbidden. The surrogate was always female. Masters and Johnson never used male surrogate partners because our culture would frown on it. The intent was admirable, but I gather from verbal reports (I have had no personal experience with the use of surrogates in sex therapy) that the attendant problems have been considerable. Ultimately the Reproductive Biology Research Foundation discontinued the use of surrogates. For a student of role behavior, conflicts would have been predictable. Is the surrogate a partner or is she to a certain extent performing a teaching or therapeutic role? If she is or considers herself to be in a therapeutic role, is she an extension of the therapeutic team? What is her obligation to observe professional standards, such as confidentiality? Controls that can be exercised more or less effectively over professional persons do not exist over surrogates. Of course, the surrogate can be dismissed if she gossips, but if this happens the damage is already done. The professional employer may have very clear ideas about such matters, but neither the surrogate nor the patient necessarily shares them. One patient referred to the surrogate as a "prostitute-lady," which implies a powerful role conflict. And how does the surrogate see herself? There is no ethical objection to the use of a surrogate as long as both patient and surrogate consent to this particular cooperative venture. I am inclined to agree with Lowry and Lowry that other ways of helping the lone male and female patient must be found [3]. The Lowrys mention assertion therapy and socialization techniques as reasonable alternative approaches to sex therapy.

The preservation of confidentiality is a very important issue in sex therapy. It may be threatened by the use of surrogates. It is even more seriously threatened by group therapy for sexual disorders. Though in principle no different from other group therapies, group therapy for sexual disorders has even greater potential for mischief. For this reason one must caution patients who wish to avail themselves of it. The intrinsic need for privacy in sexual matters has induced Masters and Johnson and other responsible therapists and clinics to use very elaborate precautions. Carefully guarded tapes, such as those the Reproductive Biology Research Foundation uses, are possibly the best safeguard. They are expensive, however, and cannot be easily administered. The need to report diagnoses of sexual disorders to insurance companies is also a threat to confidentiality, but if judiciously handled it need not be a major problem. Of course we must be wary lest the CIA, FBI, or presidential election committees get hold of our records!

In my opinion, the ethical problems facing professional sex therapy are not significantly greater than those of other psychotherapies. Our concern is not with the well-trained professional who more or less adheres to a code, but rather with poorly trained, untrained, or irresponsible persons who call themselves therapists. The other day I watched on television a brief report on sex therapy. At the end there appeared a little man (he reminded me of one of the supporting characters in the film *The Godfather*) who said: "There are millions of dollars in sex therapy, It's big business. Somebody will want to make these millions." That's where the danger lies.

Freud was concerned throughout his life with wild analysis. And sex therapy might be even wilder. The task for a small, serious professional group—to stem a tidal wave of uncontrolled and therefore potentially very harmful intervention—is gigantic and threatening. It means educating political leaders, with the ultimate goal of certification and license of well-trained, qualified persons. There need not be a restricted license for sex therapy; instead a license for professional psychotherapy could require sound knowledge in the field of sex therapy. It should also be recognized that in the future such therapies will be carried out by family physicians, urologists, and gynecologists-obstetricians. Education of professional groups is necessary. In this respect I would like to mention a very alarming finding that deserves to be addressed in medical education: Twenty-five percent of the freshman medical students at a certain medical school felt it is appropriate for therapists to have intercourse with their patients if the therapist is genuine and authentic [16]. Why not? they query. Of all the ethical problems raised, I consider this the most alarming.

REFERENCES

1. Masters, W., and Johnson, V. *Human Sexual Inadequacy*. Boston: Little, Brown, 1970.
2. Schlick, M. *Problems of Ethics*, translated by P. Rynin. New York: Prentice-Hall, 1939.
3. Lowry, T. S., and Lowry, T. P. Ethical considerations in sex therapy. *Journal of Marriage and Family Counseling* 1(3):229–236, 1975.
4. Parsons, T. *Social System*. Glencoe, Ill.: Free Press, 1951.
5. Siegler, M., and Osmond, H. *Models of Madness, Models of Medicine*. New York: Macmillan, 1974.
6. Freud, S. Further recommendations in the technique of psychoanalysis. In *Collected Papers*. London: Hogarth Press, 1948–1950. Vol. 2, pp. 342–365.
7. Redlich, F. Psychoanalysis and the problem of values. In J. Masserman (Ed.), *Psychoanalysis and Human Values*. New York: Grune & Stratton, 1960.
8. Szasz, T. *The Ethics of Psychoanalysis*. New York: Basic Books, 1965.
9. Breggin, P. Psychotherapy as applied ethics. *Psychiatry* 34:59–74, 1971.
10. Engelhardt, H. T., Jr. Psychotherapy as meta-ethics. *Psychiatry* 36:440–445, 1973.
11. Erikson, E. Growth and Crises of the Healthy Personality. In C. Kluckhohn and H. Murray (Eds.), *Personality in Nature, Society and Culture*. New York: Knopf, 1967.
12. Shakow, D. Ethics for a scientific age: Some moral aspects of psychoanalysis. *Psychoanalysis Review* 52:5–18, 1965.
13. Christensen, H., and Greeg, C. Changing sex norms in America and Scandinavia. In R. Bell and M. Gordon, *The Social Dimension of Human Sexuality*. Boston: Little, Brown, 1972.
14. Hollingshead, R., and Redlich, F. *Social Class and Mental Illness*. New York: Wiley, 1958.

15. Masters, W., and Johnson, V.   Principles of the new sex therapy. *American Journal of Psychiatry* 133(5):548–554, 1976.
16. Kardener, S., Fuller, M., and Mensch, I.   A survey of physicians' attitudes and practices regarding erotic and nonerotic contact with patients. *American Journal of Psychiatry* 130(10):1077–1081, 1973.
17. Shor, J., and Sanville, J.   Erotic provocation and dalliances in psychotherapeutic practice. *Clinical Social Work Journal* 2(2):83–95, 1974.
18. Shepard, M.   *The Love Treatment*. New York: Wyden, 1971.
19. Maugham, S.   "Rain." In *The Favorite Short Stories*. New York: Doubleday, 1937.
20. Heinlein, R. A.   *Stranger in a Strange Land*. New York: Berkeley, 1961.

DESIGNATED DISCUSSION

JUDD MARMOR

Dr. Redlich raises the legitimate question of the degree, if any, to which sex therapists should attempt to modify their patients' basic values. He emphasizes the importance of value congruence between the therapist and the patient or client and points out that it is not the function of the therapist to be a missionary. But he also recognizes that the process of psychotherapy (which he properly equates with a kind of teaching) inevitably involves imparting values to the patient and that some of these may be antithetical to attitudes the patient has long held. By its very nature, the desensitization that is such an essential component of contemporary sex therapies involves altering or at least modifying long-held values with regard to sex. The question, then, is not whether such changes are appropriate, but rather to what degree. Is there a point at which efforts to modify values held by the patient should be considered as transcending ethical boundaries? I agree with Dr. Redlich that there is, but that point is not always easy to define.

One basic criterion that might be employed in elucidating this question is the degree to which the value change the therapist is advocating is essential to help the patient achieve the therapeutic objectives that brought him or her into therapy. We could say, then, that patients' values require modification only to the degree (and no more) that will enable them to overcome the sexual dysfunction for which they have sought help. For a sex therapist to attempt more—for example, to proselytize for group sex, indiscriminate sex, bisexual behavior, or even heterosexual behavior, if that is not what the patient has come for—would certainly constitute the kind of missionary zeal that Dr. Redlich is decrying and would stretch the limits of ethical propriety to a questionable degree. On the other hand, as Dr. Redlich has implied, enabling patients to free themselves from the shackles of an archaic puritan ethos that tends to downgrade the healthily pleasurable aspects of sexuality is a prerequisite for most sex therapy. Even though, in many states, teaching or advocating a more enlightened approach to sexuality may technically be encouraging clients and patients to violate the criminal code, psychotherapists in general and sex therapists in particular should not hesitate, in my opinion, to take the lead in openly criticizing and opposing such archaic statutes.

I would sound a note of caution here, however. We know from long experience in dynamic psychotherapy that particularly rigid defenses often bespeak an underlying characterological fragility that one would be wise to respect lest one precipitate a serious decompensatory reaction. In sex therapy, too, one must be careful not to push too hard against a moral resistance that is obviously very powerful. It is neither good therapy nor sound ethics to attempt to force patients to go further or faster than they are willing to go. Incidentally, Dr. Redlich's comment that a dual-sex team often acts as a salutary check-and-balance system to prevent therapeutic excesses is probably generally true, provided the dual-sex team does not share a folie à deux! Unfortunately, there are some dual-sex teams in whom the distorted value system is shared; in such instances, the presence of two parents, so to speak, advocating some dubious practice can be a reinforcing rather than an inhibiting factor.

I cannot, of course, state strongly enough my agreement with Dr. Redlich's comment concerning sexual relations between psychotherapists and their patients. Such behavior is particularly reprehensible because of the special vulnerability of patients in this context. In many other relationships between a client and a professional, the client may be able to maintain a certain amount of personal reserve and still benefit from the relationship to a greater or lesser degree. In the psychotherapeutic relationship, however, a special emphasis is placed on the therapeutic necessity for the patient to set aside his or her customary defenses and to open himself or herself completely to the presumably benign and constructive influence of a therapist's professional skill. The implicit and explicit basis on which such total openness and trust is solicited is a solemn commitment that it will not be betrayed. Under such circumstances, a positive transference that leaves the patient uniquely vulnerable to the influence of the therapist usually develops. To exploit this iatrogenically induced vulnerability seems to me particularly reprehensible and unethical. Regardless of the rationalizations with which a therapist may attempt to justify such behavior, I have never encountered a situation of this kind in which the therapist was not clearly acting on the basis of unresolved neurotic motivations. Even granting that patients in such situations are often seductive—either actively or passively, as Dr. Redlich points out—the therapist who succumbs to such a seduction is always responding to some countertransference needs of his own—needs, incidentally, that are not necessarily always erotic in nature. For example, patterns such as unconscious feelings of hostility to women—or to men, in the reverse situation—or power drives based on reaction-formations against feelings of masculine or feminine inadequacy, or defenses against unconscious feelings of homosexuality can also be involved. None of this, of course, precludes the possibility that a therapist may genuinely fall in love with his or her patient and enter into a relationship of intimacy as a consequence. But the minimum ethical requirement under such circumstances is that the therapeutic relationship be terminated and the patient or client be referred to another therapist.

Sometimes therapists, particularly sex therapists, sublimate their unconscious needs by developing techniques that partially satisfy these needs. Into this category fall some of the voyeuristic and exhibitionistic techniques to which Dr. Redlich has referred, such as those involving erotic handling of patients under the guise of teaching or demonstration. Even though patients may be helped by some of these techniques (or perhaps in spite of them), it is my conviction that as long as there is no evidence that such techniques produce results superior to those of the more standard approaches developed by Masters and Johnson (and as far as I know there is not), the suspicion will always remain that therapists employing them are doing so to satisfy needs of their own rather than because the techniques are mandated by the therapeutic requirements of their patients or clients.

There is only one point on which I find myself in disagreement with Dr. Redlich, and that is the issue of confidentiality as it relates to group sex therapy. Needless to say, I fully share his feelings about the importance of preserving confidentiality, not only in sex therapy but in all psychotherapy. But I don't think that as psychotherapists we should take the attitude that there is anything especially shameful about sexual dysfunction. Even though our society at large tends to hold such a view—indeed, all mental disorders are regarded as shameful—it is our responsibility as professionals to do everything we can to eliminate such prejudice. One cornerstone of our therapeutic approach is the attempt to relieve such feelings of shame in our patients. Thus, although it may well be true that group sex therapy carries with it a greater risk to confidentiality than does the treatment of a single couple, the same can be said of all group therapy as compared to individual therapy. However, we as professionals should not take a different attitude toward the therapy of sexual dysfunction in this regard than we do toward the therapy of any other mental or emotional disorder. I would, therefore, find myself disagreeing that group sex therapies should in and of themselves be viewed as ethically questionable. I say this particularly because if such therapies prove useful, they would make the treatment of sexual dysfunction more accessible from an economic point of view and would enable competent therapists to help many more people. No one feels more strongly than I about the tremendous contribution Masters and Johnson have made toward the treatment of sexual dysfunction. Their model has totally revolutionized the treatment of these disorders, but it is my conviction—and I'm sure they would agree—that no theory or technique in behavioral science, no less than in any other area of science, should be considered so sacrosanct that it should not be subject to legitimate exploration and experimental modification. The application of the Masters and Johnson principles to a group therapeutic approach by qualified persons in reputable clinic settings constitutes such a legitimate effort; it would be unfortunate if it were to be discouraged on unwarranted ethical grounds.

In concluding, let me say that I'm delighted to be participating in this important conference. We inevitably raise more questions than answers, but that, after all, is the nature of the beast we are dealing with. Apart from the golden rule, very few ethical precepts are sacrosanct and eternal. Most ethical rules grow out of the homeostatic needs of the societies that promulgate them. The moral and ethical view that emphasized the reproductive aspects of sexuality, and therefore condemned such acts as extragenital sex, masturbation, and homosexuality, grew out of an historical era when high fertility was essential to human survival. Today, for reasons well known to all of you, human survival will ultimately depend on our ability to limit our fertility. Thus, it is inevitable that our ethical values are now in the process of downplaying the reproductive aspects of sexuality and emphasizing its recreational aspects. In any event, we've come a long way from the views Alice Roosevelt Longworth recently expressed when that indomitable dowager was asked what she thought about sex: "I have nothing to say about the subject of bodily function except—fill what's empty, empty what's full, and scratch when it itches!"

DESIGNATED DISCUSSION

JAY KATZ

Dr. Redlich has, as I would expect from my former teacher, given us a rich and wide-ranging presentation of the complex problems inherent in, though not necessarily unique to, sex therapy. In the limited time available to me I can do greater justice to the issues he has raised not by addressing them specifically but by extending them.

A discussion of the ethics of sex therapy immediately encounters a number of obstacles: The study of ethics, as it applies to medicine, has not been warmly embraced by medical educators or medical scholars. Questions about what is and is not ethical continue to flounder in a tangled web of opinion, often passionately held; these questions have not been submitted to careful disentanglement and analysis in seminars and scholarly journals. Thus, we do not posesss a systematic body of knowledge on an ethics for medicine. It still needs to be developed.

As a consequence, no consensus can exist on the ethical practice of any medical therapy. Here I do not wish to question the ethical behavior of medical practitioners. I only wish to assert that, in the absence of a theoretical framework, we cannot determine what is and what is not ethical behavior. What is ethical is not self-evident. This state of affairs makes it well-nigh impossible to compare sex therapy with other medical interventions in order to assess the extent to which it does or does not depart from traditional ethical practices. Indeed, in the case of any innovative therapy that is challenged by customary practice, innovators can readily point their fingers at similar uncertainties, transgressions, and ignorance in established medical procedures and ask: Why are we being singled out? This leads often to acrimonious debate but rarely to insight.

The confusion that pervades most discussions on the ethics of medicine is not rooted in a dearth of ethical principles. We have our share of them—confidentiality, injunctions against seduction, preservation of life, and the like. Such confusion, as I have already indicated, has its roots in the rarity of detailed and systematic exploration of these principles and the oft-conflicting value preferences that underlie them, as well as in the lack of conceptual frameworks for analysis of ethical medical practices.

Let me illustrate (though I will not do so systematically). One of the most ancient and revered principles governing medical practice is *primum non nocere*: First of all, do no harm. It is often asserted that fidelity to this principle serves medicine well and that little else is needed. The persistence of such simple-minded beliefs is remarkable in its own right. For what kind of harm are we talking about? Prevention of harm to a patient's physical integrity? If so, what are the consequences if prevention of such harm conflicts with psychological, religious, social, interpersonal, or dignitary integrity? How are the various facets of patients' functioning to be sorted out, and by whom?

What value preferences do we seek to safeguard with this Hippocratic commandment? Is the value preference to be based on the physician's, patient's, profession's, or state's definition of harm? If these views conflict, whose values are to be given greater weight?

If harm can be alleviated by a variety of medical interventions, each with its own particular risks and benefits, who decides which therapy is to be employed? What disclosures must be made to patients, and how far and when should we trust their capacity to make decisions on their own behalf?

As for innovative therapies, as sex therapy may still be, who decides when they are to be employed on a limited experimental scale in order to gain additional knowledge about harm and benefit, and when they can be presented to patients at large as accepted medical procedure?

If sexual intercourse with patients is viewed not as seduction but as enlightened therapy (which would at least raise questions about the applicability of the Hippocratic commandment against seduction), who ultimately approves it as therapy? Should we rely on the "courageous," "risk-taking" therapist or dual-sex team or does the employment of such therapy require, for example, approval by the profession? If the latter, by what mechanisms? Or should the decision to employ such treatment be arrived at privately between physicians and their patients? What values are preserved or undermined by proscribing such treatments for informed and consenting adults?

I hope that I have made it clear that there is more to *primum non nocere* than perhaps even Hippocrates dreamed of. In the remaining minutes, let me all-too-briefly address one prescription—better education. I share Dr. Redlich's belief that this could be an effective approach, but only if we take it more seriously than we have done until now. It is insufficient—indeed, perhaps counterproductive and even dangerous—to perpetuate our present practice of "sensitizing" students to the ethical complexities of medicine through occasional lectures or panel discussions. It is dangerous because we can become convinced that we are doing something when we are actually doing very little. We do not sensitize students to pathology or pharmacology; we teach them these subjects systematically.

What might we do? If I were to contemplate offering a seminar on the ethics of sex therapy, I would first of all stretch my canvas wide. Here I cannot even outline how such a seminar should be structured, for I do not possess sufficient knowledge in your field to do so. Thus, a few more general and suggestive comments must suffice. I might organize my teaching materials around the chief participants in the medical decision-making process—the physician, the patient, the profession, and the state—and ask: What roles should be assigned to each of the participants? I might begin this inquiry by exploring the problems that would arise if total authority were assigned to sex therapists, and by identifying their special values and qualifications to do so; then I might proceed to an examination of the competence of patients to collaborate in decision-making; and, finally, I might go on to an exploration of the roles the professions and the state should play in controlling the private decision-making between physicians and their patients.

I would spend considerable time examining the social and political organization of the medical profession, in order to discuss with students the implications of the tremendous authority that has been delegated to and assumed by professionals in our society. Here a major question would be: To what extent are either the individual's or society's interests well served by leaving the patient's protection to the professional's judgment of the patient's best interest?

The doctrine of informed consent—the extent and limits of the patient's ability and authority to make decisions on his or her own behalf—would also be a major focus of inquiry. Here I would ask: What functions, such as protecting the status of the patient as a human being or promoting individual autonomy, are to be safeguarded by the doctrine of informed consent and the jurisprudential principle of "thoroughgoing self-determination"? How can the value preference underlying these functions be implemented? And if some of the values have to be neglected, how can such neglect be kept to a minimum? What impediments to informed consent are inherent in the intellectual capacities, psychological forces, and social pressures operating in and on human beings? What restraints should the professions and the state place on informed consent in order to protect the patient from "unpleasant" knowledge and "unwise" choices or to shield society from troublesome choices, like sanctioning certain forms of sex therapy that are considered offensive to the "moral sense" of the community?

I believe I have said enough to indicate the scope of the teaching effort required in order to educate our students. A lesser commitment may be valuable as sensitivity training, but it is not education in the scholarly sense of the word.

In conclusion, let me return to the very end of Dr. Redlich's paper. He was alarmed that "twenty-five percent of the freshman medical students at a certain medical school felt that it is appropriate for therapists to have intercourse with their patients if the therapist is genuine and authentic." I am also alarmed, though perhaps for different reasons. I am alarmed about the sole emphasis on the genuineness and authenticity of the physician; how about the patient's authenticity? I am alarmed about the disregard of the psychological problems inherent in determining "genuineness" and "authenticity," especially when the imperiousness of sexual impulses needs be taken into account. I am most alarmed, though, by the students' willingness to answer the question, either affirmatively or negatively, in the first place. They should have declined and asserted instead that the question cannot be answered in the form posed, at least not without much further inquiry, thought, and specification. The incident illuminates a failure in medical education. In pathology we have taught our students well to distinguish between answerable and still-unanswerable questions, or to carefully identify, for example, the presence of Reed-Sternberg cells, abnormal lymphocytes, and normal lymphocytes before responding to questions about what to do with patients. We have not taught them well that before answering questions about professional responsibility, they must sort out when a question is not a question and distinguish between authenticity, self-deception, self-delusion, and, most important, thoughtlessness.

GENERAL DISCUSSION

VIRGINIA E. JOHNSON: The subject that we are discussing this morning is one that I think many of us have a tremendous investment in and a very deep concern for: ethical dilemmas and various psychotherapeutic approaches to sex therapy. Yesterday, Father Wilkerson mentioned that pastoral theology might be considered in one sense to be an ultimate expression of theology. Similarly, I might suggest that therapy could well be the same kind of ultimate in terms of sex research. There are certainly other research areas of equal importance, but the fact is that therapy, of course, is the connecting-point with people. For some, this represents an ultimate purpose, the quintessence of the development of scientific knowledge.

Bill and I still accept a sense of responsibility that we cannot escape for seeing this particular area of health care come of age, become stable, and acquire appropriate regulations and accreditation. This is necessary so that people who seek help can do so without assuming more than a minimal risk of exploitation—a risk that exists in any field under the heading of the human factor. At the least, we would like to be able to refer people with confidence in the competence and integrity of care they would receive—I think this is true of all health-care professionals. There's a lot of growing that needs to be done.

Our own history is interesting. The publication of *Human Sexual Inadequacy* represented one of the few major areas of contention between the two of us in the almost 20 years we've worked together. Bill felt that this material belonged in the scientific community to be shared, rejected, modified, adapted, or whatever else. I was concerned in large part because of the emotional impact of the subject. Traditional attitudes die slowly and painfully. We learned some very obvious truths, and we learned them the hard way. Professionals, with regard to sex, are human beings and individuals first and professionals second—a fact I have not seen change in recent years. That some individuals have gone on to become objective, knowledgeable, open, and willing to reach out and explore is marked by your presence here today, but there aren't many like you yet.

In 1958 we started developing ideas and approaches. The design for this work was something we were excited by. However, funding difficulties made it almost impossible to activate. Therapy was included as part of a large program because we realized that it would have to be one of the ultimate proving-grounds for the facts we hoped to develop to replace prior myths and misconceptions. During those early days, psychiatry provided a wonderful challenge to us—along with medicine, it demanded that we show the clinical relevance of our physiological work.

In 1959 we actually began a therapy program. For five years, as it was evolving, we charged no fees. People who came to us were explicitly told that this was an experimental program and that we had material that certainly was more factual than had existed in this society to our knowledge before, but that we had no sure knowledge of how to apply it.

By 1970 I wanted very much to draw on traditional techniques to help extract the dynamics of our particular therapy model so that it could be understood more clearly, more quickly, and more reliably by greater numbers of people. As I look back, that was unrealistic because of the lack of secure funding and concomitant pressures of time. The result was remarkably similar to the story of the blind men and the elephant. Each blind man described an elephant according to the part they first touched—one compared it to a snake, another to a tree trunk, and so forth. Each person who encountered this model of therapy touched a bit of it, assumed that his or her perception accurately described the whole process, and ran off to use and lecture about this strange new beast.

There is nothing we desire more than rational analysis of the model we have had the privilege to bring forth—rational analysis that can lead to either acceptance, rejection, or modification. We would have liked, above all, to have had it fully understood—and we accept responsibility for not having sufficiently distilled the essence of this work at the time of initial publication so that others could have had a broader concept of it in their own work. The model itself is infinitely more resilient than is generally appreciated by most people who are well trained in their own field. In addition to this resilience, there are so many points that we have held to meticulously in our own work but have been neglectful in sharing—such simple things as the degree to which we request and require that patients accept and share responsibility for their therapeutic destiny as it is moved along. In this regard, I must turn to the very real issue mentioned by both Dr. Redlich and Dr. Marmor: therapist modification of patient values. When our model is exercised in the way that it was conceptualized, this never becomes an issue because it is never necessary. The patient joins with the therapist in decision-making, but all decisions and suggestions are within the framework of the patient's value system.

CHARLES REMBAR: The illuminating talks this morning suggest several things to a lawyer. One is that there seems to be very little in the way of medical ethics courses in medical school. There are legal ethics courses in law school; I had one. The professor's name was Cheatham. (I had two classmates, one named Zlinkoff and one named Ketcham, and we thought it would be a marvelous law firm: Ketcham, Cheatham, and Zlinkoff.)

Dr. Redlich referred to the fact that Dr. Masters feels that therapist-patient sex constitutes rape in the traditional sense; Dr. Redlich thought that it might be better analogized to statutory rape. I think I agree with Dr. Masters on this, although I'm sure I can't cite a precedent. The definition of rape comes from a time when physical force was the principal means of accomplishing it. That sort of overwhelming power need not be physical, and I think that law, when the case is properly presented, adapts itself to the underlying consideration rather than the superficial resemblances. For example, libel, as you know, has to do with what's written, slander with what's spoken. Libel is a much more effective remedy. When radio came into being, there was a suit brought for libel that would have been successful if it was regarded as libel and would not have been successful if it was regarded as slander. The highest court of New York held that although the words were spoken, it was libel because the real distinction was not the physical one. The real distinction was that the written word always carried farther and did more harm and was more permanent than the spoken word. Radio was seen as more like the written word than the spoken word, indicating the flexibility of law.

I also want to talk briefly about the move toward what we might call the contractualization of the relationship between patient and doctor. I think this is not salutary. I think it would be much better not to rely on codification of rules, but to rely on the general traditional notion of trust. Rules that govern lawyer-client relationships are just about useless because the proper discharge of the lawyer's function is such a delicate thing that it is impossible to prove, for example, that the lawyer gave advice that was really beneficial to the lawyer rather than the client. I imagine the same sort of thing applies in the doctor-patient relationship; the area is too delicate to admit written rules.

JOHN MONEY: I'm trying to take a glimpse into history 25 years from now, and I suspect we might find that we're extraordinarily old-fashioned in our ideas about sexual intercourse in relationship to therapy—perhaps as old-fashioned by comparison as what we heard from 1872 yesterday. I might also add a little bit of history from 1900, when Howard Kelly from Hopkins made a vicious attack on an attempt to publish a paper on female sexuality, which has been recorded in the history of sex education. There already is some evidence that there are a select group of call girls who have become therapists not in the sense of belonging to a medical team or to any institutionalized team, but while belonging to their own profession. These are women who have, perhaps, an intuitive degree rather than an educated degree of understanding about the needs of their clients and do indeed perform what is in essence a therapeutic job for them! The difference for these women as compared with what we've been talking about and listening to today is that the contract between them and their client is well understood ahead of time and is not a misreading or a change of contract in midstream. The consideration of such a class of persons naturally brings up the issue of professional surrogates, which is one that's not going to be brushed under the rug simply because we ride a high, moralistic, and perhaps old-fashioned horse today. The issue of whether there will be a place for a professional surrogate in the treatment of at least some of the sexual behavioral disorders is going to be discussed more and more. I might add that we've heard only tacitly and implicitly about women surrogates for men; the issue of men surrogates for women clients has to be faced equally squarely.

This brings me to a point that I think is of the utmost importance and that has not really been clarified. We've been talking about sex instead of love; there's always a great tendency for people to do that. It's so much easier to talk about the sexual act than about this extraordinary quality of pair-bonding that goes under the name of love, falling in love, and being in love. I make this distinction because it seems to me in all the cases I've known in which the therapist has broken the initial contract, which was to talk with the patient, and begun a communication of body language in sexual contact, or sexual intercourse itself, the real problem has been that the patient wanted to fall in love with the therapist, and not just have sex. And the therapist, in a very large proportion of cases, wanted simply to have sex and not to return the strong, long, enduring pair-bonding relationship of falling in love. Here again, let me point out that implicit in all of the talks this morning has been that it's always the male who rapes the female patient. I think we ought to hear from some of the women doctors about how women feel about male patients.

And in reference to those poor students who in 25 percent of cases answered the questionnaire as they did, many may indeed have been a bit more forward than we are, although I bring this up only because I would like to know whether they had a true-false questionnaire or whether they were allowed to express themselves in their proper and complete degree of fullness.

VIRGINIA E. JOHNSON: As for the focus on the male as transgressor, I'm afraid that's almost an historical perspective; we are quite cognizant of the reverse procedure of seduction and exploitation as well. There are some realities that we have to deal with as therapists, as opposed to speculations about changing times, different values, and new roles for sexual activity between individuals. For today, we must respond in terms of the people who live in this time and place, and the kinds of values that are controlling, influencing, and reinforcing their own sense of identity. The dependency, familiarity, and reliance on those ingrained values are the things that in my experience mark the therapeutic course to success or failure. We're really talking of two things here: Yes, let's look to the future, but in considering today, next week, next month, next year, must we not also recognize the existence of prevailing values?

HELEN S. KAPLAN: I think the frequency of sexual contact between therapist and patient constitutes one of the real gender differences.

There is a relatively high incidence of male therapists having sexual experiences with female patients, in contrast with the rather rare instances when female therapists are attracted to and have sex with male patients. There is no way to determine whether this difference is primarily biologically or culturally determined. Discussions with our psychiatric residents at Cornell, about one-third of whom are now women, indicate that the male residents often have feelings of sexual desire for female patients, whereas female residents rarely have such feelings. I think the discrepancy is real and significant.

FRITZ REDLICH: Attempts to cure sexual and other ills by means of intercourse with authority figures such as priests or priestesses have a long history. In the long run, of course, it didn't work. A prostitute may help someone who needs to be accepted, who needs a little education, or who needs some titillation, but this is really different from psychotherapy. What we have to keep in mind is that usually people come to see us at the end of the road.

ROBERT C. KOLODNY: Dr. Redlich spoke in his paper of the distinction between the acute and the chronic illness, and how psychiatry has traditionally and at present focused primarily upon the chronic, which I think relates specifically to the point he is discussing now. As we take clinical histories from people who are encountering sexual difficulties, we often hear of attempts they have made either to visit prostitutes or to seek out another functional partner outside the relationship. This happens most frequently while the difficulty is acute or relatively subacute. The sex therapist rarely deals with acute problems of sexual functioning; certainly in our clinical practice, it is almost entirely the chronicity of the complaint that determines the futility and the frustrations on the part of the couple that lead them to seek therapy.

I wish that it were as simple as Dr. Money has suggested. We have heard far too often not simply of the therapist who during the course of sex therapy (in effect, after having posed the contract to talk with the patient) determines that sexual activity will take place; it is now not uncommon for a couple or an individual patient to be told by a "therapist" that a prerequisite condition of therapy in order to get over the sexual disturbance is active participation in sexual activity with the therapist. Without going into the scientific aspects of the lack of follow-up studies by prostitutes or by this type of "therapist" (which is really a moot point), I think we are talking about things that are not quite as subtle or spontaneous as Dr. Money has implied. Rather, these are deliberate instances of deception and coercion, in the sense that many of these patients do not have information about what sex therapy might entail; when they go to see someone who calls himself or herself a doctor or sex therapist, there is already, as has been hinted by Mr. Rembar and a number of other participants, an implicit trust in the sense that the authority figure is already imbued with a preordained knowledge of the subject. People don't have criteria presently available for judging the source of that knowledge or the confidence they should place in counsel they may receive.

R. CHRISTIAN JOHNSON: I think that this question of whether to have sex or not have sex with the patient is really a conflict of interests. I'd like to hold forth for avoidance of a conflict of interest as being something very basic and not likely to disappear even should attitudes toward sex change, which I'm sure they will. I think the conflict-of-interest principle applies in many different ways to the relationship between the patient and the practitioner. For example, in the medical profession, it is almost axiomatic that the physician should avoid any appearance of conflict of interest in the sense of purveying drugs to patients. In the matter of sex with patients, the practitioner has a conflict of interest in the sense of being at one time a lover or sexual partner and at another time a practitioner. Sex with the patient is simply one of a large class of potential conflicts that I think the ethical practitioner will attempt to avoid. Sex is not so special, after all, in the sense that we must make this individual case and erect a taboo about it. I would like, then, to redirect attention toward the fundamental problem of conflict of interest.

RICHARD GREEN: Perhaps ten minutes ago my comment might have been thought of as brilliant; now, unfortunately, it's a bit redundant. I think the issues yesterday regarding informed consent clearly overlap with what we're talking about right now. I want to ask whether some kinds of distinctions can be made, however, based on Dr. Redlich's earlier concern about whether we can distinguish between various kinds of professions' relationships: lawyer and client, employer and employee, teacher and student, physician and parent, sex therapist and client. I'm not sure that all of these relationships are of equal valence with respect to the appropriateness of various levels of intimacy or with respect to the degree of victimization that takes place with various levels of intimacy.

There is a sex-therapy group in California with a written contract for individual patients that states that, in addition to a primary sex therapist, a surrogate therapist is utilized as well. This contract might be seen as a type of informed consent. In an effort to avoid countertransference, there is continuous monitoring between the primary therapist and the surrogate therapist. Patients are told that the use of surrogates for people who do not have access to a sexual partner is necessary to translate interpersonal and social sexual skills into practice in order for therapy to be effective. I wonder if this is unethical if it is initially stated and agreed to. It is certainly different from the therapist who seduces his client, for that situation is both self-serving and victimizing. As pointed out, such seductions usually do not extend to the old, the infirm, or the ugly.

H. TRISTRAM ENGELHARDT, JR.: One of the issues raised by sexual activity as a part of therapy is that different professions exist by virtue of having a studied attitude of disinterest with respect to particular domains of human activity. Although priests eschew reporting penitents who violate civil laws, they enjoin religious values on the individuals who come to them. Physicians do not enjoin religious values as a part of their functions as physicians, but they do enjoin other values, namely, values related to certain concepts of disease and health. Professions define themselves by the values they do not support as well as those they do. I think what really was brought out by Dr. Redlich and others is that the traditional constellation of values which one expects from the physician, psychiatrist, or psychoanalyst includes renunciation of sexual activity with patients. Dr. Money has asked if the profession of prostitution should be more sympathetically evaluated in terms of the ways in which it can contribute to certain elements of human function. In raising such questions, one asks how, if at all, the values of the profession of medicine and the enterprise of prostitution could support each other. It may be that the values they reciprocally embrace and renounce make them incompatible.

VIRGINIA E. JOHNSON: Would you like to address yourself briefly to the fact that, even though there is a particular constellation of values around each of these particular disciplines in our professional commitments, people are first and foremost individual human beings whose personal constellation of values determine the direction of their actions and influence many of the decisions and choices that are made?

H. TRISTRAM ENGELHARDT, JR.: Professionals and patients are individuals with all sorts of idiosyncrasies, but when they assume roles, each begins to function as a typical member of a certain kind of profession. Professions offer the security of stereotypical roles. One can trust members of a profession typically to act in certain ways, and this web of typicalities in part, at least according to the sociologist Alfred Schutz, binds society together.

VIRGINIA E. JOHNSON: Thank you. One of the bridges that this conference is going to have to try to build is between the reality of what people and professionals do and the philosophies and value systems they must adhere to.

JACK WIENER: I'd like to raise another kind of question. It seems to me that sex therapy is expensive and has been, from what I've been able to gather, primarily for white middle- and upper-class people. It really has not been available for low-income groups and for minority groups. Related to this is the expression that only professional people can maintain confidentiality. We have been concerned with trying to develop the involvement of paraprofessionals in mental health, and I don't see why this cannot be done in sex therapy. I think we must try to develop a less expensive form of therapy, perhaps group therapy. I think that our paraprofessional people have a special contribution to make, particularly in relation to informed consent. Often paraprofessional people can communicate with low-income minority groups better than highly educated professionals.

PEPPER SCHWARTZ: What Mr. Wiener said relates to what I was thinking. In listening to these very excellent papers, I've been impressed by a certain pervasive theme. With all due respect for the disciplines of medicine and psychiatry, I'm impressed with the imperialism of these disciplines in the study of human sexuality. There seems to be an implication that the controls, sanctions, and ethical precepts of the field of human sexuality will be guided by medicine and psychiatry. I'd like some kind of elaboration on my feelings about this. I should also mention that I'm in sympathy with some of Dr. Katz's remarks that we seem to have pretensions as a group to more knowledge than we possess. The kinds of therapy we're talking about have had very little research done on them, very little experimentation in the classic sense of controlled kinds of research, and the medical profession as well as my own discipline is guilty of not carrying out more systematic study. Sanctions, ethics, and directions will have to come from the behavioral sciences and other disciplines as well as medicine and psychiatry.

WILLIAM H. MASTERS: I'd like to respond to several of the comments we've heard most recently. This conference was called primarily because we were firmly convinced that there was no one discipline that had a lock on human sexual functioning, its treatment, or its research development. We are gathered here with representation from almost every discipline involved in the health-care sciences for just this reason. Any ethical considerations that ultimately develop from this conference or a series of such conferences inevitably have to have application to the behavioral as well as the biological sciences. We, at least, are totally committed to a multidisciplinary approach to ethical responsibility.

I am in essential accord with John Money on the subject of surrogate partners. In 1958, when we were formalizing the concept of the surrogate partner, we thought of the possibility of male surrogates for single women. I must point out that we decided not to use them primarily because we were influenced by the mores of the times. The feminist movement did not exist except in its earliest infancy; equality of the sexes certainly was a matter of verbalization rather than actualization. The interesting thing is that, although well over 50 males were treated by our female surrogate partners before the program was discontinued, to this date we have never been asked to supply a male surrogate. The judgment that we shouldn't get involved with male surrogates in 1958 has been verified by the practical side of our actual experience.

This is not to deny the importance of the problem of treating individuals without partners, which was specifically the area we tried to address by the use of surrogates. We feel very strongly that the treatment of sexual dysfunction in a single individual cannot be accomplished as effectively on a long-range basis as when both sexes are under therapeutic scrutiny. Thus, the surrogate concept was presented and followed for almost 12 years. We got into difficulty for a number of reasons. First, we had legal difficulties, but this was of minor moment in the total structure. More significantly, no matter how hard we worked to train and orient surrogates, it wasn't long before a significant percentage of them considered themselves therapists. The construct that John Money described of the rather experienced prostitute was close to what we encountered. And we experienced great difficulty in patient relationships with the people who lost sight of their surrogate roles and assumed a pseudotherapist role. We discontinued the program as a result of these problems. But that does not mean there is no potential value in these techniques. How to handle the problems, how to control them (which is much more important) remains to be seen. I disagree with the concept that simply because one is experienced sexually, one is inevitably good therapeutically. In fact, we are now beginning to see individuals who have been traumatized rather than helped by the use of surrogate partners.

As a discipline we are in our infancy. We have so much to learn. We're going to experiment, and we're going to make mistakes. We have, and we will. Because we made a basic error in the handling of this situation doesn't mean that there isn't potential value in the concept.

MARY S. CALDERONE: This discussion is very poignant. Pepper Schwartz and John Money pointed out several things that should make us realize that, in a sense, we are in a situation analogous to the post-Freudian era when, one after another, people who had trained with or been disciples of Freud began to move away. I don't mean that Masters and Johnson are in the same position as Freud was, although some have said this. I do mean that, much as the value of techniques other than psychotherapy has been accepted even by psychoanalysts trained in the Freudian method, it's possible that 25 years from now, as Dr. Money predicted, we may have incorporated into our societal values acceptance of certain forms of therapy that might even include sexual contact between therapists and patients. Right now, we have only opinions rather than facts with which to determine that it might or might not have value. But until we know more, rather than saying "no" or "it's bad," we should simply say that we don't have enough information to say whether it's good or bad.

JUDITH LONG LAWS: Among many points this morning, one that caught my attention was an impression I got from Dr. Redlich's remarks that in the profession of medicine, the issue of ethics with respect to sexual relations between therapist and client or physician and patient was more developed—and perhaps there was even something like a consensus among practitioners as a profession about this issue. I've been very concerned about a parallel abuse in the academic setting, sexual relations between professors and students, and I found it very different as a problem from the one you describe. It is virtually impossible to get members of the academic profession to acknowledge this as a problem. This is so true that our professional ethics don't address this or anything having to do with our students. Our professional ethics are limited to research enterprises. And I wonder what on earth might be the structural factors that would account for the difference. Is there anything to be learned here?

VIRGINIA E. JOHNSON: Dr. Redlich, do you have a reply or would you like to go on?

FRITZ REDLICH: I would return to the point made earlier about conflict of interests. Enhancement of sexual pleasure seems to conflict with the objectives of mastery of a scholarly field, particularly when it clouds a teacher's judgment. One of the basic reasons, as I understand it, for spelling out this caution in the Hippocratic oath was that the temptation was always very strong. Personally, I think this is sound.

JUDD MARMOR: The question has been raised whether we have any evidence that sexual relations between therapists and patients have deleterious results. I think there is evidence to that effect. It may not be evidence as firm as some scientists would like, but I don't know any ethical way of establishing controlled studies in this matter. But let me say first that I share Dick Green's feelings that there is a difference between a therapist who openly states prior to the onset of therapy that his therapeutic approach consists of having sex with the patient and one who doesn't. (The only thing I can say about the former type of therapist is "caveat emptor.") At least the patient has been warned in advance; if the patient goes ahead voluntarily, the patient has only himself or herself to blame. With the second type of therapist, when the patient becomes involved in a therapeutic relationship with the therapist, which then becomes sexual, the patient is looking for more than just a sexual experience, as John Money has stated. The patient is looking for a love relationship. The patient has developed a transference idealization of the therapist, feels that he or she is in love with the therapist, and is looking for some element of permanence. Inevitably, when that expectation is shattered, the patient is damaged. I have yet to see one who doesn't end up with feelings of bitterness and disappointment. In a few instances that I have seen, there have been actual psychotic breaks. The evidence that we do have, at least in such instances, is that it's been very traumatic.

I am aware of the fact that people like myself see only the bad results, and I can't exclude the possibility that there may be some patients who have had such experiences and not been damaged. But judging from the dynamics of the patient-therapist relationship and the unconscious and conscious expectations that patients develop in that kind of transference relationship, I think the odds are very high that the patient is going to be damaged.

JEAN APPERSON: I think that many of the issues that have been raised concerning conflict of interest and informed consent bear on the fact that we haven't yet developed a well-differentiated concept of the function and meaning of sexual interactions between human beings. I think we need a much more differentiated view to be shared so that we can begin to look at what's going on, in order to determine whether surrogates would be appropriate, whether therapists can also be sexual partners, and whether it's damaging or not to the client to engage in intercourse with the therapist or a surrogate. We need to know what it is that these two people are doing when they come together and have sexual relations. I think that it's something that can be viewed in a more eclectic way. We must look at the matter from a psychological standpoint rather than from a religious perspective, and we must observe liaisons in behavioral terms and look at such issues as status and dominance. We really need that kind of overview to determine what would help serve the patient's needs and what's appropriate and ethical.

JAY KATZ: I very much share Dr. Johnson's concern about the conflict-of-interest issue. Though I'm generally not in favor of moratoria, I might agree to have a moratorium on sex therapy involving sexual relations with patients so that we can clarify the issues. But looking at it conceptually, I do not believe it to be a certainty that sexual intercourse with patients necessarily represents a conflict of interest. Do we know that sexual relations are harmful to *sex therapy?* Until we have gathered such knowledge, we need to ask what value preferences lead us to the conclusion that it is.

HAROLD I. LIEF: I think we must be very careful to differentiate between sexual relations between therapist and patient and the use of the surrogate partner. The surrogate partner issue is in a gray area that seems to involve different ethical concerns than that of therapist-patient sex. In this conference, we have been constantly trying to see whether there are any differences between research in this field and other fields. I think this is one striking example of a difference: The climate of opinion might make it extremely difficult to do research on the effectiveness of the surrogate partner. There are, in fact, instances in which such an approach might be quite valid. The young man who is very inhibited, to the point that he has difficulty courting and dating and is unable to find a partner, might well profit from contact with a surrogate. Dr. Redlich mentioned the use of behavioral models in socialization as one technique for dealing with this problem. I have seen cases in which it's taken three to six months of this kind of behavior therapy and socialization education for a young man to get the nerve to strike up an acquaintance with a young woman and find a partner. In contrast, a few sessions with a surrogate partner sometimes cuts through the inhibition and promotes a cure much more rapidly than this type of behavioral approach to socialization. There are the ethical issues of the amount of time and money spent in treatment, on the one hand, and the use of the partner surrogate, on the other; the latter might be a more rapid and sometimes more effective method of treatment.

VIRGINIA E. JOHNSON: This illustrates one of the pitfalls that we're constantly running into here: putting all sexual problems into one basket and overgeneralizing the care of these highly variable problems.

SEWARD HILTNER: This conference deals with many disciplines, but are we simply using health as a mythological concept? We all say we can't define sexual health. Is that simply our public-relations approach to things? Are all of the values we're concerned about subsumable under the rubric of health, however defined? I gravely question this.

ALAN A. STONE: I wish you could lock us up for two more days, because I think we're really getting up steam now. Surely that last comment gets right to the heart of our ethical conceptions. We cannot limit our discussion to the world of the health-care professions.

I don't know whether it's clear that living in Boston and Cambridge is different from the rest of the world. However, it is clear to me. The young people I know have read Masters and Johnson's books and are often functioning as surrogate partners to one another in their relationships. The quality—not to mention the quantity—of the sexual relations of these young people has changed significantly. Although there are still some who are quite naive, self-help and self-education coupled with mutual help and education are certainly proceeding apace. This is an area over which we have no control and that has no relationship to *our* ethics or *our* morals or *our* concept of health.

VIRGINIA E. JOHNSON: You have just hinted at the general direction of this work that is most important—prevention!

WILLIAM H. MASTERS: I think Dr. Stone has survived the Cambridge influence very well.

The thrust of this conference is simply to establish some concept of professional ethics for the present. This does not imply that, once some standards are set and accepted by professional consensus, they should be rigidly adhered to. History shows that once standards are established, they are modified. The difficulty at present is that there are no agreed-upon standards of ethics; in fact, there has been remarkably little serious discussion of this matter previously.

MARY S. CALDERONE: Dr. Stone, I was in Boston recently speaking to a group of Harvard medical students. They thought that the preparation in human sexuality offered by their medical school was incredibly and woefully wanting. We must bear in mind that there is an ethical duty to meet this need for future health workers in order to help them keep up with the changing social scene.

VIRGINIA E. JOHNSON: Perhaps we can close by remembering from this discussion that we must not become so enamored of our own place in history that we forget how ephemeral we are.

7

TRAINING OF SEX THERAPISTS

HELEN S. KAPLAN

I will try to outline what I think are some of the essential ingredients of the process of sex therapy and will, by implication, indicate what kinds of skills and knowledge a sex therapist should be equipped with by his training. I will not, however, address myself to the issue of just which disciplines should and can ethically practice sex therapy. That important question will resolve itself as our field matures.

There is a parallel between our present situation and past efforts of the medical profession. According to a recent description, the group of concerned physicians who gathered in Philadelphia in 1847 to found the AMA had two major objectives: to promote the art and science of medicine and to establish a code of ethics to weed out the charlatans who were then ripe in the field, peddling cures for everything from cancer to hemorrhoids. I think we are presently at a very similar stage in the development of sex therapy, and Masters and Johnson's organization of this conference, which has very similar objectives, at this particular time is an indication of their sense of social responsibility and exquisite timing.

There certainly are charlatans in this field—unskilled, incompetent, and unethical. They are not hard to weed out. But the most difficult charlatans to deal with are physicians and psychologists, protected by the licensing of their professions, whose only qualifications in sex therapy are that they have read some books on the subject and perhaps attended a workshop. Having done so, they feel that they are competent; but they are probably the most damaging, because patients expect high ethical standards from physicians and psychologists, which are not forthcoming if the professional lacks special training in the evaluation and treatment of sexual problems. Fortunately, this situation is changing and an increasing number of professionals are receiving adequate training to qualify them for work in this area.

I think we have now had enough experience to begin to talk rationally about the essential ingredients of proper evaluation and treatment of the sexually dysfunctional or sexually distressed patient. I emphasize evaluation because my experience has been that all couples or patients who present with a sexual problem are not good candidates for sex therapy. Of the patients we evaluate at our clinic, only 50 to 60 percent seem suitable for sex therapy; it is our impression that the remainder are probably best treated by other means. In this sense, the assessment of sexually dysfunctional couples is just as important as the treatment; therefore, proper emphasis on evaluation is a very important part of training. In addition to knowing how to evaluate a disorder, the therapist should understand the alternative forms of treatment that are available, including marital therapy, psychoanalytic treatment, surgical treatment, and hormonal treatment.

We can conceptualize sex-therapy training in three fundamental areas: knowledge, attitude, and clinical skills.

BACKGROUND KNOWLEDGE FOR SEX THERAPY

The fact that sex is a psychosomatic response with a biology and a psychology, as Mrs. Johnson said this morning, is the basis for understanding sexual pathology and treatment. In order to make sense out of the process of sex therapy, the therapist must be trained in the basic biology and psychology of human sexuality. Sexual responses are essentially reflex reactions, like all other vegetative responses of the body. Specifically, they consist of two sets of reflexes: the excitement reflex, which essentially consists of genital vasocongestion and which causes erection and lubrication; and the orgasmic reflexes, which are composed of the reflex contraction of genital muscles. These reflexes are subject to impairment by physical or emotional factors. In order to understand the sexual reflexes and their disturbances, an understanding of the anatomy of the genital organs, including their vascular supply and innervation, is required. The physiology of the sexual response is also fundamental to the rational practice of sex therapy. So, certainly, a good biological background is necessary. It must also be remembered that these reflexes are exquisitely sensitive to emotion. Students must have knowledge of the many kinds of intrapsychic and didactic factors that influence the sexual response.

The student must understand not only normal sexuality but also the psychopathology of sexual behavior. A significant advance in understanding the psychopathology of sexual behavior was made here in St. Louis by Masters and Johnson. Before that time, analysts and psychologists thought that only the deepest kinds of emotional disturbances could interfere with the sexual reflexes. One of the great contributions of this program was the concept that less severe problems, including superficial or more immediate causes of anxiety such as performance anxiety, were equally capable of affecting sexual responses. The penis doesn't know whether the anxiety coming from the brain is caused by castration fears or the man's fear that he won't get an erection. The penis can't tell the difference; the erection disappears because the physiology of anxiety is precisely the same. And the essence of Masters and Johnson's discovery was that, fortunately, some rather easily and relatively rapidly ameliorable causes of sexually disruptive anxiety are prevalent sources of sexual dysfunctions. A qualified person in this field has to be able both to tell the difference and to make a diagnosis of the specific source of anxiety, since this affects the conduct of treatment. Apart from intrapsychic causes, didactic variables are also important. A deep-seated partner rejection or unconscious hostilities between the couple can also cause sexual problems, and therefore have to be considered when evaluating a patient with a sexual dysfunction. Thus, a thorough understanding of both the remote and the deeper causes of anxiety that inhibit the sexual response, the intrapsychic as well as the transactional causes and dynamics, have to be part of the education of the sex therapist.

ATTITUDES OF THE THERAPIST

Complex as this all may seem, didactic knowledge is rather easily acquired, especially if you start with a student who already possesses a fundamental understanding of medicine, biology, and psychopathology. Some of the weekend seminars and brief postgraduate education courses are really sufficient for the already well-trained professional who acquaints himself with specific facts about sexuality. However, all the knowledge in the world is useless unless it is carried in the head of a person who has very specific attitudes, and I think there are two sets of attitudes that are important. First, we have devoted most of this meeting to conveying a sense of deep responsibility and concern in light of the special vulnerability in our culture of the sexually dysfunctional patient. You can't teach that in a course. Somebody from Harvard University was on a TV program talking about declining student morality and cheating, and he said, "We're taking care of that—we're giving a course now." I don't know if we can give a course in morality. I think that's something we have to start with. We have to assume the person who is in the field is well-intended but he must, as part of his training, be sensitized to the special vulnerability of his patients.

The second set of attitudes is specifically sexual, and includes the need for the professional sex therapist to be relatively conflict-free about his or her own sexuality; I say "relatively" because I think it is impossible for someone to be totally conflict-free about sex in our society. However, a sex therapist should have some awareness of the conflicts that do exist, since they can influence therapy. But more than that is required: The therapist has to have a positive attitude about sexuality; merely being conflict-free is not enough. It is not enough to be free of guilt and anxiety about sex. One should have a positive, creative feeling about sex. It is important that sex be viewed as a positively enhancing force in human life. This attitude is conveyed to the patient and is an important ingredient in successful therapy. Finally, people in this field should have a mature and, again, conflict-free and unbiased attitude about gender-role differences in love and sex.

Why are attitudes so important? I think for at least two reasons.

One is that your own comfort and positive attitude about sexuality make you much more sensitive and comfortable as a clinician. Training should foster such attitudes. After several years of training, you can say "penis" and "ejaculation" without breaking out into a cold sweat. The therapist's own positive attitude is probably an important ingredient in any therapy that is based a lot on transference and transmission of a positive emotional attitude. Furthermore, awareness of conflict areas in either gender roles or genital sexuality is important because if these conflicts are unresolved, they really are likely to be acted out in the therapeutic process. At best, one doesn't see the problems. At worst, the therapist who has unresolved sexual conflicts may be seductive, hostile, or competitive and may avoid certain areas. If one of our trainees reports more than once a year an erotic response on the part of the patient, we assume that he is doing something seductive, something countertransferential that is outside of his awareness. This is a terribly important area of training.

It is beyond the scope of this presentation to consider how to implement these complex training objectives. However, it seems clear that expertise in this field cannot be imparted in a weekend seminar. Undoubtedly, some of the sexual attitude reassessment (SAR) experiences and some of the desensitization procedures can raise a person's consciousness of his own sexual attitudes. If a person were freed from such prejudices and were relatively conflict-free to begin with, this would be an aid to become effective as a therapist. But, unfortunately, for most people it takes quite a long period of time to recognize and resolve their conflicts and biases. For example, I had a personal analysis that I think was fairly successful; even so I found myself, in the process of working with patients, underevaluating the vulnerability of the male patient as opposed to the female. I thought I was very well analyzed, that I had my oedipal conflicts all resolved, and yet I was still not quite seeing the vulnerability of the male as opposed to the female until I was confronted with this issue in the course of my clinical practice.

Sensitive supervision, experience, and sensitization to one's own therapeutic errors are indispensable tools in fostering clinical effectiveness, and I certainly think they should be part of any training program. In our own program, I and everybody on the staff periodically see patients behind a one-way mirror before our group.

Then we review the sessions very carefully and pay special attention to the influence of our personal attitudes on the conduct of therapy.

CLINICAL SKILLS AND TRAINING IN SEX THERAPY

Now we come to the most controversial area of all: skill. When I was at the World Health Organization Conference in Geneva with Drs. Lief, Calderone, and Gebhard, among others from 26 countries, we came to the conclusion that the tremendous demand for sex-therapy services could best be met by training for different levels of clinical skills. Because the procedure to train a skilled professional is so lengthy, it was thought that we should consider training three categories of professionals: sex educators, sex counselors, and sex therapists. The last should probably be reserved for the most difficult cases. I have since revised my thinking a little bit. It seems to me that our patient population is changing—that the easy cases are disappearing. We used to have more cases with isolated sexual problems of the type that would probably respond to counseling and education. When I evaluate a patient, it is my custom always to give some advice for the interim and to make some interpretation of the evaluation so the patient feels he is gaining something from the session—so that he perceives it as having positive value. It used to be quite common, when we called the patient three months later to say that we now have room in the program, for the patient to say, "Everything's okay now. You really helped me."

Occasionally, I still get very easy cases. I remember one involving a couple who complained of an unconsummated marriage. At the initial evaluation, it turned out that the husband thought it was not very masculine to take a bath or shower before sex. She was too delicate to speak up, but his body odor was repellent to her. This became immediately apparent in the session, and I commented on the situation and encouraged him to pay heed to his personal hygiene. Two weeks later, they called and reported successful intercourse. This type of problem, which can benefit from counseling, is disappearing, although it used to be quite common.

Also becoming extinct is the couple who respond to merely behavioral interventions. Of course, I still see patients with premature ejaculation for whom Seman's exercises are effective. The patients don't resist and therapy proceeds smoothly. After ten sessions, there's good control and good communication. But these cases too are becoming rare. The cases are getting tougher, by which I mean that instances in which purely superficial anxieties or misinformation is the prime cause are disappearing. It may be speculated that improved education, more and better books, and more sophistication on the part of the public in the area of sexuality has eliminated some of the simpler problems. What we now see more often are the harder cases, in which deeper marital and intrapsychic problems play a more active role, requiring more sophisticated and tougher kinds of psychotherapeutic interventions. Perhaps our experience is specific to a large metropolitan center; I'd certainly be very happy to hear what people are experiencing in other geographic areas.

To do sex therapy with a case in which intrapsychic and transactional factors are important, you have to be extremely skilled. You have to be able to use behavioral methods, marital methods, and intrapsychic methods. You have to be able to amalgamate and integrate those three approaches. Resistances arise and must be dealt with. The sexual tasks evoke intense emotion. You advise a woman to masturbate, and terrifying dreams occur, along with overt anxiety and guilt. The issues that have to be dealt with in this situation extend beyond performance anxiety. You have to know when to stop, when to leave something alone, when to focus on the obvious, and when it's absolutely essential to work on a deeper and more subconscious level. That's quite a task for a therapist. But again and again I have cases that require complex intervention. Our principle is to stick to the behavioral model as much as we can and to deal just with the communications and behavior of the patient. Only if obstacles and resistances arise do we deal with the deeper issues. However, it now seems that an increasing number of cases demand deeper kinds of therapy.

TRAINING RECOMMENDATIONS

The conclusion suggested by this kind of experience is that sex therapy, at least with the more difficult cases, demands that the therapist be a really good clinician before he even begins his training. Psychopathology and therapy cannot be taught in a year or six months. Unless a candidate already starts with a high degree of clinical skill, training becomes difficult or impossible. Now this is admittedly a prejudiced opinion, because I am a psychiatrist and I have no control studies that show me that psychiatrists or psychotherapists trained in this field are any more effective than someone coming from another discipline. My attitudes derive from clinical experience. However, I think that this issue should be considered seriously. It is very tempting to take people with significantly lesser degrees of training, people who don't understand the biology, people who are not that well-versed in psychotherapy and psychopathology. It is tempting to train them and to admit them to this field because the need is so great—because there is such a tremendous demand, both public and professional. But my own prejudice is to opt for the more difficult, the more expensive, the lengthier, and the more tedious and demanding kind of training to produce a therapist who is truly equipped to treat sexual dysfunctions.

In my experience of conducting a training program, it usually takes two years before the therapists themselves feel comfortable and secure doing this kind of work. After a year, most feel they are formally in training, but almost all of them elect to stay a second year before they feel competent as sex therapists.

My recommendation is to make the standards as tough and as difficult as need be to produce competent professionals. I am aware that this attitude may be unpalatable to many people. However, I think our long-range aims to promote excellence in this field will best be served in this manner.

DESIGNATED DISCUSSION

CARL S. SHULTZ

One of the issues that we have not dealt with sufficiently, and which is very relevant when we are discussing training for sex therapy, is institutional responsibility. We've been speaking about individual professional responsibility to the patient and the public, but I think when we consider training, particularly, we must think in terms of institutional responsibility, the responsibility of the training agency or the training school. Now, one of the complications cited earlier is that many of the people—in fact, most of the people—who enter into sex-therapy training are coming from some previous professional background. Thus, most of these people are licensed or accredited in some way or other in their basic profession. This may be assumed to mean that the institution that offered basic training has provided an ethical background or some knowledge of what was expected of this individual with regard to professional behavior and etiquette. However, I think that is too easy an assumption, particularly in an area as sensitive as sex therapy. In this field, it is extraordinarily important that the training agency or institution take active responsibility for communicating some form of ethical code to the trainee.

It isn't just a matter of knowledge, as Dr. Kaplan has said; it's also an exploration of the attitude of the trainee with regard to ethics. The example cited by Dr. Redlich, a study of medical students, is particularly salient because it shows that the institution had some ongoing responsibility to deal with ethical perceptions and attitudes before it provided those students with a diploma. Then again, I think this touches on the area of skills because it's in the actual demonstration of how an individual functions in relation to a patient that one can even learn more about his or her ethical approach. This brings me to the point of stressing the necessity—which Dr. Kaplan dealt with very directly—of the supervised practicum, the necessity of both the clinical clerkship and supervised practice if we are to be comfortable discharging upon the public those we have trained, the professionals we take credit for.

At this conference I am representing a multidisciplinary professional group that took on the responsibility of believing that it could certify some of its members as qualified sex educators or qualified sex therapists. In the process, the question was very quickly raised: Is it possible, particularly in the area of sex therapy, to have individuals go forth as certified by this organization without the organization promulgating a code of ethics with regard to the behavior expected of those certified? A distinguished group of practicing therapists came together at the behest of the organization to develop some ethical standards, and I want to share these with you because I think they are relevant to the discussion this afternoon. When I look at the order of these, I'm really not too pleased because this is the order in which they were developed by the group. However, I will share them directly with you rather than doing any editing on my own.

The first standard has to do with the duration of training. Two hundred hours of supervised training need to be completed under the supervision of a qualified sex therapist who does not function in the relationship of either co-therapist, husband, wife, professional, or social partner. The second item is that patient and/or therapist nudity in an alleged therapeutic modality is prohibited, except that group meetings and therapeutic group processes involving female or male sexuality problems within a recognized nudist colony are considered professionally acceptable. So, in other words, nudity may be acceptable if it's regarded as the norm, but in one-to-one relationships it is not accepted by the group. The third point is that the therapist and/or sex educator shall not be judgmental in promoting or propagandizing a given sexual point of view. It is essential that the therapist and/or educator create a climate of openness and trust relative to the client's or patient's sexual value system, and respect his or her right to express and value it—irrespective of conflict between sex value systems. That basically means that the patient's views are to be respected and that the therapist is not to impose his views on the client. The fourth point is that the therapist shall refrain from examining male or female patients for the purpose of stimulating the patient in order to elicit a sexual response; however, the therapist can familiarize the patient-client and partner with a procedure for stimulating a response by suggesting ways in which the couple experience various responses to sexual stimuli. Fifth, the therapist shall refrain from any bodily contact with a patient for the purpose of either giving or receiving erotic stimulation. Sixth, all information, records, and communication received about the patient are considered confidential unless the patients waives his or her rights in writing. We certainly established that point yesterday when it was made clear that confidentiality was determined by the patient, not the therapist. Seventh, sex therapists are encouraged to use traditional, professional forms to announce their practice; however, announcements of special workshops, courses, clinics, or professional meetings sponsored by health, education, or social institutions may be made by paid advertisement. Eighth, an individual or group of individuals who misrepresents by trade names specific professional functions performed, or misrepresents explicitly or by inference the number of professional persons involved in the performance of sex therapy, shall be censored or subject to other appropriate actions. Ninth, it shall be unethical for any sex therapist to pass judgment on the practice of another sex therapist without substantial research and data on the value of the other therapist's work. Nor shall the sex therapist claim that his or her work is superior to that of other therapists without hard data to support such an allegation.

This leads to a slightly different issue: the need to avoid a cult approach within any institution or agency. This is my own view and not that of the group I was just alluding to. It's very easy to fall into the belief that my disciples and I have the very best approach and that all others should be disregarded. Again, I think it is the institution's or agency's responsibility to familiarize students with a variety of approaches to the therapeutic interaction. To do so is like following the European model, in which the student travels from place to place in order to absorb the best thoughts of various professors in various institutions. I think this is something we have to keep in mind with regard to our own institutions and not let pride of professional success spoil for the student the opportunity for breadth of experience and knowledge. Otherwise, I don't see how we can accomplish the kind of amalgamation or synthesis of approaches that Dr. Kaplan has mentioned, which allows one, after evaluating the patient, to recommend the therapy and to try the therapeutic intervention most likely to meet with success.

I think that we're in a very difficult area. A great deal of our success and acceptance by the public and throughout society today is going to depend on how well we meet these challenges. This in turn will depend on the manner in which we stress to the trainee the importance of communicating to patients the risks involved in taking certain courses of action within our current society. I think there is an institutional and agency responsibility for making sure the trainee understands and can communicate to his patients the principles of informed consent, so that the patient understands the risk he or she is assuming by engaging in a therapist-patient relationship.

GENERAL DISCUSSION

HAROLD I. LIEF: I can't let the occasion pass without saying a word about the effect that Masters and Johnson's method of sex therapy has had on the whole field of psychotherapy. It is my impression, and I think this is often overlooked, that this work has revolutionized not only sex therapy but also psychotherapy of people who do not have sex problems per se. It has given impetus to new methods of psychotherapy. There was a small book called *Direct Therapy* by Hertzburg, published in the 1930s, in which he advocated that the therapist assign certain tasks to patients and not be content with basing therapy only on what happened in the consultation room between therapist and patient. Very few people paid any attention, and this approach was felt by those who were analytically trained or influenced by psychoanalysis to be an attenuation of the doctor-patient relationship and to interfere with the development of transference. The work that Masters and Johnson have done has shifted the focus, I think, to the here-and-now and to what takes place in vivo—in the real lives of the people who come for help. More and more people have turned to forms of psychotherapy that make use of the various kinds of behavioral strategies, including assignment of tasks. I just wanted to get this on the record because I think it's an important aspect of the work that has been done here in St. Louis. Now, there have been a number of important issues raised by Dr. Kaplan and Dr. Shultz. Let me open the floor to discussion.

MAE A. BIGGS: I certainly agree with Dr. Kaplan that adequate evaluation is very important prior to initiating sex therapy. An additional area that was not touched on and needs to be given consideration is the therapist's awareness of when to stop therapy during a treatment course. Sometimes we must recognize that patients are not being helped or that they do indeed need a different modality of treatment. This type of continuing assessment should also be stressed during training.

ROBERT C. KOLODNY: I would like to go back to the observation that in many of our practices the easy cases seem to be disappearing. I wonder if this reflects any major change in the general population or if it is more of a shift in the distribution of these cases. From our educational programs we know that patients are now doing the same things they used to do—that is, going to the office gynecologist or internist or family practitioner—but now they are beginning to be met by a little more knowledge, a lot more receptivity, and a much more positive attitude that permits such a practitioner to address very practical aspects of sexual function and dysfunction. This also seems to be the case with many nonmedical professionals, such as the pastoral counselor, the psychologist, or the social worker, who are better educated in the area of sexuality than they were 10 years ago and are therefore "curing" the simple problems and referring the more difficult ones. In many instances, professionals are able to combine simple reassurance, factual advice, and a chance for ventilation to help people resolve sexual problems very effectively. There is a marked difference in the population our clinic sees now in contrast to the few years prior to the publication of *Human Sexual Inadequacy*. In the past two years, about 85 percent of the couples we have seen have been prior psychotherapeutic failures in the sense that one or both members have gone through six months or more of psychotherapy and have not solved the problems they perceive in their lives. This population is different from the one we treated in 1967 or 1968. One final point may be of interest. Although I agree that experience in psychotherapy can be a very valuable background for training in sex therapy, our experience has been that training psychiatrists who are used to individual therapy in our dual-sex therapy team model has often been extremely difficult, since so many professional habits and attitudes are already set. Sometimes professionals who have experience with people outside of formal psychotherapy are more flexible and therefore easier to train.

ROBERT L. STUBBLEFIELD: I would like to make a comment and ask a question. I have served on the board of directors of the American Board of Psychiatry and Neurology for eight years, so I have been involved in trying to decide how you establish clinical competence. We had several conferences about the evaluation of competence in psychiatry, neurology, and child psychiatry. We have evaluated people who are certified already, to see if we could recertify them at regular intervals. Some of the factors we tried to identify were basic intelligence, the ability to assess clinical skills, the level of empathy, the ability to make observations and integrate them, and intervention skills. We looked at some records of physicians in practice. We tried to go in to see how people are actually behaving in ordinary practice. We also read reports from testing services such as the National Board of Medical Examiners, the Educational Testing Service at Princeton, and others. Our conclusion is that it is very difficult to define training by time—it is easy to say that a person needs two years, or three years, or five years, or 200 hours. Often this has a little bit of the flavor of trade unionism—"because I have gone through it, you have to go through it." I am not belittling what Dr. Kaplan said; however, I think if one is going to talk about 100 or 200 hours, or one or two years, one needs to go beyond that to the definition of general goals and a specific body of knowledge and agree on what it is you are assessing in the certification process.

Now, my question. Would some of you who are involved actively in training sex therapists talk some about the ones you have not selected? I have learned a little bit in psychiatry by looking at those individuals we choose not to train as psychiatrists; one of the tragedies in American medicine has been that when you select and later terminate a trainee, he can go somewhere else and enter a training program. We have made efforts to stop that. Could you tell us some of the positive things you want in sex therapists by telling us about the kinds of people you have trained? Are there some you wished you had not trained, or had dropped, or not accepted in the first place?

HELEN S. KAPLAN: So far, I have never had to drop anybody from the training program. The way I interview applicants is very simple.

I will admit only psychiatrists, psychologists, or psychiatric social workers in the program, since I am not equipped to give adequate training in psychotherapy. I will train obstetricians, urologists, neurologists, and internists, but only in the evaluation aspect of the field, not in therapy. Our interview procedure is simple. We invite applicants to join our seminar for one or two weeks and then, as a group, we decide if they would fit in. That is not a very scientific method, but so far it has worked. All our trainees have gotten along well in the program and seemed to feel comfortable with their skills.

There was a problem with one person. I'm training two homosexual counselors (a man and a woman) who are psychologists so that they can apply these methods to a homosexual population. It was my feeling that homosexual counselors could apply these skills within their own value systems and without a heterosexual bias. A problem arose with one of these individuals when she applied her homosexual value system to the heterosexual couples and encouraged them in homosexual practices. I wanted this person dropped, but as a group we decided not to. She did have to remain in training for an extra year while we worked with her and tried to resolve her conflicts. I don't think there was any basic change in her attitude.

Most people who have been trained have found the experiences to be personally enhancing to the extent that they don't want to leave. Everybody stays on as volunteers. This kind of training, I think, when properly done, has a positive influence on a person's whole life.

PEPPER SCHWARTZ: I'm fascinated by this both as a consumer advocate and as a professional scientist. Personally, I have no idea which of the various professions would be best suited for therapy. I am interested in the kinds of preferences people from different disciplines have. It is also interesting to see the lack of systematic comparative data here. Valid answers can't be derived from just the theoretical level. What seems to be needed is less reliance on being simultaneously the therapist and the researcher of one's own work. I understand why that has been important, and I'm sure we're all in favor of that kind of scientific endeavor, but much might be gained by outside research on individual therapies and groups. Perhaps it would be worthwhile to initiate a working relationship with evaluation research and social science research on these clinical populations and the different backgrounds of therapists in order to get more data. This might create small problems in the area of confidentiality, but not insurmountable ones.

RICHARD GREEN: Three major issues trouble me: the training issue, the quality-control issue, and the research evaluation issue. I've been trying to think of some logical way to approach this to produce some order. First of all, there must be recognition of the entity of sexual help, with treatment of sexual dysfunction being one component of that entity. This requires standards of professional competence, which would at least open the door for quality control and licensing. Whether the quality control and licensing come from a professional organization or from a federal or state agency is less relevant. The essential first step is recognition of a particular field of competence as a field for health professionals. Next comes the decision on licensure. At the present time there are about a half-dozen diverse groups in this country, with different criteria, giving out slips of paper that certify people as "competent" sex therapists. Presently, few clients know whether or not a therapist is licensed, and no one group recognizes another group. Yet the spirit is good and the requirements make sense. However, without universal recognition, all of this is essentially meaningless. You don't have control over the people you don't accredit. You're merely saying that a particular person *is* accredited; that doesn't mean that clients will go and seek that person.

Those of us who have medical or clinical psychology backgrounds bear the responsibility of demonstrating that it is a necessary requirement for everyone to have a medical degree or a clinical psychology degree to be competent in this field. This may in fact be so, but I don't think we can assume it and I don't think we can advance it as a given rule. Unless we can demonstrate that people with a certain training background are in fact better therapists, I think we will be seeing many people with lesser training entering this field. I don't think we can merely fall back on our degree credentials, as we have in the past, and say that by virtue of those credentials it is axiomatic that we are more qualified.

The issue of the biological interface with sexual dysfunction is very real. But so is the biological interface with many kinds of emotional disorders. Consider neurology. How many psychoanalysts with medical training do neurological examinations of their patients? God help them if they touch their patients! There is an assumption that some of these medical things can be performed by someone else. There are screening procedures that we rely on, and we would like to think that when clients come to us, other professionals with different skills have already ruled out other factors as contributing to the problem we're dealing with. We don't have to have all the skills ourselves, so long as we exist in a professional network that allows for full evaluation.

In another direction, I don't think that we can separate the issue of surrogate therapists from our concerns over quality control, training, licensing, and certification. Whether we like it or not, the fact is that there are people in this country today training sexual surrogates, there are groups that are licensing sexual surrogates, and there are clinicians of considerable sophistication utilizing sexual surrogates. It's like trying to outlaw prostitution. The fact is that the surrogates are out there and you can't ignore them, and if we're going to be increasingly responsive and responsible to patients and clients, we're going to have to have quality control of therapists at various levels utilizing various strategies.

My last point is somewhat disconnected. It was brought up by the issue of gay people treating gay people. It brings up the question of whether black people should treat black people, and women should treat women, or men should treat women. We don't know for sure that gay people can treat gay people, and men can treat women, and blacks can treat whites, and Hispanics can treat native Americans, and God only knows who else. If that isn't bad enough, maybe we ought also to know a little bit about the sexual functioning of therapists. What is the best kind of prior sexual biography of a therapist? In psychoanalytic institutes, there is screening for the best candidates. It's supposed to be good if you have had some (but not too much) depression, so that you have some capacity for experiencing depression and some capacity for insight and personal retrieval. Would the best therapist for a man with premature ejaculation be someone who himself has been a premature ejaculator? Should the woman treating a nonorgasmic woman have had difficulty herself with orgasmic attainment? Would she then have a better feel for the issues surrounding orgasmic attainment in females? Or should she be a female whose first orgasm was at age 8 riding horseback?

EMILY HARTSHORNE MUDD: I've been interested in training, and I'm very impressed by what's been said here. It seems to me that one of the things that hasn't been explored very much is the criteria for acceptance in training. I know Dr. Kaplan specified that it must be a person who has trained in psychotherapy. I didn't hear Dr. Shultz state what specific criteria his group had. I remember the struggles that Dr. Waggoner and I went through when we began working with continuing education at the Reproductive Biology Research Foundation. We went through endless applications and tried to figure out criteria for acceptance into our training program. Many professional associations with representatives at this conference have committees that have spent a great deal of time on the criteria for acceptance into training. But one thing I haven't heard anybody address himself to is this: Aside from the professional criteria for training, what kind of a person, what kind of personality, is most desirable? Is it the person who believes in people, who can work with their strength, who has enough humility to know when he or she can be helpful and when to refer? What about the person who's in this for self-aggrandizement? I put in a big plea for the person who really believes in helping, and who can share, and who has a certain degree of humility rather than too many godlike qualities.

HAROLD I. LIEF: One of the very difficult issues is whether the personal characteristics of a good psychotherapist, a sex therapist, or any other professional makes any difference. There's been a considerable amount of research on this question, conducted by Hans Strupp, Lester Luborsky, Jerome Frank, and others, and it's extremely difficult to assess those personal characteristics that make a competent therapist. For some years we believed that empathy and warmth and several other characteristics were essential to the good therapist. Jerome Frank has recently said that all the data disprove this. In other words, empathy and warmth have no correlation with the outcome of therapy. So we're still really at the point of trying to find out what makes a good therapist.

JUDD MARMOR: I think we've veered off a little bit to the issue of selection, and I think it's one of the most difficult of processes, as any dean of a medical school, chairman of a psychiatric training program, or dean of a psychoanalytic institute can tell you. Some years ago, the Menninger Foundation went through an elaborate ritual in trying to select their residents and psychoanalytic trainees. They had them all take a battery of psychological tests, and they were all interviewed by three experienced analysts. After a three- or four-year research project, they came to the conclusion that none of their predictive formulas had worked at all. So I don't think we know the answer to this.

I'd like to return to the issue of the training and clinical skills necessary for sex therapists. Dr. Kaplan has outlined what she considers to be—and what is, in many respects—a kind of optimal program. It would be nice if every sex therapist had all of these skills. In fact, one could add a few: Perhaps they should also be gynecologically trained and neurologically trained, and possess a lot of other skills that are beyond the capacity of any one person to have. However, I think we must look at the issue of training sex therapists in a more limited way if we're going to be realistic about it. We find the same problems in training any psychotherapist. Ideally, we would like psychotherapists to have a medical, psychological, sociological, and anthropological background. We'd like them to have all kinds of skills because the more they have, the better psychotherapists they will be and the broader their purviews would be. But we also know that there is a limited-skills approach that can be taught to qualified people with a certain kind of competence. In continuing education, psychiatrists have been involved for many years in training general practitioners in the basics of psychotherapy and psychiatric evaluation, not in the expectation of making them psychiatrists, but in the hope that they could function in a limited capacity to cut off at the bridge, so to speak, some of the emergent critical problems they encounter, and to know better what they couldn't help. Now there is a broad area of need for the treatment of individuals who have rather simple sexual problems. It may be that experts like Dr. Kaplan are getting the tougher ones because many of the others are being handled more or less competently, more or less adequately, by less well-trained individuals. But the kind of model that Masters and Johnson have elaborated can be utilized by a number of different professionals, given an adequate training program and an amount of training sufficient to ensure that they know their limitations. The important thing is to teach them the limitations that will prevent them from trying to do the kind of psychotherapy they're not trained to do, and also to teach them to recognize a psychotic or severely neurotic individual. But once that is done, if they are dealing with simple cases of sexual dysfunction, I see no reason why we can't give them that kind of training and thus perform a useful social function. The problem then becomes one of teaching qualified selectees limited clinical skills, rather than trying to train them broadly in psychotherapy. Above all, they need to know what their limitations are so that they will not transcend those limitations.

MARY S. CALDERONE: Dr. Marmor made a distinction that I think corresponds to the differentiation between educators, counselors, and therapists that was made in the WHO Technical Report [1]. But I was concerned about Dr. Shultz's presentation because I thought that he was going to be talking about the qualifications for entering the field and then for accreditation. It seemed to me that what he mostly talked about was a code of ethics for those who are already accredited in the field.

CARL S. SHULTZ: That's quite true. I did emphasize the ethical practice aspects. With regard to steps toward certification, academic preparation at the graduate level is required prior to certification as a sex therapist by AASEC. However, there are problems involving equivalency. Obviously, there are individuals whose experience and training were not obtained in formal graduate schools and who are highly skilled and highly able to function as sex therapists. Also, as Dr. Green has stated, there are individuals who, no matter how many certificates or academic titles they have, are wretched therapists. There is just no escaping it: They really are not qualified. One of the points I was trying to emphasize in my presentation was the fact that it is the responsibility of the sex-therapy training institution to try to weed these out and keep them from being inflicted on the general public. The difficulty is, as we stated earlier, that if they don't get what they want from you, they'll go somewhere else and get it, and you have a major problem on your hands. You can only protect any institution so far, and then they become more and more paranoid in their total behavior and you're in all sorts of trouble for slander or one thing or another. Nevertheless, some graduate academic experience is the basic requirement, unless equivalency can be demonstrated to a group of qualified individuals in the field. Furthermore, there is a necessity for a certain period of experience and training under a skilled therapist in order to acquire skill. Then there is the question, How many hours? Some people acquire skills very rapidly; others are rather awkward in their acquisition of skills. So it's a very difficult issue again. Unfortunately, I think any organization has to be somewhat arbitrary in deciding whether it's so many hours or so many degrees or this or that or the other thing, because that's the only way an institution can function.

SALLIE SCHUMACHER: I'd like to comment on the earlier observations that the easy cases seem to be disappearing, which suggests that the cases we're treating now are harder than those that were treated before. I think that's only part of the reason why cases are harder. There seems to be a problem that's recurrent in almost all areas of medicine and is sometimes stated humorously: Whenever some new procedure or therapy is presented, we must hurry and use it before it doesn't work anymore. That is, most new areas of medicine seem to go through certain developmental stages, and initially there is a lot of enthusiasm that sometimes leads to oversimplification and interpretation of procedures and results. So far, we've been talking about issues of confidentiality and protection of patients and we've been talking about doing something about the charlatans out there, but I think another part of our ethical responsibility is an objective look at what we are doing. Following what Dr. Schwartz said, let's see if we can't come up with some more systematic and comparative data to help sex therapy really become a more adult area of medicine.

HELEN DARRAGH: I think that we have to look beyond what we're talking about in terms of training. We're talking about training in graduate schools, internship, and clinical experience, but it seems to me that one of the real points Dr. Kolodny brought up earlier in reference to objectivity and values was the role of peer review. The field of social work, as you know, has almost been too sticky in terms of its appraisal of its practitioners' work. However, ongoing evaluation, which gives therapists an opportunity for peer consultation, peer relationship, a chance to be perceived as perhaps they don't perceive themselves, is a terribly important area and issue in any discipline.

VIRGINIA E. JOHNSON: I want to respond to Dr. Schumacher's comment, with which I firmly agree. As expertise develops and awareness develops, so we become less simplistic. This is readily apparent in training situations, where professionals under close supervision for the first time, making all the mistakes they can possibly make and seeing so little because of the stress of the situation that it's remarkable, may still find that the cases work out beautifully. One thing we have to remember and feed into this discussion of the evaluation of therapy, quality control, and admission to our ranks is that the motivation of the patients themselves accounts for a significant percentage of success. Patients who are highly motivated in the face of this oversimplistic type of therapy will almost do it for you. As your own skills and ability to see the complexities grow, you are going to approach these people in a more complex way and they're going to seem much more difficult. Of course, there are also the truly complex cases that require a wide range of judgment and intuitions in addition to knowledge, but this matter of motivation must be kept in mind when you think in terms of dividing people up into different levels of training and competence. The reassuring, merely informative counselor who can reverse many problems and get credit for reversing them when he or she has done very little— this is not a sex therapist in any way. This is your kind next-door neighbor who's a little better informed than you are; this is the kind of caring person who is going to respond to needs. This is a vastly different matter from some of the questions raised yesterday about definitions of therapy and of research.

We should also recognize that the issue of training includes a question of economics. In our pilot program, such as it was, the length of training was much too short, but it was determined by the amount of time people were willing to give to it.

We wanted to start somewhere. This pilot training must be differentiated from people like Dr. Schumacher who were on our staff for some time, and from the full-time year-long fellowship program we now have. The participants in these short-term training periods encountered very real difficulties. These people, who were chosen as carefully as Drs. Mudd and Waggoner could, were, with one exception, from academic settings. It was our express purpose to share whatever we could share in a short period of time so that it could be taken back to their academic environments and worked with and expanded and modified, remaining in a research-oriented environment. Regrettably, this was not always the case, and their commitment to continue their professional interests in sexual response as a learning, teaching, and research process sometimes faltered. This is a field that can be lucrative, which bears directly on people's willingness to follow Dr. Marmor's very apt suggestion that people must be trained to recognize their limitations. But will they accept their limitations?

HAROLD I. LIEF: What has become clear to me is that we could have a two-day conference on training alone, and there wouldn't be much wasted time. So many issues have been raised. I want to make three quick comments. It is very interesting to hear from Dr. Kolodny that psychiatrists prove to be the most difficult trainees here.

ROBERT C. KOLODNY: I was speaking of the experience of the trainer, not talking about the end product.

WILLIAM H. MASTERS: I think he's right here.

VIRGINIA E. JOHNSON: I disagree with Dr. Kolodny. I recognize what he has encountered, and it is very real, but there are many other disciplines I consider much more difficult.

HAROLD I. LIEF: Well, I think there's a common factor here, and I would go back to the issue of flexibility. There is a famous paper by

Lawrence Kubie in which he explored all the varieties of things that might be involved in neurosis and finally came up with only one thing that was a hallmark of neurosis, and that was inflexibility. I think the same thing is true of the selection of candidates for training. It's flexibility that we're concerned with. You have psychiatrists who are locked into a certain mode of approach, you have physicians who are locked into a medical model and can't move from that, and so forth. It's the degree of flexibility that determines whether or not someone is a good candidate for a new form of treatment. With regard to the level Dr. Marmor and others spoke of, I have a chapter on sex counseling in a recent textbook called *The Health Care of Women,* and I use an instrumental or operational kind of approach for gynecologists. After giving them a way of screening out patients who should obviously be referred to a psychiatrist, marital counselor, or more skillful sex therapist, I advise them to do what they can within six sessions, and then, if they're really stuck, really in over their heads, to make an appropriate referral. That's a very practical approach to the problem. Finally, with regard to the question of quality control, to which Bob Stubblefield and Dick Green addressed themselves, I wonder whether we'll ever get to the point with our techniques that the National Board of Medical Examiners is now experimenting with, and that is to use simulated patient examination instead of other kinds of criteria for evaluating quality control.

REFERENCE

1. "Education and Therapy in Human Sexuality: The Training of Health Professionals." WHO Technical Report #572. Geneva: WHO, 1975.

8

SUMMARY AND FUTURE CONSIDERATIONS

WILLIAM H. MASTERS

The stated purposes of the conference have been not only met but generously exceeded. As one mulls over the formal presentations and enjoys the flavor of the discussions, the ethical dimensions of sex research and sex therapy come into reasonable focus. There are generally accepted ethical standards germane to all interaction between the patient or research subject and the clinical or research professionals of the health-care world. These ethical principles have been succinctly reidentified during this conference. But we have also considered the intangible pressures inevitably placed on these accepted ethical standards by both public and professional discomfort with the entire area of human sexuality.

What modifications of ethical principles can and do occur under these sociocultural pressures, how these modifications or interpretations vary from discipline to discipline, and how best to come to terms with the widely variant views of individual professionals are issues that have intrigued the conference participants.

We have also identified ethical issues specifically related to this field—specific training and treatment standards, accreditation demands, surrogate partners in sex therapy, and the multifaceted aspects of human sexual function are but a few of the areas considered.

A review of the highlights of material exchanged at this conference may serve to underscore established ethical precepts and to identify variations on accepted ethical themes engendered by either the uniqueness or the immaturity of this new discipline. I will follow the format of reporting the thoughts that particularly intrigued me in the presentations and discussions and will take advantage of the reviewer's privilege of inserting a few words in context, in summary, or as the mood strikes.

"The Historical Background of Ethical Considerations in Sex Research and Sex Therapy" was presented by Dr. Emily Mudd and amplified by Dr. Paul Gebhard. I don't know two people who are more qualified to provide us with a firsthand account of the genesis of this new discipline.

It was fascinating to hear of the legal problems arising from the establishment of the first birth control clinic in Pennsylvania in 1927 and the ethical issues surrounding the development of the Marriage Council of Philadelphia in the 1930s and 1940s. This account underscores both the frequent confusion between ethical concerns and moral precepts and the social prohibitions that have handicapped every pioneer attempting to provide enrichment for marital interaction. When we realize the bitterness of strife between the general public and those attempting to educate the same public in basic principles of population control, and when we recognize that this battle is only a little over 50 years in the joining, we have some frame of reference for judging how far we have come. The social trauma endured by Kinsey and Gebhard in their battles to establish fact and abolish fiction and taboo in the 1930s, 1940s, 1950s, and even in the 1960s, emphasizes for us the existence of an extraneous but powerful influence on all studies in the field of human sexual interaction.

Paul Gebhard provides additional historical insight in his discussion and raises a number of themes that are also of a contemporary nature. For instance, he comments on the element of deceptiveness that may exist when subjects who are being interviewed assume that the interviewer shares their value judgments and feelings. We have a strong awareness of problems arising from deception in research and have attempted to handle them by openly stressing our *interest* in subjects' or patients' values, experiences, and attitudes, without stating or implying agreement or endorsement. I suspect that in actual practice our interviewing styles may not be very different.

Deception of a different sort may occur when we acquire information without informed consent, as in studies involving participant observation. Although Dr. Gebhard does not offer a solution to this problem, it appears to require particular attention to the ethical risks involved.

A broad, central, and extremely important ethical consideration is confidentiality in a clinical setting. Paul Gebhard states that the Institute for Sex Research has always insisted on maintaining confidentiality, even at the cost of becoming "amoral at best or criminal at worst." He gives as an example of amorality the refusal of the institute's personnel to inform a wife that her husband has confessed to having an active venereal disease. In using this example, Paul Gebhard successfully underscores the marked variations in the definitions of confidentiality subscribed to by the different disciplines involved in this field. While anthropologists or sociologists can, without penalty, refuse to inform a wife of a husband's confession of active venereal disease, a physician-researcher would be caught in a bind. Every physician is specifically required by law to report the existence of any new cases of venereal disease he encounters. If he doesn't inform the involved marital partner or cooperate with the Public Health Service in conveying the information, not only to the spouse but also to all other potentially involved sexual partners, he is subject to legal action. Thus, matters of confidentiality are subject to modification by different professional disciplines functioning within this field. The broader point—that is, beyond the simple question of legality—has to do with concepts of confidentiality and ethical responsibility that were discussed in greater detail by many speakers during this conference.

The importance of a broad approach to ethics is brought out by the interesting theological presentations of Dr. Seward Hiltner, Rabbi Robert Gordis, and Father Jerome Wilkerson. When we were planning this conference, we were well aware that scientists are often overwhelmed by theological philosophy. Regrettably, this means that the valuable perspective afforded by religious thinkers is all too often dismissed or ignored because it does not easily fit the scientific method. The decision was therefore made to invite articulate representatives of theology to this conference—a decision we stuck to despite some criticism. I am glad that we did not change our position because I think these papers have presented unique insights.

Shortly before this conference was held, the Vatican issued a brief but comprehensive statement on human sexual ethics. Seward Hiltner discusses the implications of this document from a variety of viewpoints, emphasizing that although the term *sexual ethics* is used in the Vatican statement, the framework is primarily one of morals rather than ethics. Although it is not my intention to discuss this in further detail, one must wonder about the practical impact that a theological edict such as this will have at a time when a majority of Catholics in this country are ignoring the teachings of the Catholic church with regard to contraception.

While acknowledging some similarities in Catholic, Jewish, and Protestant views of sexuality—for example, each religion regards sex as a serious matter and views it within the context of God's intent for humans—Dr. Hiltner also focuses on some major differences in outlook. Catholicism stresses the procreative potential of each morally "right" sexual act, viewing nonprocreative sex as contrary to natural law. Judaism, on the other hand, views sexuality in a more positive way: Sexuality is seen not as a divine concession to human weakness but as one facet of human creativity. Protestants share certain elements of both of these views of sexuality; their more permissive theological positions on matters such as masturbation, contraception, and abortion are of relatively recent origin.

Dr. Hiltner points out that the response of church leaders to Kinsey's work was either negative or silent. As I remember those days, it seems to me that the response from most quarters, including academia, was either negative or silent. More recently, our own work has met with considerable support from a variety of religious leaders, especially since it has been realized that this work has practical clinical relevance. But I heartily agree with Dr. Hiltner when he advises that we all "take care of the context in which findings are presented."

Dr. Hiltner also points out that studies involving human sexuality are quite likely to continue to find predetermined enemies both in and out of churches. Our collective recognition of this circumstance is unfortunately all too acute, as many of you at this conference realize. However, negative attitudes are slowly changing. One way in which professionals in this field can foster such change is by including theologians in our work, both as advisors and as collaborators. Another way is by providing appropriate educational opportunities to this audience, without attempting to alter values and with the major objective of transmitting factual information.

Times are changing. This new discipline is achieving reasonably full acceptance at both professional and public levels. We must continue to emphasize the overwhelming need for adequate basic research and to underscore the direct ties of such research to the therapeutic field. If this is done within a context of judicious and responsible professional ethics, we need only a little tincture of time.

Father Wilkerson's comments about the Vatican declaration on sexual ethics and its implications for sex therapy and sex research are of considerable interest. To add a practical observation that seems to confirm his interpretation, a sizable number of the married couples we treat for sexual problems are on the verge of divorce. While we have no precise statistics to cite, it seems to me that many of these couples achieve improvement not only in the sexual component of their lives but also in other dimensions of their marriages. A somewhat more dramatic illustration is the fact that in the past six years we have treated approximately 100 unconsummated marriages. These individuals did not have the freedom to pursue their procreative goals until after successful completion of a course of sex therapy.

In his contribution to this conference, "Ethical Requirements for Sex Research in Humans: Informed Consent and General Principles," Dr. Robert Kolodny poses a vital question: Is sex research different from other types of research? He believes sex research *is* different from other types of research, particularly in terms of public, political, and professional attitudes—a view with which I must concur after more than 20 years in this field. It should be emphasized that Dr. Kolodny is *not* arguing that a different set of ethical principles be applied to sex research; he is, instead, urging a particularly rigorous adherence to sound ethical precepts because of the greater degree of sensitivity that is involved in sex research. Because this is a relatively new science, because the potential for misunderstanding in this area is so great, and because such strong emotional responses are elicited from many people by matters pertaining to sexuality, we will indeed profit from a major focus on our ethical responsibilities as researchers.

Dr. Kolodny discusses the major elements that comprise informed consent: disclosure of study procedures and their risks, comprehension of those facts, freedom of choice as to participation, and freedom to withdraw from the study. There are many nuances that present practical and theoretical obstacles to full attainment of this ideal, even when the researcher makes a wholehearted effort. It seems to me now, as I look back, that even when "informed consent" was less visible in the field of medicine, it was a goal that we reached for in our studies. My point is that, because of the types of inherent problems Dr. Kolodny explores, we will seriously jeopardize the future of our work unless we all make an effort to pursue vigorously the ideal of informed consent. The late Dr. Henry Beecher pioneered medicine's recent renewed attention to ethics with a disquieting article in the *New England Journal of Medicine* in 1966 that described unethical—and often frightening— studies done under the guise of science. I strongly hope that we will not someday read about such injustices committed in the name of sex research.

Dr. Ruth Macklin correctly points out that the ethical principles of sex research are not different from those of other kinds of investigation. As I said earlier, I do not believe that this point invalidates Dr. Kolodny's view that sex research is different from other types of research, although there was a lively discussion of this point. Dr. Macklin's suggestion to heed Kant's ethical precept, "Always treat other persons as ends and never solely as means," is an excellent summation of the spirit of this entire conference. Unfortunately, Kant does not provide us with a ready method for fulfilling this precept.

To appreciate the pressures of public and professional opprobrium that this field engenders, one must have worked in this area for a while. There is a great danger that overreliance on formal ethical rules, rigidly adhered to, will be constrictive rather than constructive. A new field of endeavor in a controversial area cannot develop or grow without flexibility and innovation. But responsibility for ethical decisions must never be put aside by the researcher. The essential ethical precept in human sex research is, of course, that of all health-care investigation: "Above all, do no harm." It takes an emotionally stable, competent, experienced investigator to meet this criterion while being both productive with and protective of his study-subject population. Unless every conceivable effort is made to protect the study subjects in a sex research program, the investigator is but a short step from charlatanism.

Dr. Miriam Kelty presented a superlative paper about issues of confidentiality. I don't know of a better repository of information, complete with case references and legal precedents, broadly applicable to the subject of confidentiality with special applicability to sex research and sex therapy. One of the most important ingredients in the progress of our own research work was careful attention to details of matters of confidentiality, without which I am quite sure our efforts would never have gotten off the ground floor. For similar reasons, any clinical program of sex therapy also requires meticulous responsibility in this regard.

Dr. Kelty discusses the complexities of privacy and confidentiality in a world that has moved from the days of Brandeis to the age of computers. Federal legislation seems to increase exponentially the paradoxes and dilemmas of these issues. However much we consider the broad constitutional issues and matters of law, we should not forget that seemingly minor details of confidentiality may have more impact. For example, we go to great lengths to be certain that two couples who are in our therapy program are not put in a waiting room together. We have our offices in a general medical building so that patients who arrive at the building cannot be identified as "our" patients. Concern for details of confidentiality extends to matters such as filling out patients' insurance forms and maintaining medical records.

I was particularly impressed by Dr. Kelty's suggestion that professionals in this field might begin systematically and collaboratively to design experiments to test different methods of protection for both researchers and research participants. If we could also shed some light on the abysmal ramifications of state law relative to sexual behavior and in time encourage some degree of national codification of laws pertaining to sex, it would indeed be a memorable achievement. Sex researchers must demonstrate the efficacy of the processes and procedures they have developed to enforce adherence to codes of ethics within their specific field. Then it is obviously incumbent on these researchers themselves to communicate to policymakers and to the general public the importance of gaining further understanding and knowledge of sexual behavior.

In his discussion of Miriam Kelty's paper, Dr. Richard Green observes that current methodologies for maintaining confidentiality of research data are more sophisticated than methodologies for collecting the data. I agree wholeheartedly with this observation. Dr. Green also raises some important questions about the responsibilities of the patient who receives extensive medical care that requires long-term follow-up to allow for full assessment of outcome. The conflicts between individual needs for privacy and the social needs (and needs of future generations of patients) that may temporarily weigh against such privacy are uncomfortably thorny.

Before I leave the topic of privacy and confidentiality, one further perspective might be of interest. Despite all of our attention to matters of confidentiality, whenever we speak before a large audience someone invariably stands up during the question-and-answer session and begins talking about his or her own sexual difficulties. This openness is of relatively recent vintage, but it supports Miriam Kelty's point that what today is carefully controlled specifically to protect privacy may tomorrow be of little or no consequence.

Dr. John Money presented an interesting, challenging paper about research and treatment of variant forms of human sexual behavior, beginning with some general remarks about ethical issues in sex research. For example, he correctly points out that it is impossible to get a genuinely random sample of human subjects for any type of medical study today because of the constraint of informed consent. Dr. Money also explores the problem created by those who use the banner of medical ethics as camouflage for ideological constraints, often political in origin. He notes an erosion of power in medical decision-making, which he traces to anti-scientism that may represent a backlash from the profound influence of scientific research and technological advances. Whatever one's level of acceptance of these observations, I think everyone in the field will agree with Dr. Money's point that researchers in human sexuality have not united in any meaningful way. Those who should be allies have all too often been involved in petty rivalry; there is not a single department of sexology in an American medical school.

In considering ethics and homosexuality, John Money points out that there are no absolute criteria by which to evaluate a bisexual cultural tradition as either superior or inferior to a monosexual one.

Yet few physicians would accept as ethical the idea of treating the heterosexual person so as to bring about a homosexual response, even briefly and reversibly. However, most of the same professionals would agree that the homosexual should be treated to become heterosexual, if possible. Some would even insist that such treatment be enforced by edict.

The ethical issue is not denial of psychotherapy or counseling to people whose homosexual responses distress them. Rather, it is recognizing that many homosexuals can function better, or at least well enough, by not being forced into a sexual orientation that they do not desire. This is a position that we have held to for many years.

John Money also discusses transsexualism, as further evidence that professionals must sometimes assume the burden of responsibility for the ethics of a decision for which no custom or precedent exists. No one can speak with more authority on this point than Dr. Money, since his pioneering work in the area of transsexuality and gender identity was most instrumental in developing a major field of human sexuality. These professionals then have a responsibility to educate their colleagues and the general public in the rationale and outcome of their decisions. Without guidance or explanation, professional and public response may too easily become negative. A positive strategy can influence public opinion and policy in favor of the ethics of the new decision.

Some of the liveliest discussions of this conference grew out of Dr. Fritz Redlich's intriguing presentation on the ethics of sex therapy. Tracing the historical antecedents of medical and psycho-therapeutic role models, particularly as they relate to the therapist-patient relationship, he portrays an evolving system that has moved from the older fiduciary-authoritarian relationship to a new working alliance. Within this new relationship, informed consent is a major new concept.

Examining the question of values in sex therapy, Fritz Redlich points to the social changes we have witnessed in recent years and the continued wide variability in people's values with regard to sex. He argues that the sex therapist should not attempt to influence patients to change their values beyond the prerequisites for therapy, unless the patient wishes to change. At the Foundation, we agree heartily with this concept. In fact, treatment of sexually dysfunctional couples is always controlled by the patients' value systems. The essence of the rapid-treatment technique is to help the clients define both their social and sexual value systems and then to keep all therapeutic endeavors in consistent harmony with these values. The therapists' social and sexual value systems are necessarily subordinated. Of course, alterations in value systems necessary to the success of treatment must be identified when appropriate, since the client(s) must then decide what they can accept or tolerate. The sex therapist has no right arbitrarily to impose his or her own values, or an idealized set of values, on the couple.

Dr. Redlich also discusses the topic of sexual relations between therapists and their patients, which I consider a pivotal question in establishing an effective ethical position for our field. He points out the interesting fact that the original Hippocratic oath states, "I will abstain from . . . the seduction of females or males or freemen or slaves," although the modern version of the oath has deleted this reference. Dr. Redlich develops a compelling position against therapist-patient sex by pointing out the exploitation implicit in this situation of particular vulnerability, as well as the breakdown of trust that invariably accompanies termination of such a relationship. He also briefly notes that sexual involvement between therapist and patient is likely seriously to damage therapeutic objectivity and effectiveness (thus impinging on the therapist-patient contract) and to traumatize the exploited individual.

Dr. Judd Marmor also speaks strongly against sexual involvement between psychotherapists and their patients, noting that the psychotherapy patient is expected to set aside his or her customary defenses in order to become open to the therapeutic experience. He feels that exploitation of such an iatrogenically induced vulnerability is particularly reprehensible.

On another subject, Fritz Redlich questions whether actual observation of sexual activity is ethically justified. He believes that although such observation is permissible in the specific context of research, it is clearly not permissible as a component of sex therapy. These views exactly coincide with my own. Although some people have not realized our precautions in this matter, in physiological studies involving observation of sexual functioning, we never utilized dysfunctional subjects; the potential emotional pressures and traumas were too great to risk. The sex therapist who demands observation of sexual activity as a part of treatment is more likely to be doing so for reasons of personal titillation than of professional concern.

Dr. Redlich also examined the role of surrogate partners in sex therapy; this discussion was extended by many comments from conference participants, who were not always in agreement. Our original program involving use of surrogate partners did not involve them as therapists; although we have now discontinued our use of surrogates, other institutions have initiated programs in which the surrogate functions as a teacher or therapist.

The ethical issues, including matters of confidentiality and informed consent, that arise in connection with the use of surrogate partners were examined; the majority expressed the opinion that as long as there is mutual consent, this practice is ethically permissible.

Dr. Judd Marmor's remarks on the ethics of sex therapy were characteristically cogent and comprehensive. He points out that all psychotherapy involves imparting values to patients, sometimes producing conflict with attitudes the patient has previously held. Thus, he suggests that the degree of value modification that is deliberately brought about in sex therapy be determined by assessment of the patients' specific therapeutic requirements to reach their treatment goal. Dr. Marmor also discusses the matter of group therapy of sexual dysfunction, which he believes to be a legitimate ethical approach to a problem of economics and accessibility. He concludes his comments by observing, "Apart from the golden rule, very few ethical precepts are sacrosanct and eternal. Most ethical rules grow out of the homeostatic needs of the societies that promulgate them."

Dr. Jay Katz discusses the lack of systematic preparation for ethical decision-making on the part of physicians and health-care professionals. He questions the value of *primum non nocere* as a nebulous and rather simplistic ethical concept and argues for the development of more detailed methods of uniformly analyzing ethical problems. In many ways, these remarks point toward a process that will need to occur as follow-up to this conference.

Dr. Helen Kaplan presents us with some of the concepts and problems that must be considered in the training of sex therapists.

She notes a problem that has not previously been widely recognized: that incompetence in sex therapy may be more difficult to contend with in physicians and psychologists than among the professionally unqualified, since the formal licensure of these individuals protects them and allows them to work in this field without any specialized training. In our own experience, we have become aware of numerous instances in which professionals utilized their licensure as a kind of immunity against requiring any adequate and comprehensive training in sex therapy. Such situations are particularly difficult to deal with since there are presently no broadly effective mechanisms for peer review in this field.

Dr. Kaplan discusses in detail the major aspects of the training of sex therapists: knowledge, attitudes, and clinical skills. I strongly concur with the stress she places on an adequate understanding of the physiological and pathophysiological elements that are essential to full comprehension of human sexuality. It is, of course, possible to do sex therapy without such knowledge (as Dick Green suggests, one may draw on the expertise of consultants), but there are at least two consequences: The scope of the therapy is diminished and, in my opinion, the quality of therapy declines. It is not possible to separate or compartmentalize the biological and the psychosocial, ignoring one while dealing with the other, without often miscomprehending the actual situation.

Dr. Kaplan considers the clinical skills necessary for evaluation and diagnosis of sexual disturbances, as well as for competency in the conduct of sex therapy. Although it was concluded at the WHO Conference in Geneva that the need for clinical services in this area could be met by practitioners with different levels of training and competence, she has changed her opinion and opts for a higher level of training because the easy cases seem to be disappearing.

A necessary adjunct to knowledge and clinical skills is the set of attitudes a therapist possesses. Dr. Kaplan delineates two groups of attitudes that are of critical import to this field: attitudes relating to professionalism, including ethical conduct, and attitudes relating to sex, including one's own sexuality and gender role differences. These are difficult matters to teach, but we cannot ignore their importance in our training programs or we will not be meeting our full training responsibilities. One possible solution to this problem,

I might suggest, is to consider for training only individuals who already manifest a suitable degree of attitudinal maturity. The danger here, unfortunately, is that some might take this as a mandate to train only those whose attitudes agree with their own. We cannot afford an unduly restricted range of people and ideas in this field, which is still so very young.

Dr. Carl Shultz talks about the training issue from two major perspectives: that of institutional responsibility and that of the code of ethics formulated by the American Association of Sex Educators and Counselors. It is indeed heartening to see that a number of groups are attempting carefully thought-through solutions to the difficult questions of what constitutes responsible and efficacious sex therapy, who should do it, and how we can best serve the public interest.

Our discussion of treatment and training standards is an open demand for adequate training facilities and treatment programs. Until our behavioral and medical centers acknowledge that human sexual function is a legitimate area for basic research and clinical investigation, it will not be possible to implement adequately whatever training or treatment standards are established. Since we continue to be embarrassed by the fact that to date in this country there is no department of human sexology in any medical school or university graduate school, where is our academic political power base?

Ever the optimist, I do believe these academic acknowledgments will come. Meanwhile, we must set our house in order. Charlatanism is rampant. No state has adequate laws to protect its sexually dysfunctional citizens from the fake experts, the sex faddists, or even from the well-meaning but professionally inadequate "experts." It is only with the impetus that a conference such as this inevitably provides that the concerned professionals in this field can develop a sounding board of political consequence. We must make ourselves heard. But we must also have something to say—consensus is a powerful weapon when arrived at through creative, objective discussion in a receptive climate such as that created by this conference.

The task of reviewing the information exchanged at this conference has been a pleasant one, for there is indeed a wealth of material. Doubtless, another reviewer would apply different priorities to the constructs and concepts I have underscored. And with good reason, for there is much important information that has not been included in my obviously biased review.

We plan to continue the work of the Reproductive Biology Research Foundation quite actively in this area, with a follow-up conference of expanded size and format to be held in January, 1978. The proceedings of this conference will be disseminated to interested professionals and to the public in book form, allowing ample discussion and consideration prior to our next meeting. Our aim at that time will be to formulate a set of ethical guidelines for both the sex researcher and the sex therapist. It will not be an easy task.

This conference is but a first step toward creating some sense of professional order out of the chaotic topsy-like growth of this new discipline. More—much more—must follow before acceptable ethical standards are widely incorporated both in research and in treatment. A natural growth in major training centers and the acceptance of strict accreditation procedures will inevitably follow. All of this must occur before this discipline will be fully accepted by both public and professional worlds. So—let's get on with it.

INDEX

Adolescent sexuality, problems in research of, 65–66

Affectionate behavior, between therapists and patients, 151–153

Allport, G. W., 27

Apperson, J., 178–179

Aquinas, Thomas, 39–40, 133

Assignment tasks, in therapy, 193

Autonomy, as therapeutic goal, 146

Bank, E., 91

Barnard College, 12

Barth, K., 25

Beam, L., 5

Beck, A. T., 5

Beecher, H., 211

Benjamin, H., 129

Biblical references, to sexuality, 24, 25–26, 34, 37, 51

Birth control clinic, first in Pennsylvania, 2, 207

Boruch, R. F., 98, 99, 100

Bourke, V. J., 41

Brandeis, L. D., 86, 115

Branzburg v. Hayes, 88, 89

Breggin, P., 146

Briggs, M. A., 193–194

Bronowski, J., 2, 9, 44

Brown, E. G., Jr., 113

Brunner, E., 25

Calderone, M. S., 46–48, 117, 142, 176–177, 181, 201

Caldwell v. United States, 88

Campbell, D. T., 98, 99, 100

Catholicism
and historical views on sexuality, 133–134
and Vatican statement on sex ethics, 20–29, 39, 40, 42, 47, 208–209, 210

views compared to Protestant tradition, 24–25, 209

Changes
in standards for behavior, 2, 103, 113, 124–125, 136
in types of patients in therapy, 187–188, 194

Childhood sexuality, problems in research of, 65–66, 81

Christian tradition of ethics, 21–22
compared to Judaism, 35–36, 209

Chromosome abnormalities, research in, 120, 137–138
attacks against, 111, 121–122
and confidentiality, 110–112

Coitus interruptus, biblical reference to, 37, 51

Committees, for review of research, 60–61, 76

Computerized data systems
and confidentiality of information, 90–92
and individual privacy, 93–94

Confidentiality, 84–104, 208, 212–213
and changing standards of sexual conduct, 103, 113
and chromosome abnormalities, 110–112
and computerized data systems, 90–92, 93–94
concepts of, 84–85
and educational records, 94–95
federal regulations for, 92–93
and freedom of information, 97–98, 113
and future concerns with privacy, 101–104
and group therapy, 155, 160
as issue in research, 85–86

221

Confidentiality—*Continued*
  legal aspects of, 86–87, 100–101,
    116, 208, 212
  problems with, 13, 15, 16–19, 55,
    69–70
  proposed solutions for, 98–101
  and regulations for federal agen-
    cies, 95–97
  and rights of news reporters, 87–
    90, 115
  and rules of privilege, 102–103,
    114–115
  and technological protections of
    data, 98–100
  in therapeutic procedures, 154–
    155
  and transsexuality, 107–110, 116
Consent. *See* Informed consent
Contraceptive information, attitudes
    toward, 2
Corner, G., 11
Crime Control Act of 1973, 94
Curran, C., 42
Curran, W. J., 91

Darragh, H., 141–142, 202–203
Davis, K. B., 5
Davison, G., 113
Deception of study subjects, in re-
    search, 13, 64, 207
Democratic National Committee v.
    McCord, 89
Dickinson, R. L., 5, 6
Drug Abuse Office and Treatment
    Act of 1972, 93
Drug research, and confidentiality of
    data, 88, 92, 93

Education, medical
  on ethical issues, 53, 163–165, 168
  on human sexuality, 181
  and lack of sexology departments,
    213, 218
  and neutrality of behavior, 152
  and training of sex therapists, 182–
    189. *See also* Training of thera-
    pists
Educational programs, compared to
    therapy, 148

Educational records, confidentiality
    of, 94–95
Eisenstadt v. *Baird*, 87
Ellis, A., 6
Ellis, H., 5
Engelhardt, H. T., Jr., 74–75, 132–
    136, 139, 146, 173–174
Engelhardt, R., 41
Erikson, E. H., 6
Ervin, S., 94

Family Educational Rights and Pri-
    vacy Act of 1974, 94–95
Federal Reports Act of 1970, 98
Fetal research, value of, 116
Fielding, L., 106
Fitzgerald, F. S., 5
Flexner, S., 2
Foote, N., 8
Freedom of Information Act of 1966,
    97–98, 113
Freud, S., 5, 27, 144, 146, 149–150,
    155

Gaylin, W., 54
Gebhard, P. H., 11–14, 16, 17–19,
    50, 207–208
Goethe, 152
Gordis, R., 32–38, 49, 51, 75–76,
    133, 139–140, 208
Gorovitz, S., 54
Graham, B., 12
Green, R., 82–83, 106–114, 172–173,
    197–199, 213
Gregg, A., 6, 11
Gregory the Great, 133
Griswold v. *Connecticut*, 87
Group therapy, for sexual disorders,
    155, 160–161, 216

Hamilton, G. V. T., 5
Häring, B., 42, 43
Harvard University, 11, 47, 113, 121,
    181
Heinlein, R. A., 151
Hermaphroditism, sex reassignment
    in, 129–130
Herr, D., 43

Hiltner, S., 20–32, 49, 180, 209
Hippocratic oath, 145, 149, 163, 215
Historical aspects of sex research, 1–9, 207
Hollingshead, R., 147
Homosexual therapists, 196
Homosexuality, 213–214
   public announcements of, 113
   research on, attitudes toward, 29
   theological views on, 24, 25, 26, 37–38
   therapy for, attitudes toward, 30–31, 126–129
Horney, K., 6

Indiana University Medical School, 12
Information retrieval systems, and confidentiality of data, 90–92, 93–94
Informed consent, 61–66, 210–211
   and constraints on research, 120–121
   and prisoner studies, 122–123
   problems with, 13, 15, 17, 64–66, 70, 72–73, 164
   proxy consent for minors, 65–66, 73, 81
Ingelfinger, F., 53
Institute for Sex Research, 208

Janvier, V., 2
Jefferson Medical College, 4
Jewish tradition of ethics, 21–22, 33–38
   compared to Christianity, 25–26, 209
   and views on sexuality, 25, 34–36
Johns Hopkins University, 11, 122, 123, 169
Johnson, R. C., 15, 74, 138, 172
Johnson, V. E., 8, 44, 50, 76–77, 139, 165–168, 170, 174, 180, 181, 203–204
   and Masters, 31, 43, 47, 143, 146, 147, 153, 154, 155, 160, 184, 193, 201
Jones, H. W., Jr., 129, 130

Kant, I., 74, 211
Kaplan, H. S., 75, 91, 170–171, 182–189, 195–196, 216–218
Kardener, S., 150, 151
Karyotype variants. *See* Chromosome abnormalities, research in
Katz, J., 141, 161–165, 179, 216
Katz v. *United States*, 86
Kelly, H., 169
Kelty, M. F., 84–104, 212
Kinsey, A., 6–8, 11, 12, 23, 27–28, 114, 207
Klerman, G., 65
Kohlberg, L., 47
Kolodny, R. C., 52–68, 77, 78–80, 116–117, 138–139, 171–172, 194, 210–211
Kubie, L., 205

Labeling of research subjects, effects of, 59, 72
Laska, E. M., 91
Lawrence, D. H., 5
Laws, J. L., 177
Lee, R., 11
Legal principles
   and changing values, 2
   and confidentiality, 86–87, 100–101, 116, 208, 212
   and information in data files, 91–92
   and involvement in legal suits, 16
   and laws on sexual behavior, 71, 148, 158, 212
   and new therapeutic procedures, 130
   and sex research, 14
Lerman, N. M., 100
LeRoy, E., 44
Levi, E. H., 85
Lief, H. I., 7, 17, 48, 77–78, 116, 140, 179–180, 199, 204–205
Lombard, P., 134
Longworth, A. R., 161
Love, concepts of, 35, 36–37
Lowry, T. P., 150, 154
Lowry, T. S., 150, 154

Macklin, R., 16, 41, 69–74, 75, 133, 211
Manson, C., 151
Marmor, J., 157–161, 178, 200–201, 215
Marriage
  and concerns of churches, 29–30
  and Jewish tradition, 34–36
  and sexuality, 134
  Vatican statement on, 23
Marriage Council Service, Philadelphia, 3–4, 7, 207
Maryland legislation, on confidential records, 91–92
Masters, W. H., 8, 76, 79, 80, 149, 168, 175–176, 181, 206–219
  and Johnson, 31, 43, 47, 143, 146, 147, 153, 154, 155, 160, 184, 193, 201
Masturbation
  as natural function, 47
  and problems in research, 78, 79
  theological views on, 24, 25, 26, 37, 48
Maugham, S., 151
McCormick, R., 42
McIntosh, M., 12
Medical education. *See* Education, medical
Meyer, A., 11
Miller, A., 94
Minors, and informed consent for research, 65–66, 73, 81
Monell Institute, 78
Money, J., 81, 116, 119–132, 138, 169–170, 213–214
Morality
  and changing standards of behavior, 2, 103, 113, 124–125, 136
  compared to ethics, 21, 39, 74
Mudd, E. H., 1–9, 16, 44, 79, 199, 207
Mudd, S., 2

National Institute of Mental Health, 80, 90
National Research Council Committee for Research in Problems of Sex, 11

Natural law theory, 22–23, 24, 32–33, 39, 40–41, 133, 135
Nejelski, P., 87–88, 89, 100
New York Academy of Medicine, 6
New York State, legislation on confidential records, 91
News reporters, and protection of information sources, 87–90, 115
Niebuhr, R., 12, 30, 39
Nielsen, K., 41
Noonan, J., 134
Nudity, and therapy, 153, 191

Osmond, H., 144

Paraphilias, tolerance or intolerance of, 125–126
Paraprofessionals, in sex therapy, 174
Parsons, T., 6, 144, 145, 152
Pellegrino, E. D., 41
Pennsylvania, University of, 2, 7, 78
Personnel for sex research and education, problems with, 12
Peyser, H., 87, 89
Philadelphia County Medical Society, 3–4
Placebos, used in research, 58, 71
Premarital sexual behavior
  attitudes toward research on, 29
  and Jewish tradition, 37
Prevention of disorders, ethical issues in, 127–128
Prisoners, as research subjects, 17–18, 64–65, 73–74, 122–123
Privacy. *See also* Confidentiality
  concepts of, 84–85, 115
  need for, in sexual matters, 153, 155
Privacy Act of 1974, 95–97
Professionalism, in sex research, 15
Prostitution, 154, 169, 171, 172, 173–174, 176
Protestant tradition of ethics, 21, 26
  compared to Catholicism, 24–25, 209
Psychological concepts of sexuality, 5, 6, 183–184

Rape, and sex between therapists and patients, 149, 151, 168

Records of patients, safeguarding of, 155, 212

Redlich, F., 41, 143–156, 171, 177, 214–216

Registries of patients, need for, 112

Religious concepts. *See* Theological concepts

Rembar, C., 18–19, 51, 75, 80, 81, 83, 115–116, 168–169

Reporters, and protection of news sources, 87–90, 115

Repression, reactions to, 44

Reproductive Biology Research Foundation, 44, 66, 154, 155, 199, 219

Research on sexuality
  abuses in, 61, 72
  allocation of funds for, 140
  attitudes toward, 28–32, 43
  attitudes and values in, 66–68
  in childhood and adolescence, 65–66, 81
  in chromosome abnormalities, 120, 121–122, 137–138
  and confidentiality. *See* Confidentiality
  and conflicting loyalties of physicians, 69–70
  constraints in, 120–121, 123–124
  and deception of study subjects, 13, 64, 207
  decisions against, 81, 111, 114, 116, 121, 131
  design of studies in, 54–59
  and dilemmas from data analysis, 58–59, 71
  individual versus group ethical issues in, 140–141
  and informed consent. *See* Informed consent
  and interpretation of information by subjects, 77
  and Jewish tradition, 38
  and labeling of participants, 59, 72
  legal aspects in. *See* Legal principles
  long-term effects of participation in, 62–63
  and other types of research, 52, 69, 76, 77–78, 79, 210

prisoners as subjects in, 17–18, 64–65, 73–74, 122–123

and provision of services, 131–132

review procedures in, 59–61, 76, 82, 114

and rights of subjects, 57–58

risk factors in, 62–63

and role of decision-makers, 129–130, 139–140, 141

and selection of study populations, 55–57

and sex therapy, 29–32, 166–167

and training in ethical issues, 53

unethical areas in, 58, 70–71

in variant forms of sexual behavior, 119–132

Review procedures, in research, 59–61, 76, 82, 114
  and problems with committees, 16

Rice, T., 12

Risk factors, in research, 62–63

Roe v. *Ward*, 87

Role models, 144–146
  psychoneurotic model, 145
  sick role, 144
  and values in sex therapy, 146–149

Sanger, M., 2

Sanville, J., 150

Scheffey, L., 4

Schlick, M., 143

School records, confidentiality of, 94–95

Schultz, C. S., 49–50, 77, 189–193, 201–202

Schumacher, S., 202

Schutz, A., 174

Schwartz, P., 18, 48, 82, 114, 175, 196–197

Schwartz, R. D., 98, 99

Scientists, value judgments of, 49

Sex education of youth, effects of, 12

Sex offenders, consent for therapy of, 122–123

Sex therapy. *See* Therapeutic procedures

Sexuality
  biology and psychology of, 5, 6, 183–184

Sexuality—*Continued*
  childhood, problems in research
    of, 65–66, 81
  historical views on, 4–6, 133–136
Shepard, M., 150
Sherfey, M. J., 16
Shor, J., 150
Shultz, C., 218
SIECUS, position on masturbation,
  47
Siegler, M., 144
Social attitudes on sex, evolution of,
  4–6, 133–136
Southern Illinois University, 114
Stein, M., 5
Steinberg, J., 98, 99
Stone, A. A., 76, 114–115, 116, 117,
  137, 139, 141, 180–181
Stubblefield, R. L., 50–51, 82, 140–
  141, 195
Student records, confidentiality of,
  94–95
Supreme Court decisions, on confi-
  dential information, 88–90
Surrogate partners, 154, 169, 173,
  175–176, 179–180, 216
  attitudes toward, 31
  conflicts with, 154
  training of, 198
Szasz, T., 146

Talmudic references to sexuality, 33–
  36
Theological concepts, 20–32, 208–
  210
  and differing views on sexuality,
    24–26
  historical aspects of, 21–22
  and views on scientific research,
    26–28, 39
Therapeutic procedures
  assignment tasks in, 193
  attitudes toward, 30–32, 44–45
  background knowledge for, 183–
    184
  and change in types of patients,
    187–188, 194, 202
  clinical skills in, 187–188, 200–
    201, 217
  compared to education, 148

  and confidentiality, 154–155. *See
    also* Confidentiality
  dual-sex teams in, 153, 158, 194
  and education of medical students,
    152, 163–165, 168
  ethical problems in, 153–156,
    214–216
  goals of, 145–146
  group therapy in, 155, 160–161,
    216
  paraprofessionals in, 174
  and research, 29–32, 166–167
  and safeguarding of records, 155,
    212
  surrogate partners in. *See* Surro-
    gate partners
Therapists
  affectionate behavior with pa-
    tients, 151–153
  attitudes of, 185–187, 217–218
  dual-sex teams of, 153, 158, 194
  ethical standards for, 191–192,
    201–202, 218
  homosexuals as, 196
  personal characteristics of, 199
  role of, 50
  sex with patients, 149–151, 156,
    158–159, 165, 168, 170–173,
    177–178, 215–216
  sexual background of, 198–199
  training of, 182–189, 203–204,
    217–218. *See also* Training of
    therapists
  values of, 147–149, 157–158, 168,
    173, 191, 196, 214–215
Thielicke, H., 25
Training of therapists, 182–189,
  203–204, 217–218
  and clinical skills, 187–188, 200–
    201, 217
  duration of, 189, 191, 195, 202
  and flexibility of candidates, 205
  and institutional responsibility,
    190, 192, 218
  quality control and licensing in,
    197
  and selection of applicants, 195–
    196, 197, 199, 200
  short-term periods of, 204
  for surrogate therapists, 198

Transsexualism, 214
and confidentiality, 107–110, 116
and ethics of sex reassignment,
129–131, 136

United States v. *Liddy*, 89

Value judgments
and changes in standards for behavior, 2, 103, 113, 124–125,
136, 147
and problems in sex therapy, 147–
149, 157–158
and professional nonjudgmentalism, 125
and role of decision-makers, 129–
130, 139–140, 141
by scientists, 49

and values of therapists, 147–149,
157–158, 168, 173, 191, 196,
214–215
Vatican statement on sex ethics, 20–
29, 39, 40, 42, 47, 208–209, 210

Walzer, S., 110
Warren, S., 86, 115
Wells, H. B., 12
Wiener, J., 15, 80, 118, 174
Wilkerson, J. F., 38, 49, 166, 210
Wilkins, L., 129–130
Women
sexuality of, 4, 6, 8
views of female orgasm, 6, 31, 59

Yerkes, R., 11